The Rise of Political Advisors in the Westminster System

Political advisors have risen in significance in Westminster countries, and have been increasingly thrust into the limelight by headline scandals and through their characterisation in various television series. This increased prominence has led to greater scrutiny of their role and influence. This book demonstrates that the introduction of political advisors into the structure of the executive has led to the erosion of the Westminster doctrine of ministerial responsibility.

Adopting a comparative approach, the book analyses the rise in the power and significance of political advisors in the Westminster jurisdictions of the United Kingdom, Australia, New Zealand and Canada. It shows the fundamental shift of the locus of power from the neutral public service to highly political and partisan ministerial advisors. Tracing the divergent paths for legal and political regulation of political advisors, Yee-Fui Ng illuminates the tensions that they pose within the Westminster system in terms of the media/politics and faction/opposition interfaces.

Providing insights for those researching or engaged in politics and public administration, this work will interest scholars and students of politics and public law, policy and administration.

Yee-Fui Ng is a Senior Lecturer at Monash University, Australia. She has worked as a Policy Advisor at the Australian Department of the Prime Minister and Cabinet, a Senior Legal Advisor at the Victorian Department of Premier and Cabinet, as well as a Manager at the Victorian Department of Justice.

The Rise of Political Advisors in the Westminster System

Yee-Fui Ng

Routledge
Taylor & Francis Group
LONDON AND NEW YORK

First published 2018
by Routledge
2 Park Square, Milton Park, Abingdon, Oxon OX14 4RN

and by Routledge
711 Third Avenue, New York, NY 10017

Routledge is an imprint of the Taylor & Francis Group, an informa business

British Library Cataloguing-in-Publication Data
A catalogue record for this book is available from the British Library

Library of Congress Cataloging-in-Publication Data
Names: Ng, Yee-Fui, author.
Title: The rise of political advisors in the Westminster system / Yee-Fui Ng.
Description: Abingdon, Oxon ; New York, NY : Routledge, 2018. |
Includes bibliographical references and index.
Identifiers: LCCN 2017059727 | ISBN 9780415787482 (hardback) |
ISBN 9781351020541 (e-book)
Subjects: LCSH: Political consultants–Commonwealth countries. |
Ministerial responsibility–Commonwealth countries. | Government
accountability–Commonwealth countries. | Commonwealth
countries–Politics and government–21st century.
Classification: LCC JF1525.C6 N4 2018 | DDC 351–dc23
LC record available at https://lccn.loc.gov/2017059727

ISBN: 978-0-415-78748-2 (hbk)
ISBN: 978-1-351-02054-1 (ebk)

Typeset in Times New Roman
by Out of House Publishing

Contents

Figures

Tables

Acknowledgements

First of all, I would like to thank Greg Taylor, for critically commenting on a draft of the entire manuscript, and for his support and encouragement to carry on when the going was tough. I am also indebted to Jonathan Craft, who read and commented on the whole manuscript, Maria Maley, who read and commented on one chapter, and Anna Esselment, who helped me verify aspects of the Canadian material. I am very grateful to Ellen Bicknell, who assisted with the underlying research for the project and carefully proofread and commented on the manuscript at the end. I would also like to thank Elsie Loh, who provided research assistance, and Mari Fitzpatrick, Claire Kaylock, and Simon Williams for their proofreading of the text.

One of the great pleasures in undertaking this project is getting to meet and discuss ideas with the incredibly friendly and helpful community of academics across the globe who research in this area, particularly Jonathan Craft, Anna Esselment and Paul Wilson in Canada, Chris Eichbaum and Richard Shaw in New Zealand, Ben Yong in the United Kingdom, Athanassios Gouglas in Belgium and fellow Australian Maria Maley. I appreciate their generosity in time and spirit in assisting my understanding of their respective jurisdictions.

The research for this book is underpinned by 22 interviews with current and former Ministers and Members of Parliament in Australia, as well as Access to Information requests in Australia, New Zealand and Canada. In addition, I had productive discussions in the United Kingdom with various academics and practitioners who research in the area of special advisors when I was a Visiting Researcher at the University College London. Monica Pfeffer helpfully facilitated introductions to academics.

I also appreciate the permission of Federation Press to reproduce some of the material in my book *Ministerial Advisers in Australia: The Modern Legal Context* (2016).

As always, I am extremely grateful to my partner, Simon Williams, who has supported me along this journey, with much home-cooked food, reassurance and love.

1 Introduction

Drunk with their newfound power, they are often in the full bloom of youth, deeply ambitious and mired in the dirty world of politics. Partisan political advisors have become a potent force in the Westminster system in the last 40 years. As partisan advisors have increased in power and prominence, the power of the civil service has correspondingly waned. We have moved from an age of 'Yes Minister', where the imperial civil servant subtly and cleverly manipulates a hapless Minister, to an era reminiscent of the popular British programme 'The Thick of It', where a powerful political advisor berates both Ministers and civil servants alike with magnificent bouts of swearing and bile. Although the caricatures are extreme, the basic illustration is apt.

Although political advisors have increased in power and influence over the years, they are largely able to escape accountability as the law has not kept pace with political developments. In addition, Ministers have utilised their advisors as scapegoats to avoid their own ministerial responsibility to Parliament. This has led to numerous large-scale scandals that have appeared on the headlines of the news. As a result, there has been increasing scrutiny of the role and influence of political advisors in traditional Westminster advisory systems.

Several questions arise. Why have these political advisors come to prominence across the Westminster jurisdictions? How has this trend played out across the different jurisdictions? Has the rise of the political advisors created any schisms within the traditional Westminster system? And how do we realign Westminster values and principles, created more than a century ago, to a new and ever-changing world?

These questions are important because the Westminster system is predicated upon the binary relationship between Ministers and civil servants. Nevertheless, the injection of hundreds of new people into the structure of the executive has fundamentally changed the traditional interactions between Ministers and civil servants. The scandals and controversies that have erupted show that the traditional Westminster system is poorly adapted to dealing with a significant new actor within the executive. In an era of declining public trust in political institutions, governments have the impetus to rebuild public confidence by reforming and adapting the Westminster system to improve the legal and political accountability of Ministers and their advisors.

Ministers, as our elected representatives within the Westminster executive, have unrivalled power in our democratic system. They run the country. They alone effectively exercise executive power. Yet it is lonely at the top. Ministers are faced with silky-tongued mandarins who command a vast and bewildering bureaucratic machine, who may not have their best interests at heart. The omnipresent media are perpetually hungry for blood, looking to turn against them at any moment. Factional opponents within their own party are constantly searching for opportunities to bring them down, so that the opponents themselves may rise up, not to mention the opposition parties biting at their heels. Ministers also have to appease the Prime Minister and fight for the priority of their agenda against those of other Ministers.

It is impossible for one person to shoulder all of these tasks single-handedly. This means that Ministers must have a strong advisory system to allow them to carry out their constitutional, policy and legislative duties. Understandably, Ministers reach out to trusted partisan advisors, loyal to them, to bolster their position.

This book analyses the rise of political advisors in the United Kingdom, Canada, Australia and New Zealand: the classic liberal Westminster jurisdictions. The Westminster system refers to a 'British-inspired version of parliamentarianism', as opposed to legislative or other presidential systems (Rhodes, Wanna and Weller 2009, p. 2). These jurisdictions were chosen because they share a liberal democratic framework within a common constitutional heritage derived from the Westminster tradition. This study does not include non-liberal, autocratic Westminster countries within its scope, as there are many complicating factors, possibly including corruption, that create accountability issues in those countries, beyond the institution of political advisors within the system of government. The liberal democratic Westminster countries chosen in this study are generally seen as exemplars for the rule of law and have high scores for transparency and lack of corruption. For instance, all of the jurisdictions in this book are seen to have high-quality civil services according to the 2016 World Bank government effectiveness indicator, with each country scoring a high percentile ranking: New Zealand (97.1 per cent), Canada (95.2 per cent), the United Kingdom (92.8 per cent) and Australia (92.3 per cent).

The countries examined in this book do have significant variances in their governing structure. Britain and New Zealand have flexible constitutions, while Australia and Canada are characterised by inflexible constitutions. The United Kingdom and New Zealand are unitary states, while Australia and Canada have a federal system of government. Despite these differences, the Westminster countries covered in this book do share a common heritage from the British tradition relating to executive organisation and its relationship to the legislature and civil service (Rhodes and Weller 2005, p. 7). This includes a constitutional fusion of the executive and legislature, the accountability of the executive to Parliament, and a professional career civil service (Rhodes,

Wanna and Weller 2009, pp. 13–14). It is these aspects of the Westminster system that will be explored in this book.

The Westminster civil service tradition

The modern day Westminster civil service tradition stems from the Northcote–Trevelyan Report of 1853. In the eighteenth and early nineteenth century in Britain, it was difficult to be appointed to government office unless you were an aristocrat with the right connections to a very small elite (Fukuyama 2014, p. 127). This patronage-laden system was transformed in a small span of 15 years through the cohesive campaigning of a few powerful elites: Thomas Babington Macaulay, Charles Trevelyan, William Gladstone (Chancellor of the Exchequer), Stafford Northcote (his private secretary), as well as Benjamin Jowett, master of Balliol College in Oxford University. They first reformed the Indian Civil Service, then the British one. This group had varying motivations for seeking the end of the patronage system, some less noble than others. In seeking open competition and educational qualifications as a basis for service in India, Macaulay had imperialist interests to ensure that 'India was governed by a like-minded elite – a cadre of liberally educated and class-conscious Englishmen posted abroad' (Sullivan 2009, p. 423). Likewise, Gladstone wanted to solidify the governing caste: 'one of the great recommendations of the change in my eyes would be its tendency to strengthen and multiply the ties between the higher classes and the possession of administrative power' (Sullivan 2009, p. 423). Northcote echoed his boss Gladstone in wishing to consolidate the civil service through the appointment of educated gentlemen. Jowett was concerned about the future of the Universities of Oxford and Cambridge, and wanted to transform them 'from ecclesiastical to national institutions' (Sullivan 2009, p. 423). On the other hand, Macaulay's brother-in-law Trevelyan had idealistic reformist ambitions. Trevelyan was an energetic man from a baronet's family who worked in the East India Company. He was disgusted by the incompetence of the aristocrats in that company, deriding India as the 'sink to which the scum and refuse of the English professions habitually gravitates' (Bourn 1986, p. 32).

To reform the British civil service, Trevelyan, who despite being a beneficiary of patronage when he was elevated to Permanent Secretary of Treasury at the youthful age of 32, collaborated with Northcote towards ending the system of patronage they both benefited from. Together they wrote the Northcote–Trevelyan Report: a searing critique of the patronage system that characterised the British civil service. The slender document of 20 pages became the bedrock for the ideals of the civil service in the Westminster system.

The report stridently criticised the civil service as currently being the home to:

> the unambitious, and the indolent or incapable … [t]hose whose abilities do not warrant an expectation that they will succeed in the open

professions ... and those whom indolence of temperament or physical infirmities unfit for active exertions (sic), are placed in the Civil Service.
(Northcote and Trevelyan 1854, p. 4)

The report concluded that a permanent body of public servants who were subordinate to Ministers was necessary for effective government administration. It argued that the appointment of junior staff based on patronage, combined with an absence of competition, led to difficulties in getting a good supply of employees in the public service compared to other professions. The report also condemned recruitment external to the public service based on patronage over the promotion of public servants with merit:

[N]umerous instances might be given in which personal or political considerations have led to the appointment of men of very slender ability, and perhaps of questionable character, to situations of considerable emolument, over the heads of public servants of long standing and undoubted merit.
(Northcote and Trevelyan 1854, p. 7)

The Northcote–Trevelyan Report forms the basis of the Westminster public service today, where civil servants are expected to be neutral, apolitical, and recruited and promoted on the basis of merit. The intention was very much to rid the system of patronage.

The system recommended by the Northcote–Trevelyan Report, with its fixation on higher educational qualifications for higher 'intellectual' posts, was not beyond reproach. Although theoretically open to all classes, in reality this very much confined the ranks of the civil service to the aristocracy and upper middle class who had the money and connections to send their sons (for only men were considered for those positions at the time) to Oxford or Cambridge (Fukuyama 2014, p. 129). Indeed, some of the reformists did have the intention that only the higher echelons of British society would be appointed to the civil service.

Nevertheless, the Northcote–Trevelyan Report was ground-breaking in its day, as the aristocracy preferred the status quo that benefitted them. Queen Victoria herself had reservations about opening up the civil service to public competition, fearing that this would allow into high office low people without the 'breeding' or 'feelings' of gentlemen (Kellner and Crowther-Hunt 1980, p. 105). Modern commentators such as Peter Hennessy proclaimed that the Northcote–Trevelyan reforms were 'the greatest single transformation the British Civil Service has ever undergone, and, in their day, they were wholly beneficial' (Hennessy 1989, p. 31). The report also left an enduring legacy. As Hennessy noted, Northcote–Trevelyan:

created the country's first true meritocracy, a genuine aristocracy of talent. Its bone structure is clearly visible in the higher Civil Service

> of today. Despite two world wars, the complete extension of the franchise, a social revolution or two, the rise and fall of the British Empire and the decline of the country as the world's leading manufacturer and exporter, the Home Civil Service today is … still fundamentally the product of the nineteenth-century philosophy of the Northcote–Trevelyan Report.
>
> (Hennessy 1989, p. 31)

The modern civil service thus operates on the values of impartiality and accountability within the framework of ministerial responsibility. The traditional conception of the civil service rests on three main tenets:

- the recruitment of government officials should be made on merit, that is, 'the ability to perform the work rather than any form of personal or political favouritism';
- since jobs are filled on the basis of merit, those employed should be granted tenure regardless of political changes; and
- the price of job security should be 'a willing responsiveness to the legitimate political leaders of the day' (Heclo 1977, p. 20).

The rise of political advisors appointed not on the basis of merit, but patronage, thus poses a significant challenge to the Westminster civil service, which was constructed as a bulwark against patronage.

Features of Westminster advisory systems

The Westminster traditional ministerial advisory system is predicated on a binary relationship between Ministers and civil servants. Two fundamental assumptions underpin this relationship. First, there is a clear delineation of roles: Ministers are responsible for politics, while civil servants are responsible for administration; that is, the classic but discredited politics/administration dichotomy (Wilson 1887, pp. 201, 204). The politics/administration dichotomy was conceived of by Woodrow Wilson a century ago. Wilson advocated for the strict separation between politics and administration, stating that:

> administration lies outside the proper sphere of politics. Administrative questions are not political questions. Although politics sets the tasks for administration, it should not be suffered to manipulate its offices.
>
> (Wilson 1887, pp. 201, 204)

The politics/administration dichotomy deeply pervaded public administration discourse over many decades. However, this dichotomy is rather unfashionable today, after being derided as being too simplistic in the demarcation of the roles of public servants and politicians. Indeed, the insertion of political advisors as an additional layer between Ministers and public servants problematises the politics/administration dichotomy. Political advisors play significant roles in both the procedural and substantive dimensions of policy advice (Craft 2016, pp. 32–40). They also operate across the technical/administrative and partisan/political dimensions. As Pat McFadden, former Deputy Chief of Staff in the British Prime Minister's Office, stated:

> Special advisers operate on the terrain ... which crosses between the administrative function and the political function. You cannot remove that.
> (Committee on Standards in Public Life 2003, p. 16)

The second assumption in the Westminster conception of the relationship between Ministers and the civil service is that there is a unity of mind between Ministers and civil servants, where civil servants are assumed to act as the agent of the Minister and the Minister absorbs any mistakes of their agent, that is, the concept of individual ministerial responsibility. Further, according to the Westminster ideal, civil servants operate in the long-term interests of their country. They are to display 'neutral competence', that is, to perform the work expertly and objectively (Aberbach and Rockman 1994, p. 461). In this way, civil servants are able to serially serve politicians of all stripes across the political spectrum.

Over time, however, Ministers grew dissatisfied with large and powerful bureaucracies. There was a suspicion that bureaucrats did not in reality serve the public interest but instead, according to public choice theory, operated on the basis of their own self-interest. The public choice principal-agent literature suggests that public servants will 'shirk' from their duties and sabotage their Ministers in a self-serving way (Downs 1967; Niskanen 1971).

In addition, conservative governments suspected that the bureaucracy was secretly biased against them and were progressive at heart, while progressive governments chafed against the passivity of the civil service and doubted that a sluggish bureaucracy could implement innovative and ambitious reform agendas (Rourke 1992, p. 541). This meant that Ministers started to clamour for their advisory system to shift towards one of loyalty or 'responsive competence', to better serve the needs of the elected politicians. The move to a 'new public management' approach, with its structural changes to destabilise the bureaucracy, and the rise of political advisors in the Westminster system in the 1970s and 1980s is a direct manifestation of the desire for the Westminster advisory systems to move from neutral competence to responsive competence.

There are questions about how this new class of political advisors could be accommodated within the Westminster advisory system. To this end, a strand of literature on policy advisory systems has developed that examines various internal and external sources of policy advice beyond Ministers and civil servants, and explicitly seeks to incorporate the position of political advisors into the system (Craft and Howlett 2012, p. 80; Halligan 1995, p. 138). In contemporary times, the civil service no longer holds the monopoly on advice to Ministers. Rather, a range of stakeholders now provide policy advice to Ministers, including internal governmental advisors, such as partisan political advisors, as well as external advisors, such as non-governmental organisations, think tanks, universities and political parties. Proponents of the literature on policy advisory systems argue that political advisors have become one element of an overarching policy advisory system to Ministers, that is, an interlocking set of actors who provide information, knowledge and recommendations to policy-makers (Craft and Howlett 2012; Halligan 1995).

Yet these developments have not escaped criticism. Peter Aucoin asserts that we have moved into an era of 'new political governance', where an aggressive media, increased demands for transparency and increased partisanship has led to four distinct shifts in governance: government conducted as a continuous campaign, partisan-political staff as a third force in governance, a personal-politicisation of appointments to the senior civil service, and an assumption that public service loyalty means being promiscuously partisan (Aucoin 2012). Thus, external pressures have led to the politicisation of the civil service as well as the rise of political advisors. The essential argument advanced by proponents of 'new political governance' is that we have moved to an era of hyper-politicisation and tipped too far into the 'responsive competence' end of the spectrum at the expense of 'neutral competence'. The structure and evolution of Westminster advisory systems thus reflect the tension between the traditional Westminster concept of political neutrality and the 'new public management' imperative of responsiveness. The rise of political advisors results in the system moving towards responsive competence.

Alternatives to Westminster advisory systems

The Westminster advisory system that cleaves a strict division between the apolitical civil service and partisan advisors is not the only option for ministerial advisory systems. I will outline two main alternative systems: the American system and the European *cabinet* system. Many proponents of reform of the Westminster advisory system have referred to the American and *cabinet* systems as a template for reforms, so this discussion provides a basis for understanding these proposals.

America: the legacy of the spoils system

Britain and the United States started the nineteenth century with aristocrat-dominated patronage-ridden governments, but took divergent paths towards bureaucratic reform, with Britain pioneering the career-based professional bureaucracy and America moving to the spoils system. In the spoils system, based on the catch-cry 'to the victor belong the spoils', high and low official positions were used to reward friends, cronies and supporters, and as incentives to work for the political party (Page 1992, p. 27). The spoils system is generally associated with the presidencies of Andrew Jackson (1829–37) and Martin Van Buren (1837–41), and was developed as a reaction against elite factions and the entrenched upper class. In the early nineteenth century, federal public servants were landed gentry who held the office until they were old, and were often succeeded by their sons (Schultz and Maranto 1998, p. 35). The spoils system was justified idealistically as a way for the ambitious non-elite to get ahead and to have a more representative bureaucracy. In practice, it created opportunities to place party loyalists in bureaucratic positions (Fukuyama 2014, pp. 217, 223). David Schultz and Robert Maranto (1998, p. 39) found that, even under Jackson, the majority of political appointees came from elite backgrounds. Although there were a higher percentage of middle class appointments, 'the common man', such as the farmer, was not represented. Max Weber has criticised the American system for its low level of competence and endemic corruption:

> [T]here were 300,000–400,000 party members, who could show no other qualification than their good service to the Party. This situation could not persist without enormous disadvantages; corruption and waste without any parallel which could only be tolerated by a country with at the time unlimited economic opportunities.
>
> (Weber 1972, p. 846)

Sure enough, problems soon emerged with the spoils system. Corruption was rife, including embezzlement and bribery. A notorious example was Jackson's New York City Customs Collector, Samuel Swartout, who absconded to Europe with $1.25 million, at that time 5 per cent of the federal budget. Spoils also created friction in the political party as 'each appointment could spawn ten enemies and one ingrate' (Schultz and Maranto 1998, p. 58).

As a result of these issues, the spoils system was reduced in the mid-twentieth century. The *Pendleton Act* in 1883 (based on the British Northcote–Trevelyan reforms) was a watershed moment, shifting towards a tenured and merit-based public service with competitive entrance examinations (Gely and Chandler 2000, p. 798; Fukuyama 2014, pp. 229–232). The Pendleton Bill was passed amid much drama. President James Garfield, who pushed for the reform, was assassinated by a disappointed office seeker hoping for a federal job under the spoils system; consequently, Garfield's term only lasted 200 days. The Bill was finally passed by Congress and signed into law by his successor, Chester Arthur. Despite the Pendleton reforms, until today there remains the option of appointing public servants on either a merit or patronage basis. The number of political appointees has varied over time across different presidencies.

American presidents have always had large numbers of political staff at a scale that exceeds the Westminster political advisory system due to the concentration of executive power in one person, rather than a ministry, as well as the complete separation between the legislature and executive. These institutional arrangements justify stronger support for the executive in order to pass legislation. The Executive Office of the President has about 1,500 employees who are mostly political appointees (Peters 2015, pp. 790–791). Due to the large numbers, many staff do not have direct contact with the President. The quality of political appointees has diminished over time, as partisan loyalty has come to outweigh competence in making political appointments (Edwards 2001).

In addition to the positions in the Presidential Office, the President can appoint over 3,000 employees at the top of federal public service organisations (Cohen 1996, p. 6). The *Civil Service Reform Act 1978* allows up to 10 per cent of the Senior Executive Service to be political appointees. Although this is a small fraction of the 2.1 million civilian career employees, the political appointees are concentrated at the top ranks of the public service (Cohen 1996, p. 6). Peter Schroth contends that 'party service and a relationship with the President often weigh far more heavily than other qualifications' and a significant number of civil service hiring decisions appear to be made based on party affiliation (Schroth 2006, p. 576). Many high-level administrative positions and ambassadorships are given to friends, contributors and supporters as a form of reward. Hugh Heclo found that during the Kennedy administration in the 1960s, there was a combination of traditional recruitment through 'the intricate network of friends and friends of friends' and a network of evaluators who compiled patronage files containing more than 5,000 names: 'a motley collection of information on who had scratched whose political back' (Heclo 1977, p. 90). Despite the professionalisation of the civil service, the legacy of the spoils system persists in the attitude that political leaders should be able to appoint a significant number of allies to public sector positions (Ingraham 2005). The continuation of patronage appointments was justified on the basis of a democratic ideal: ensuring that the electorate's policy choices would be protected against an entrenched and unresponsive bureaucracy (Peters 2010, p. 187).

This level of patronage means presidents have been pressured to make dubious appointments where the person was spectacularly unqualified for the job. The White House tends to place unqualified people in agencies that were perceived to be less strategically important such as the Federal Emergency Management Agency, considered to be a backwater agency at the time (Horton and Lewis 2010). However, this backfired with the appointment of Michael Brown as Director of the Federal Emergency Management Agency. Brown, who previously worked in a private law practice and for the International Arabian Horse Association, botched the response to Hurricane Katrina. He was ultimately forced to resign from his position. Other appointees have had a conflict of interest with their previous employment. For example, a former lobbyist for a pharmaceutical firm was appointed as counsel for the Food and Drug Administration, a key regulator for the industry (Peters 2010, p. 191). This may undermine the public interest.

According to Guy Peters, those appointed under the spoils system are less qualified than professional bureaucrats. Being mainly interested in their political careers, they meddle in the affairs of government without having the necessary policy or managerial expertise. There is also a rapid change-over of managerial staff, which deprives the government of necessary stability. These issues have continually re-surfaced throughout American political history (Peters 2015, p. 795).

Thus, a major difference between the American and traditional Westminster systems is that, with the former, partisan political appointments are pervasive and incorporate the top layer of each department in the bureaucracy, where public servants find themselves at a ceiling for promotions within a department unless they take a political appointment (Heclo 1977, pp. 116–120, 133–134). In the need to balance the values of 'neutral competence' and 'responsive competence', the American system has placed greater emphasis on the responsive competence dimension for civil servants (Peters 2010, p. 187).

European cabinet *system*

Another main alternative to the Westminster advisory system is the long-standing *cabinet* system of nations such as France and Belgium. The *cabinet ministériel* system consists of a formal group of personal advisors attached to each Minister that comprise a mix of public servants and political advisors. The *cabinets* are interposed between the Minister and the civil service. The *cabinet* system is different across nations, with large ministerial *cabinets* that are staffed mostly by public servants in France, and smaller, more politicised *cabinets* in Belgium. This account will focus on the French *cabinet* system.

In France, some *cabinet* advisors are partisan or parliamentary collaborators from outside the administration but most (66 per cent) are high-level career civil servants on temporary secondment (Krynen 2015, p. 24), receding from the high-water mark of the 1960s and 1970s, where 90 per cent of *cabinet* members were civil servants (Searls 1978, p. 171). In contemporary times, civil servants dominate the senior levels, with almost 100 per cent of senior managerial staff in the French *cabinets* being civil servants (Krynen 2015, p. 84), creating a quasi-monopoly of the civil service in all aspects of government decision-making. The political structure in France has thus shifted from professionals in politics alone towards professionals in administration (Gaborit and Mounier 1987, p. 115).

By comparison, in Belgium about half of the *cabinet* members are from the public service (Göransson and Eraly 2015, p. 717). Perhaps due to this secondment process, it is not uncommon for senior civil servants to be known for their political affiliations (people talk about civil servants having 'colours', such as red for socialists). The appointments process in Belgium is also more politicised, with *cabinets* seeking to control recruitments, promotions and nominations, or to find jobs in the administration for collaborators in recognition of their work, sometimes with flagrant disregard for the requirements of the job.

The size of the French *cabinet* system is substantial. In 2016, under the Valls Government, there were 39 cabinets with a total number of 2,983 ministerial *cabinet* advisors (Republique Française 2017). There are almost as many ministerial *cabinet* staff as there are senior civil servants. For example, in 2015, there were about 600–650 advisors in the ministerial *cabinets*, compared to approximately 600 high-level bureaucrats in the civil service (130 directors, 17 managing directors, 452 heads of service or deputy directors) (Krynen 2015, p. 64).

The ministerial *cabinets* are 'politico-administrative' entities with limited formal legal status. In France, membership of the *cabinet* is not so much about political partisanship but is the result of competencies and complex networks. It allows senior civil servants to get a taste of power at the centre, without compromising or stigmatising themselves as political hacks. In this way, the *cabinet* system is a form of rational and reasoned politicisation of senior public servants, like a civilised spoils system. It also results in a technocratisation of public life (Krynen 2015, pp. 89–91). *Cabinet* members drawn from the civil service benefit from being plugged into the bureaucratic machine and are better able to manoeuvre than outsiders are. Although the *cabinet* dissolves when the Minister is dismissed, there is no wholesale US-style purge of staff, but rather a reshuffling of *cabinet* staff based on their known political allegiances. Staff with sympathy to the outgoing party will be transferred to 'less sensitive' areas, but remain in the senior civil service (Duggett and Desbouvries 2011). Thus, *cabinet* members involved in political matters can return to the civil service, blurring the divide between politics and administration.

Yet the story is a familiar one. Ministerial *cabinets* undertake similar functions to Westminster political advisors as they have roles encompassing public policy, media and coordination. *Cabinet* members supervise the activity of the ministry's central administration, intervene (sometimes decisively) in strategic choices and the development of public policy, participate in the drafting of bills, conceive of and implement the media plan, as well as engage in inter-ministerial coordination (Krynen 2015, pp. 24, 86–87). *Cabinet* members have the power to direct officials and speak on behalf of the Minister. In exercising their functions, *cabinets* wield significant influence, and can be even more influential than Ministers in certain spheres (Searls 1978, p. 168).

Similar issues also arise in the French *cabinet* system that are endemic to the Westminster one. The French *cabinet* advisors do not have the democratic legitimacy of elections, and they do not have open competition for employment, unlike the bureaucracy (Krynen 2015, p. 50). The system is also not immune to nepotism. For example, Claude Chirac was communications advisor to her father for 20 years (Krynen 2015, p. 83).

Clearly there is less emphasis in the European systems on the divide between politics and administration. The *cabinet* system creates a porous barrier between administrative ranks and the political centre: the 'flexible bridge that joins politics and administration' (Paul Morand, *La Nuit de Babylone*, quoted in De Lamothe 1965, p. 365). Thus, *cabinet* systems are different in terms of institutions (professional structures, decision-making processes), the social division of roles (between the political world and the administrative world), and the political values of the actors involved (Rouban 2007, p. 499).

To sum up, the American system involves politics permeating bureaucratic structures, creating a politicised bureaucracy without any essential structural change within the civil service. By contrast, the European model includes a new structure, the *cabinet*, composed of both non-partisan civil servants and partisan political advisors carrying out partisan functions. Thus, both the American and European models incorporate some form of politicisation of the bureaucracy, with the American system appointing partisans into the civil service, while the European system has civil servants undertaking partisan functions in the *cabinet*.

On the other hand, the Westminster solution is to interpose an additional structure, the ministerial office, between the Minister and bureaucracy. The ministerial office is staffed by partisan advisors, while the civil service remains impartial. Several jurisdictions, such as Australia, have removed the security of tenure for senior public servants, allowing partisan appointments to the top of the bureaucracy, which is a step towards the American system. The move towards increasing partisan support for Ministers reflects an emphasis towards enhancing the 'responsive competence' of civil servants.

Approach

This comparative study has three purposes. The first is to trace the rise of political advisors in each jurisdiction, and examine the different regulatory trajectories taken by each country and the consequences in terms of scandals and controversies. The second is to analyse the efficacy of legal and political regulation of political advisors in various countries, encompassing legislation, 'soft law' such as guidance and codes of conduct, parliamentary scrutiny, as well as monitoring by oversight bodies and the media. This will enable policy-makers to design and evaluate a range of regulatory options for political advisors. Finally, the book will consider how the traditional Westminster principle of ministerial responsibility can be realigned to the modern world. This includes developing an accountability framework for political advisors based on current political realities.

One question is why it is beneficial to adopt a comparative perspective in relation to political advisors, that is: what is the importance of Elsewhere? First of all, it is interesting to see how countries can start at the same point and diverge into completely separate paths and to examine why this happens. Also, Westminster jurisdictions have made major reforms to the regulation of political advisors in recent years – and these discussions inform us about how different legal and political systems view the role of political advisors, the relationship between advisors and Ministers and civil servants, as well as the power of advisors.

Outline

This book investigates the situation in various Westminster jurisdictions. Each chapter is written so that it can be read independently for those interested in specific countries by clearly delineating the jurisdictions in headings within each chapter. The comparative themes are discussed and analysed at the end of the chapters.

Political advisors have come to prominence in the last 30–50 years in the Westminster jurisdictions. Chapter two will look at the rising profile, numbers and entrenchment of the position of political advisors in the Westminster system. It explains the factors that led to the rise and increasing influence of these advisors, and examines their varied roles within the system of governance, from administration to policy and media management. The Westminster jurisdictions have shown a general increase in numbers of advisors, as well as a remarkable similarity in the roles of the advisors. Political advisors have also become very powerful and influential within the Westminster system, due to both internal factors such as the position of advisors within the system, and external factors such as the 24/7 news cycle.

Chapter three examines the interaction between political advisors and the civil service in the jurisdictions, which has at times been characterised by tension. Civil servants have been deeply destabilised by the 'new public management' movement and have complained that political advisors intrude into bureaucratic advice. As the power and significance of political advisors has increased, there has been a corresponding decline in the influence and job security of the senior civil service in Westminster jurisdictions.

The integration of political advisors within the traditional Westminster model has not been entirely smooth sailing. Chapter four canvasses the various scandals and controversies involving advisors that have plagued each jurisdiction. It identifies and categorises the common trends across jurisdictions. I argue that a major reason for these scandals erupting is based on issues that arise from the media/politics and faction/opposition interfaces.

Chapter five examines the legal and political regulation of political advisors in each jurisdiction. Canada and the United Kingdom have proved to be the jurisdictions with the greatest regulatory intensity. Although there are fewer special advisors in the United Kingdom compared to other jurisdictions, there is significant public scrutiny of their actions in terms of parliamentary committees and media commentary. Canada has the largest number of advisors compared to other jurisdictions. Large-scale scandals have led to the implementation of a sophisticated regulatory regime of legislation and codes of conduct overseen by independent commissioners.

New Zealand has recently bolstered its regulatory framework by introducing a code of conduct for political advisors to supplement the previously sparse regulation primarily based on contracts of employment. Despite the prior minimal regulation, advisors in New Zealand have largely avoided the major controversies that have plagued other jurisdictions. Compared to the other jurisdictions, Australia has the lowest level of regulation, which has led to significant controversies and accountability failures linked to the refusal of advisors to appear before parliamentary committees.

This discussion is integrated in chapter six, where common themes are further developed and analysed. This chapter challenges the traditional Westminster precepts of individual ministerial responsibility and how these relate to the accountability of advisors. It shows that parliamentary accountability has been deeply unsatisfactory in holding political advisors to account due to strong party politics. As vertical accountability through Parliament has proven deficient, the chapter argues that horizontal accountability mechanisms, such as independent statutory officers and the media, are the key to holding advisors to account.

Chapter seven concludes the book and provides recommendations for reform, including reform of legislation and codes of conduct, enhanced parliamentary accountability for both Ministers and their advisors, the integration of political advisors into horizontal accountability mechanisms and improved managerial accountability of Ministers and chiefs of staff for the actions of political advisors. The focus of this book is thus at once exploratory and normative. Utilising a comparative approach, this book explores the rise of political advisors through a broad-scale analysis of the evolution of the roles, influence, regulation and accountability of political advisors across the Westminster jurisdictions. It also provides concrete proposals for reforms of the legal and political framework for political advisors within the Westminster system towards achieving a stronger and more robust system of governance that aligns with contemporary political realities.

References

Books and journal articles

Aberbach, J D, and Rockman, B A, 1994, 'Civil Servants and Policymakers: Neutral or Responsive Competence?', *Governance*, vol. 7(4), pp. 461–469.

Aucoin, P, 2012, 'New Political Governance in Westminster Systems: Impartial Public Administration and Management Performance at Risk', *Governance*, vol. 25(2), pp. 177–199.

Bourn, J M, 1986, *Patronage and Society in Nineteenth Century England*, Edward Arnold, Baltimore, MD.

Cohen, D, 1996, *Amateur Government: When Political Appointees Manage The Federal Bureaucracy*, CPM Working Paper 96–1, The Brookings Institution, Washington.

Committee on Standards in Public Life, 2003, *Defining the Boundaries within the Executive: Ministers, Special Advisers and the Permanent Civil Service*, Ninth Report.

Craft, J, 2016, *Backrooms and Beyond: Partisan Advisers and the Politics of Policy Work in Canada*, University of Toronto Press, Toronto.

Craft, J, and Howlett, M, 2012, 'Policy Formulation, Governance Shifts and Policy Influence: Location and Content in Policy Advisory Systems', *Journal of Public Policy*, vol. 32(2), pp. 79–98.

De Lamothe, A, 1965, 'Ministerial cabinets in France', *Public Administration*, vol. 43(4), pp. 365–381.

Downs, A, 1967, *Inside Bureaucracy*, Little Brown, Boston, MA.

Duggett, M, and Desbouvries, M, 2011, 'The Civil Service in France: Contested Complacency?' in A Massey (ed), *International Handbook on Civil Service Systems*, Edward Elgar, Cheltenham, UK, pp. 347–346.

Edwards, G C, 2001, *Why Not the Best? The Loyalty–Competence Trade-off in Presidential Appointments*, Brookings Institution, Washington, DC.

Fukuyama, F, 2014, *Political Order and Political Decay: From the Industrial Revolution to the Globalization of Democracy*, Farrar, Straus and Giroux, New York.

Gaborit, P, and Mounier, J-P, 1987, 'France' in W Plowden (ed), *Advising the Rulers*, Basil Blackwell, Oxford, pp. 92–117.

Gely, R & Chandler, D, 2000, 'Restricting Public Employees' Political Activities: Good Government or Partisan Politics?', *Houston Law Review*, vol. 37, pp. 775–822.

Göransson, M and Eraly, A, 2015, 'Les cabinets ministériels en Belgique' in J Eymeri-Douzans, X Bioy, and S Mouton (eds), *Le règne des entourages: Cabinets et conseillers de l'exécutif*, Presses de Sciences Po, Paris, pp. 703–720.

Halligan, J, 1995, 'Policy Advice and the Public Sector' in B G Peters, and D T Savoie (eds), *Governance in a Changing Environment*, McGill-Queen's University Press, Montreal, pp. 138–172.

Heclo, H, 1977, *A Government of Strangers: Executive Politics in Washington*, Brookings Institution, Washington, DC.

Hennessy, P, 1989, *Whitehall*, Fontana, London.

Horton, G, and Lewis, D E, 2010, 'Turkey Farms and Dead Pools: Competence and Connections in Obama Administration Appointments', Paper prepared for 2010 meeting of Midwest Political Science Association, Chicago, IL, April 22–25.

Ingraham, P W, 2005, *Foundations of Merit*, Johns Hopkins University Press, Baltimore, MD.

Kellner, P, and Lord Crowther-Hunt, 1980, *The Civil Servants: An Inquiry into Britain's Ruling Class*, MacDonald General Books, London.

Krynen, J, 2015, 'Le conseil du roi, siège de la prudence royale' in J Eymeri-Douzans, X Bioy, and S Mouton, (eds) *Le règne des entourages: Cabinets et conseillers de l'exécutif*, Presses de Sciences Po, Paris, pp. 113–140.

Niskanen, W, 1971, *Bureaucracy and Representative Government*, Aldine-Atherton, Chicago.

Northcote, S H, and Trevelyan, C E, 1854, *Report on the Organisation of the Permanent Civil Service*, House of Commons. Available online: www.civilservant.org.uk/northcotetrevelyan.pdf.

Page, E C, 1992, *Political Authority and Bureaucratic Power: A Comparative Analysis*, 2nd edn, Harvester Wheatsheaf, Hertfordshire.

Peters, G, 2010, 'The United States', in C Eichbaum and R Shaw (eds), *Partisan appointees and public servants*, Edward Elgar Publishing, Cheltenham, pp. 180–197.

Peters, G, 2015, 'Les hommes du président', in J Eymeri-Douzans, X Bioy, and S Mouton, (eds), *Le règne des entourages: Cabinets et conseillers de l'exécutif*, Presses de Sciences Po, Paris, pp. 787–798.

Republique Française, 2017, *Personnels Affectés Dans Les Cabinets Ministériels*.

Rhodes, RAW, Wanna, J and Weller, P, 2009, *Comparing Westminster*, Oxford University Press, Oxford.

Rhodes, RAW, and Weller, P, 2005, 'Westminster Transplanted and Westminster Implanted: Exploring Political Change', in P Weller, J Wanna, and H Patapan (eds), *Westminster Legacies*, UNSW Press, Sydney, pp. 1–12.

Rouban, L, 2007, 'Public Management and Politics: Senior Bureaucrats in France', *Public Administration*, vol. 85(2), pp. 473–501.

Rourke, Francis E, 1992, 'Responsiveness and Neutral Competence in American Bureaucracy, *Public Administration Review*, vol. 52, pp. 539–546.

Searls, E, 1978, 'The fragmented French executive: ministerial cabinets in the Fifth Republic', *West European Politics*, vol. 1(2), pp. 161–176.

Schroth, P W, 2006, 'Corruption and Accountability of the Civil Service in the United States', *The American Journal of Comparative Law*, vol. 54, Fall, pp. 553–579.

Schultz, D A and Maranto, R, 1998, *The Politics of Civil Service Reform*, Peter Lang Publishing, New York.

Sullivan, R E, 2009, *Macaulay: The Tragedy of Power*, Harvard University Press, Cambridge, MA.

Weber, M, 1972, *Wirtschaft und Gesellschaft*, 5th edn, JCB Mohr, Tubingen.

Wilson, W T, 1887, 'The Study of Administration', *Political Science Quarterly*, vol. 2(2), pp. 197–222.

Legislation, codes, case law, government and parliamentary reports

United States, Civil Service Reform Act 1978.

United States, Pendleton Act 1883.

2 Genesis and rise

The constitutional systems of Westminster jurisdictions are set up envisioning a dualistic relationship between Ministers and civil servants. Political advisors have gradually crept on to the scene over the years and are a relatively new player within the executive. This chapter traces the rise of political advisors in the liberal democratic Westminster jurisdictions of the United Kingdom, Canada, Australia and New Zealand, from their genesis to the current period. It examines the changes in the numbers and roles of these advisors over time. As their numbers have increased and they have taken on increasingly extensive and diverse roles, political advisors have gradually become institutionalised and entrenched in the governmental system and are now an indispensable part of the executive.

United Kingdom

Before the 1960s, there was no doubt that the British civil service was the main advisory system for Ministers. Appointments of advisors outside the civil service tended to be on an ad hoc, rather than systematic, basis. The foundations of a neutral and impartial civil service recruited and promoted on merit, based on the Northcote–Trevelyan Report, was seen to be the 'ideal' model of public administration. There was a general complacency about the British civil service tradition; indeed in 1947 the Fabian Society claimed that the British civil service was 'probably the best … in the world' (Fabian Society 1947, p. 5).

The first emergence of advisors outside the civil service happened in periods of war, where the exigencies of war necessitated a broader advisory system to Ministers beyond that of the civil service. In the First World War, Prime Minister David Lloyd George (1916–1922) introduced a Prime Ministerial Secretariat of about five temporary advisors, dubbed the 'Garden Suburb' as they were located in huts behind Downing Street (Blick 2004, p. 36). These staffers were responsible for advisory work in allocated policy areas, speech-writing, coordination between departments and the modern-day spin-doctoring or leaking information to the press.

During the Second World War, the large-scale British response to the war necessitated a range of expert, specialist advisors outside the civil service.

A Central Register was specifically established to provide thousands of temporary staff to Whitehall departments (Milward 1980, p. 102). Then Prime Minister Winston Churchill (1940–1945, 1951–1955), who replaced Neville Chamberlain, distrusted the Treasury Department as its Permanent Secretary was associated with Chamberlain's appeasement of Nazism. Rather than rely on the Treasury for coordination and advice, Churchill established a Ministerial Cabinet body headed by the Lord President of the Council, staffed by a maximum of 12 temporary advisors from the Economic Section of the War Cabinet, as well as a Prime Minister's Statistical Section of six economists (Churchill 1948, p. 368; Blick 2004, p. 39). The new advisory system was deliberately set up separately to the civil service to provide independent advice. Several well-respected academics such as the famous economist John Maynard Keynes were also appointed to assist the Treasury Department in both world wars. After the wars, these groups were disbanded and, by and large, the temporary advisors returned to their previous occupations.

As the British Empire declined and its international influence waned in the 1950s, there was a growing disenchantment with 'the establishment', including the civil service (Blick 2004, pp. 47–9). Significant groups such as the Fabian Society changed their previously sanguine tune and began campaigning for civil service reform. The civil service was seen to be too powerful and insularly dominated by privileged graduates from the Universities of Oxford or Cambridge, with an excessive focus on generalist rather than specialist skills. Parliamentarian Thomas Balogh criticised the typical senior official as being a 'smooth, extrovert conformist with good connexions and no knowledge of the modern problems, or of up-to-date techniques of getting that information' (Balogh 1959, p. 110). The Fabian Society recommended political appointments of two types of temporary advisors: experts to help implement particular policies, and personal aides to provide general help to Ministers. They favoured a model akin to the European *cabinet*, where Ministers are able to appoint three or four assistants in their private offices, and rejected the American model as promoting excessive patronage (Fabian Society 1964, pp. 39–40).

The cries for reform fell on particularly receptive ears with the new Labour Prime Minister Harold Wilson (1964–1970). Wilson himself had been a temporary advisor in the War Cabinet Secretariat and saw appeal in such arrangements. Wilson expressed concern about the 'amateurism of the central direction of Government' (Blick 2004, p. 87). He established the Fulton inquiry into the civil service, which supported the appointment of external experts and recommended the introduction of departmental planning units comprising both civil servants and outsiders (United Kingdom, Committee on the Civil Service, 1968, pp. 104–6).

Wilson's appetite for change, alongside broader Labour governmental concerns about the ability of the civil service to adapt after 13 years of serving a Conservative government, sparked the special advisor as we know it today. Wilson announced that he wished to implement the Fulton Committee's recommendations, calling his initiative the 'Political Advisors Experiment'.

Although Wilson rejected the European *cabinet* model, when he took power in 1964 he appointed five special advisors to the Cabinet Office and Treasury, with three appointed at a senior level (Blick 2004, pp. 62–122). Most of the advisors recruited between 1964 and 1970 were academic economists. They were experts, rather than political apparatchiks, although a few did play a role in media management. There was some friction with the permanent civil service, with resistance to special advisors being given access to top-secret departmental papers. Although the special advisors failed to achieve some of their objectives, they 'comprised a substantial, radical force within government' (Blick 2004, p. 122).

Special advisors faced a decline in influence under the subsequent Heath government (1970–1974). Heath's biographer stated that 'as a group they quickly sank without trace' as they were 'too few and too isolated' and they were mainly Conservative apparatchiks (Blick 2004, p. 124). Still, in this period some public administration reforms sought to strengthen coordinative capacity at the centre. A Central Policy Review Staff (CPRS) was introduced in 1971. The CPRS was tasked with reviewing the country's economic performance, undertaking studies of major long-term issues beyond departmental boundaries, and providing collective briefs to Cabinet or personal briefs to the Prime Minister. After some resistance amongst Ministers, the remit of the CPRS was broadened to advising Cabinet as a whole, not just the Prime Minister. Further, following pressure from the civil service and the difficulty of finding a suitable appointee, the CPRS was headed by a permanent civil servant, rather than a partisan appointee. The CPRS was generally a non-partisan body that consisted of a 50:50 ratio of civil servants versus prestigious outsiders such as academics and business people, but there were certain staffers who were active Conservatives (Blick 2004, p. 136). Despite the existence of the CPRS, the civil service was very influential in this period. Heath was particularly reliant on William Armstrong, the head of the Home Civil Service, to the extent that Armstrong was informally called the 'Deputy Prime Minister' (UK, House of Commons, 1964). In short, special advisors in the Heath government (1970–74) were less influential, and were eclipsed by the civil service.

The position of special advisors was institutionalised into the British governmental system in the second term of the Wilson government in the 1970s. Wilson considered political advisors to be necessary due to ministerial overload and thought that the educational background of senior civil servants was too narrow and that their privileged status meant that they 'can become isolated from changes to the mood and structure of society' (Wilson 1976, p. 99). Wilson described special advisors as 'an extra pair of hands, ears and eyes and a mind more politically committed and politically aware than would be available to a Minister from the political neutrals in the established Civil Service' (Wilson 1976, p. 99). In his paper, Wilson set out the role of special advisors:

- acting as a 'sieve', examining papers and drawing attention to problems and difficulties, particularly political issues;

- a 'deviller' function of checking facts and findings outside Whitehall, spotting obstacles and ensuring that sensitive political points were dealt with appropriately, and chasing up ministerial wishes;
- preparing 'think pieces' engaging in medium and long-term planning;
- participating in policy planning in departments through departmental committees and contributing ideas that may originate 'from outside the Government machine, and perhaps contrary to long-established departmental views';
- liaising with the party and interest groups; and
- speech-writing and research work. (Wilson 1976, p. 99)

Accordingly, Wilson established a Policy Unit: a group of about 30 expert advisors that advised the Prime Minister directly and were politically committed to the government. The Policy Unit scrutinised departmental policies from a political angle and played a role in governmental coordination. This Unit aimed to extend the range of policy options available to the Prime Minister towards achieving the government's political goals. The entrenchment of special advisors was not just limited to the centre of government. Special advisors also infiltrated every department by 1974, as all Ministers were allowed to appoint up to two special advisors with Prime Ministerial approval (Darlington 1978). In addition, a new category of special advisors was introduced: political aides, as opposed to expert appointments. These purely political appointments were of 'young people with no administrative experience or academic expertise' (Bishop 1974). Parliamentarians and civil servants were suspicious of this new breed of advisor. Parliamentarian Iain Sproat stated that it was 'totally repugnant that special advisors on political matters should be paid out of taxpayers' money' (UK, House of Commons 1976, cols 887–8), while then Minister Barbara Castle explained that 'the idea of bringing party activists into the inner citadel of ministerial power was totally alien' (Castle 1993, pp. 460–1).

Out of 34 special advisors appointed in 1974, 19 were drawn from academia (Blick 2004, p. 160). Since 1975, when public money was made available to parliamentarians and Opposition spokespersons, special advisors have tended to have experience of working for a political party or as a parliamentary research assistant (Fawcett and Gay 2010, p. 34). As their numbers grew, so did their influence. Wilson acknowledged that the proliferation of special advisors was 'of considerable significance and Political Advisors now play a definite role in our affairs' (Wilson 1976, p. 99). The Policy Unit was also seen to have an extensive influence, particularly in the areas of health and social administration, as well as economic and financial policy (Pimlott 1993, pp. 620–1).

The Thatcher government (1979–1990) placed a lesser emphasis on special advisors and reduced their numbers. Thatcher showed a distinct preference for expert advisors, compared to political aides:

> I do not like political advisers as such and have discouraged them. Nevertheless, some Cabinet ministers feel they would like a personal assistant who they know and who can help them tackling that side of their work which is partly government and partly party political ... Professional Advisers, I welcome these.
>
> (quoted in Yong and Hazell 2014, p. 62)

Nevertheless, Thatcher's Chief Press Secretary Bernard Ingham was well-known and was notorious for regularly using 'off the record' Downing Street lobby meetings to brief against other Cabinet Ministers. Structurally, Thatcher introduced the position of Chief of Staff and abolished the Heath government's CPRS in 1983, but retained the Policy Unit and had a number of additional external aides directly attached to her (Blick 2004, p. 186). The number of political advisors declined under Thatcher, although the number of staff in the Policy Unit grew during her Prime Ministership (Yong and Hazell 2014, pp. 23–24).

Under both Thatcher and John Major (1990–1997), advisors were mainly focused on policy issues, with media communications being a secondary aspect of their role (Yong and Hazell 2014, p. 115). A 1991 Order in Council stated that special advisors are appointed 'only for the purpose of providing advice', and were not to direct officials. By this stage, all Conservative Ministers had one or two special advisors (Yong and Hazell 2014, p. 24).

The second resurgence of special advisors occurred under Tony Blair (1997–2007). After 18 years in Opposition, Labour Ministers had a profound distrust of the civil service. The general attitude was that 'senior civil servants were part of the establishment and therefore not to be trusted' and had a 'Thatcherite bias' against the government (Barber 2007, p. 45; Richards 2007, pp. 148–54). Labour also questioned the competence of the civil service. Former special advisor, Lord Lipsey, stated:

> When the Labour Government got in ... things did not rub down quite as well as they might have done, and you will still get a lot of senior Ministers grumbling about their civil servants not being up to it.
>
> (UK, Committee on Standards in Public Life 2003, p. 33)

Under the new Labour government, the numbers of special advisors swelled from 38 to 84. The centre was strengthened, with the Prime Minister's Office staff increasing from 8 to 28 (Fawcett and Gay 2010, p. 32–3). Blair defended the increase in numbers, stating that in the United States 'there were 3,500 or even 4,000 political appointments; we have 80 special advisors for the whole of government. There are 3,500 senior civil servants; there are 80 special advisors' (UK, Liaison Committee 2002). Blair also lamented the inflexibility and inaction of the civil service: 'You try getting change in the public sector and public services, I bear the scars on my back after two years in Government' (quoted in Seldon 2005, p. 423).

It is in the Blair period that special advisors were increasingly formalised in the system. For the first time in 1997, there was a *Model Contract for Special Advisers*, setting out the roles of special advisors, agreed upon by both major parties. The roles were based on Harold Wilson's paper in 1976, with significant additions being encouraging presentations by the party, briefing party MPs and officials on government policy and adding party-political content to material prepared by civil servants for inclusion in speeches. As a change from the Wilson era where advisors only provided political advice, Blair's advisors were increasingly involved in policy formation. The differentiation between the political advisor and expert advisor was dropped, as many advisors performed mixed roles.

The position of Chief of Staff was created in the Prime Minister's Office to coordinate operations between the political advisors and civil service and Jonathan Powell was appointed to the position. Powell described the role as:

> [T]o bring together the different parts of Downing Street; to bring together the foreign and domestic, the political and the Civil Service, the press and the policy bits of Number 10 [the Prime Minister's Office]. Our analysis was that, under previous Number 10s, there had been a problem of not having anyone underneath the Prime Minister who could bring together all the different parts, who could coordinate it ... It is a bit of a jack of all trades and a master of none. There is a slight problem with it, but it is a useful coordinating function.
>
> (Powell 2010b, p. 2)

This period also marked the advent of the media advisor, pejoratively called the 'spin doctor'. Although special advisors had taken an interest in public relations since 1964, the Blair government's approach was distinctive in its aggressive focus on selling positive stories to the press. Former BBC journalists were employed as advisors and the number of advisors dealing directly with the media increased (Jones 2002, pp. 72–74). In 2002, about half of the total number of advisors (approximately 40 staff) dealt with the media (UK, Public Administration Select Committee 2002).

Special advisors were initially prevented by a 1995 Order in Council from acting in an executive role. This was overturned when the Blair government introduced a controversial Order in Council in 1997 that gave special advisors the power to instruct civil servants. Alastair Campbell, Blair's Chief Press Secretary, and Jonathan Powell, Blair's Chief of Staff, were empowered to give directions to any civil servant (UK, Committee on Standards in Public Life 2002b). Both Campbell and Powell were widely considered to be the most powerful unelected officials in the country.

The new Order in Council was meant to put on a legal footing a practice that was already prevalent (House of Lords Select Committee on the Constitution 2010, p. 20). Sir Richard Wilson claimed that the change to the

Order in Council was 'in reality a technical change' since 'there has been a certain amount of management by Special Advisors going on in Number 10 under previous governments' (UK, Public Administration Select Committee 2002, Q424). Powell, Blair's Chief of Staff, likewise stated he did not think that the Order in Council made any difference as political appointees had been managing civil servants for decades (Powell 2010a, p. 21).

Alastair Campbell became a public figure who was incredibly powerful; dubbed 'Deputy Prime Minister' and the 'unofficial 23rd Cabinet Minister'. Campbell's role was divided into two categories: Prime Minister's official spokesman, where he gave on-the-record and non-attributable press briefings, in addition to playing a coordinating role; and, more significantly, exercising control over Ministers through centralised media management across departments. This media control was achieved through new institutional structures. In 1997, the *Ministerial Code* (UK, Cabinet Office 1997) required all major interviews and media appearances to be cleared with the Number 10 Private Office. In 1998, a Strategic Communications Unit was formed, located at Number 10, comprising about six staff with a mix of civil servants and special advisors. This body coordinated central media management of policy announcements. The Research and Information Unit was established in 1999 to rebut hostile press items. A Conservative Minister thought that Campbell's approach to media management undermined public confidence:

> The appointment of Alastair Campbell has done the reputation of the body politic no good whatsoever. Putting someone who is in effect a politician in that role is simply wrong. You suspect he is going to lie. I know that is an overstatement. But you can expect a civil servant to respect the truth and know where the boundaries are, whereas a party apparatchik will simply try and present everything to his party's short-term advantage.
> (quoted in Yong and Hazell 2014, p. 122)

In addition to paid advisors, Blair also had an unpaid strategic advisor, Lord Birt (former Director General of the BBC), who looked at criminality and long-run social trends (UK, House of Commons 2000). Birt provided private internal advice to the Prime Minister and other Cabinet Ministers. The government claimed that Birt's advice was exempt from public disclosure under the previous *Code of Practice on Access to Government Information*, on the basis that disclosure of the advice might harm the frankness and candour of internal discussion (UK, House of Commons 2002). There is a similar exemption under the current *Freedom of Information Act* (s 36(2)). It is easier to use this justification when an advisor is unpaid and not formally classified as a special advisor, as special advisors are subject to the investigation of the Information Commissioner (as discussed in chapter five).

Blair's Prime Minister's office was not the only one with powerful advisors. Then-Treasurer Gordon Brown had strong special advisors at Treasury, including Ed Balls, Charlie Whelan, Sue Nye and Ed Miliband. Balls and Whelan were:

> an operation that had as much interest in preserving and enhancing Brown's political power in the government and the party as worrying about the next spending round or the preparations for entering the euro. They weren't Treasury men, they were 'Gordon's men'.
>
> (Naughtie 2002, p. 247)

Balls' influence on economic policy was remarkable. He was 'reckoned by Whitehall insiders to be the most influential outsider in the Treasury since John Maynard Keynes' (Routledge 1998). Brown's right-hand woman, Shriti Vadera, was also enormously influential; known as 'Gordon Brown's representative on earth'. However, she was also dubbed 'Shriti the Shriek' for her notorious bullying behaviour that reduced junior members of staff to tears (Yong and Hazell 2014, p. 177).

Hence special advisors were ascendant in the Blair era and their positions were institutionalised into the system. They had significant power and influence. Senior advisors, particularly media advisors, were often more powerful than many Ministers and MPs. Nevertheless, there were concerns about the lower expertise of these increasingly large number of advisors compared to their expert predecessors in the Wilson era (UK, Committee on Standards in Public Life 2003, p. 44).

When Gordon Brown became Prime Minister (2007–2010), he vowed to reduce the spending on special advisors and usher in a new spin-free era. Brown revoked the Order in Council giving special advisors executive power. He appointed a career civil servant, Tom Scholar, as Chief of Staff and Principal Private Secretary. Despite his initial pledge, the number of advisors grew steadily as Brown's premiership continued. Brown instituted a comprehensive regulatory framework for special advisors by introducing for the first time legislation to govern the appointment and conduct of special advisors: the *Constitutional Reform and Governance Act 2010*. The Act was significant as it enshrined in statute both the Code of Conduct for Special Advisors, first introduced in 2001, and the Order in Council that governed their role as temporary civil servants. The legislation imposed substantive restrictions on special advisors that are policed by an external body, the Civil Service Commission (discussed in chapter five).

David Cameron managed to cobble together a Conservative-Liberal Democrat coalition to form government from 2010–2015. Cameron's pledge to keep the number of advisors low was thwarted by the exigencies of Coalition government. Coalition governments have to be carefully managed, which requires coordination and political negotiation between the coalition parties to broker policy positions. As a result, the number of special advisors rose rapidly throughout Cameron's premiership to a peak of 100 in 2014. When Cameron was elected with a majority government in 2015, he fulfilled his promise to reduce the number of special advisors in government and culled the number of staff to 87.

Cameron started off with a small Policy Unit of only five special advisors answerable to both him and the Deputy Prime Minister. With so few advisors, Cameron was unable to oversee the policy activities across government, which led to a weak centre (Yong and Hazell 2014, p. 203). In 2011, a new Policy and Implementation Unit was set up, with five civil servants and six outsiders from the private sector, which Yong and Hazell considered to be too weak as the unit was composed of civil servants. The Policy Unit was reorganised again: this time it was headed by an MP, with eight political advisors and an advisory board of six MPs. After the resignation of Andy Coulson as the Prime Minister's Director of Communications following the *News of the World* phone hacking scandal (discussed in chapter four), Cameron introduced a policy of only employing civil servants as his strategy advisors.

In 2013, the Cameron government introduced a new but short-lived innovation in ministerial advisory systems where Ministers would be able to establish Extended Ministerial Offices (EMOs). An EMO is an extended private office staffed by civil servants, special advisors and external appointees. The external appointees are employed as civil servants for a maximum of five years and must comply with the Civil Service Code, but they do not have to be recruited through open competition. This can be seen as a step towards the European *cabinet* system, with a more fluid interface between the political and administrative elements of government. However, the ability to introduce EMOs was abolished in 2016 as the take up of EMOs was low. No EMOs were set up under the Coalition in 2013, while five were set up under the 2015 Conservative government led by David Cameron.

Like her predecessors, Prime Minister Theresa May (2016 to present) was interested in reducing the number of special advisors. She intended to limit each Cabinet minister to just two special advisors, and to remove instances of nepotism or incompetence. Advisor appointments were vetted by May's joint chiefs of staff, Fiona Hill and Nick Timothy. May also introduced a new a pay cap on the salaries of Conservative Ministers' special advisors of £72,000 a year, unless she authorised otherwise. The cap did not apply to Prime Ministerial staff. Some of May's former Ministers complained that she relied on her advisors more than her colleagues in government (Hardman 2016). May's former director of communications was scathing of May's chiefs of staff:

> The chiefs of staff were great street fighters but poor political leaders. Great leaders lead by bringing people with them, not alienating them before having even digested breakfast. What I could never work out was whether Mrs May condoned their behaviour and turned a blind eye or didn't understand how destructive they both were. For all the love of a

> hierarchy, the chiefs treated Cabinet members exactly the same – rude, abusive, childish behaviour. For two people who have never achieved elected office, I was staggered at the disrespect they showed on a daily basis.
>
> (Perrior 2017)

The joint chiefs of staff were sacked following May's poor performance in the 2017 UK General Election, where she lost majority government despite strong polls predicting a resounding Conservative victory.

A contemporary statement of the roles of special advisors is set out in the *Code of Conduct for Special Advisers* (2016), stating that special advisors may:

- assist on any aspect of departmental business, and give advice (including expert advice as a specialist in a particular field);
- undertake long-term policy thinking and contribute to policy planning within the department;
- write speeches and undertake related research, including adding party political content to material prepared by permanent civil servants;
- liaise with the party, and brief party representatives and parliamentarians on issues of government policy;
- represent the views of their Minister to the media (including a party viewpoint), where they have been authorised by the Minister to do so; and
- liaise with outside interest groups (including those with a political allegiance).

Thus, the main roles of advisors are providing policy advice, liaising with various stakeholders and media functions.

As seen in Figure 2.1, in general, the number of political advisors in the UK has increased over the ten years to 2015, with a steep increase in the Cameron coalition-government period, due to the difficulties in coordinating a minority government. In 2015, there was a slight dip, reflecting Cameron's newly elected majority government's pledge to reduce spending on special advisors. Publicly available data shows the number of advisors increased by almost 32 per cent in the ten years from 2005 to 2015. This equates to an average of 3–5 advisors per portfolio, although these are concentrated in the Prime Minister's and Deputy Prime Minister's offices. Despite the increase in numbers, the UK has the lowest number of political advisors compared to the other Westminster jurisdictions.

Although the number of special advisors is low in the United Kingdom, those who are close to the centre of power in the Prime Minister's Office or the Treasury are able to influence the Minister to make interventions that pivot the whole system (Yong and Hazell 2014, p. 98). Special advisors who had the confidence of their Minister were able to influence priorities, as well as policy direction, implementation and presentation. A former permanent secretary stated:

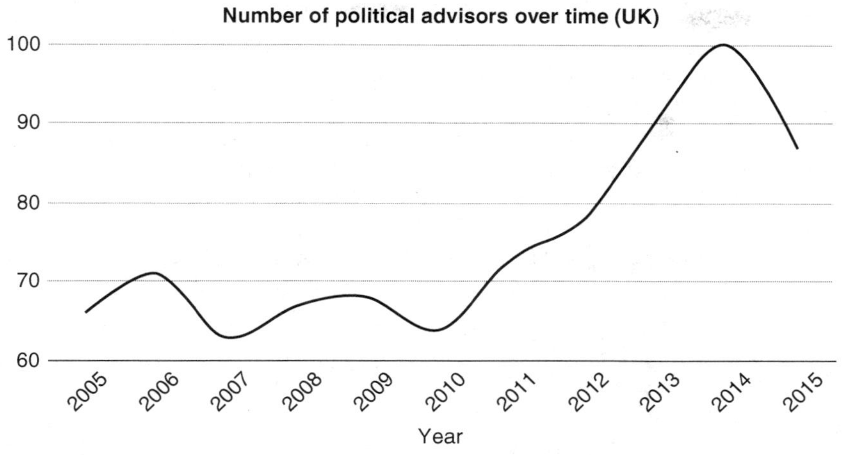

Figure 2.1 Number of political advisors in the United Kingdom from 2005–2015

Note: Where the numbers of political advisors are not publicly available, these figures have been obtained through Freedom of Information requests in the various jurisdictions. The figures calculated for the graphs are limited to advisors to Ministers/assistant ministers and parliamentary secretaries, and exclude non-ministerial roles such as whips and leaders of the House. The political staff figures also exclude non-advisory staff where possible, such as administrative staff, support staff and drivers.

> I think that often good special advisors were more influential and powerful than junior ministers in a department. This is primarily because they had been chosen by the Secretary of State and junior ministers had not been.
> (quoted in Yong and Hazell 2014, p. 76)

The British experience shows that there are three main catalysts for the resurgence of numbers of special advisors: times of crisis such as wars; when a new government takes over after a long drought of being outside government and distrusts the civil service (Wilson and Blair governments); and in periods of coalition or minority government, where additional brokering and coordination is needed between political parties (Cameron coalition government).

Canada

Before the 1950s, there was minimal staff in ministerial offices in Canada, comprising one private secretary, two stenographers and a secretary (Mallory 1967, pp. 27–28). Political staffers played a very limited role that did not intrude into the bureaucratic-ministerial relationship.

The rise of Canadian political advisors began during the Pearson government (1963–1968), which 'set the mould for contemporary political office' (Benoit 2006, p. 151). In this period, executive assistants (equivalent to the modern day chiefs of staff) were 'celebrities' and became a political force in their own right. Political staff often took a lead role in the government's most controversial and innovative policy initiatives, such as the unification of the armed forces. Liane Benoit (2006, p. 152) described them as a group of:

> highly partisan, passionate young men, infused with the rebellious spirit of the times, anxious to champion the most progressive of the social policies and … willing to do whatever it took to ensure the electoral success of the Liberal party.

These young staffers had immense power, including to act on behalf of the Minister. At the age of 27, Harold Gordon, as an executive assistant to a Minister, felt he 'ostensibly, had the authority to represent the Minister' (quoted in Benoit 2006, p. 151). In 1964, the Commission of Inquiry on the Rivard affair (discussed in chapter four) was told that it was 'customary practice' for a Minister's executive assistant to give instructions to departmental staff; in this case, the political staffer of the Minister of Justice was intervening in the handling of a case by a departmental prosecutor. The Commission condemned the practice, stating:

> … it is now high time that this practice cease … Counsel for the Federal Government may expect the Minister's instructions to be conveyed to him not by the Minister in person, but through the intermediary of a senior official in the Department concerned. Does it not logically follow that an intervention coming from an Executive Assistant may be interpreted as an intervention coming from the Minister himself, or, at the very least as an intervention taken with the Minister's full approval?
>
> (Canada, Dorion Inquiry Report 1964, pp. 95–96)

In this period, political staff were also institutionalised within the system, as the *Public Service Employment Act 1967* codified the 'special advisor' category of exempt staff, as a category distinct from the public service. The rise of these young and highly partisan advisors did, however, lead to controversy. Indeed, the Rivard investigation led to the imprisonment of a political advisor who offered a bribe to a government prosecutor to release a drug smuggler on bail, on the basis that the smuggler would donate large sums to the Liberal party. This scandal sparked a debate between two prominent commentators about the position of political advisors in the Canadian system: J R Mallory and Paul Tellier. Mallory disapproved of the presence of political advisors within the Westminster model of democracy:

> It is clearly undesirable that a considerable number of persons not a part of the civil service should be interposed between a Minister and his department. They lack the training and professional standards of the public service: it may even be the peculiar nature of the appointment means they escape the security screening which is an unpleasant accompaniment of most candidates for responsible posts in the public service. Not only do these functionaries wield great power because they control access to the Minister and can speak in his name, but they may wield this power with ludicrous ineptitude and in ways that are clearly tainted with political motives.
>
> (Mallory 1967, pp. 26–7)

Mallory thought that the Minister's private office had been 'inflated beyond recognition' and that political advisors should stay out of policy or program development, and their roles should be limited to media and coordinative functions, which he described as 'such mundane matters as supporting the Minister's public image by cultivating the goodwill of the press gallery' and as a gatekeeper 'to act as a buffer between a busy Minister and his constituents and political followers' (Mallory 1967, p. 25).

On the other hand, Paul Tellier thought that political staff served an important and necessary function and their policy capacity should be enhanced. Tellier thought that these positions should not be given to anyone over the age of 40, as these advisors could bring policy input that was young and innovative, compared to the seasoned and bureaucratic advice to Ministers (Tellier 1968, p. 423). This debate over the role of political staffers would rage on over the coming decades.

Pierre Trudeau (1968–1979, 1980–1984) set out to build a strong centre of government by bolstering the Prime Ministerial office capacity: 'One of the reasons why I wanted this job, when I was told that it might be there, is because I felt it very important to have a strong central government, build up the executive, build up the Prime Minister's Office' (quoted in Radwanski 1978, p. 146). As such, Trudeau formally institutionalised political advisors into the Prime Minister's Office in 1968 by moving to partisan appointment of the principal secretary, regional desks and a policy team (Schacter 1999, p. 6). His staff were 'largely bright, young people in their 20s and early 30s who … had no pre-eminent expertness in particular policy fields' (Tellier 1968, p. 341; Wearing 1977). Political staff took on increasingly specialised and differentiated roles in research, administration and departmental liaison (Lenoski 1977, p. 170). Previously an executive assistant would single-handedly conduct all duties.

Nevertheless, the bureaucracy successfully managed to reduce incentives to political advisors. Michael Pitfield, Clerk of the Privy Council (head of the Civil Service), persuaded Trudeau to stop raising the salaries of political staff, which were about $15,000 a year, roughly equivalent to that of a high school principal, to discourage them from staying too long (Benoit 2006, p. 159). Despite this, the number of political staff increased due to the growing sophistication of government and media demands, as well as the substantial increase in the total number of Ministers in Cabinet. With the exception of the Chrétien government (1993–2003), which differentiated between senior and junior Ministers, all Ministers sat in Cabinet. The low wages led to the appointment of a majority of 'recent and highly partisan graduates cutting their teeth in a world of *realpolitik*' (Benoit 2006, p. 159).

The victory of the Mulroney government (1984–1993) led to another resurgence of political staff. The Tories entered government with a deep distrust of a bureaucracy that had served the Liberal government for a long time, and were concerned about being 'in office but not in power' (Benoit 2006, p. 160). The new government set out to strengthen political staff with senior appointments that could stand up to the mandarins 'eye-to-eye and belly-button to belly-button' (Benoit 2006, p. 160). This decision was a deliberate move to check the power of the public service and countervail an 'ossified public service' (Benoit 2006, p. 161).

Structurally, Mulroney introduced the chief of staff position, describing the position as 'an official in the American style' (quoted in Savoie 2003, p. 124). The position was created to secure greater ministerial control over the bureaucracy. The chief of staff was to offer policy advice above that provided by the department, with a significant increase in pay; an act that was seen by civil servants as 'revolutionary' to the point of 'high treason' (Savoie 2003, p. 124). Despite the increase in pay and prestige, the Mulroney government failed to recruit high calibre staff. A deputy minister (equivalent to departmental head) stated:

> I think Mulroney adopted the Lévesque method. When he arrived, his team did not have confidence in 40 years of Liberal power and the public servants associated with this regime. When Lévesque outfitted himself with French-style ministers' offices in Quebec, he was looking for people who were sympathetic to their political agenda. The Parti Québécois were at first suspicious of the senior public servants they had inherited. The ministers' offices became a funnel, a security filter for the program. But the essential difference with the Parti Québécois was that the Conservatives weren't able to attract the brains that Lévesque had attracted.
>
> (quoted in Plasse 1994, p. 33)

Chiefs of staff were responsible for liaison between the Minister and their own department as well as other departments, the Prime Minister's Office, other Ministers' offices, the caucus, Parliament, the party, departmental client groups and the media (Plasse 1994, p. 37). There was also some semblance of inter-departmental coordination, as chiefs of staff met every 15 days to discuss major issues (Plasse 1994, p. 42). Thus, in this period, political staff interacted with a whole range of stakeholders across the political system, vertically with

Ministers and public servants, and horizontally with other ministerial offices. In addition, political advisors dealt with external stakeholders, such as the political party, parliamentarians and the media.

Micheline Plasse found that Canadian chiefs of staff in the Mulroney era had influence at three levels: first, with the department, through discussions with senior public servants as the Minister's main representative; second, with the Minister, through the advice they provide; and third, with the government as a whole, through the advice they give the Minister on major national issues (Plasse 1994, p. 71). For example, a former chief of staff stated:

> We can influence the minister almost all the time because we are the ones who have the last word with the minister. Often, when the minister goes to meetings, he or she will meet with us just before. We have short talks just before and the minister will especially consult the chief of staff if he or she isn't sure of the position to be adopted.
>
> (quoted in Plasse 1994, p. 70)

Thus, chiefs of staff influenced the Minister directly as the final port of call and the Minister's sounding board, and influenced departmental advice through their proximity to the Minister.

The Mulroney administration also solidified centralised policy functions by increasing the policy capacity of the Prime Minister's Office and creating the Deputy Prime Minister's Office (Craft 2016, pp. 51–52). The number of political staff increased significantly, with 40 Cabinet Ministers, and often 30–40 ministerial staff in each office supervised by a chief of staff (Larson 1999, p. 57). Nevertheless, in the Mulroney period, the policy contribution of political advisors was limited. They coordinated policy advice, but lacked the expertise to provide long-term strategic advice (Plasse 1994; Bakvis 2000, p. 79).

The Chrétien Liberal government (1993–2003) reduced the numbers of political staff in 1993 to counter the objections of the Reform Party that there were too many unelected officials with influence in Ottawa (Aucoin 2010, p. 70). Gradually, however, the numbers crept upwards again towards the end of Chrétien's term. Chrétien also abolished the position of chief of staff in all ministerial offices except for the PMO, and changed the title back to 'executive assistant'. This was, however, just a symbolic move as there was no change to the job or level of influence (Aucoin 2010, p. 72). The title of chief of staff was restored by Paul Martin (2003–2006).

Political advisors in the Chrétien (1993–2003) and Martin (2003–2006) periods were young and inexperienced, 'acting like little puppies going around chewing on everything and peeing on the carpet to identify their turf' (Benoit 2006, p. 162). These advisors were, nevertheless, greatly influential despite their lack of experience due to their proximity to the Minister. Benoit explained:

> ... it is the younger, often less experienced, political advisors who come to the process bearing the weight of ministerial authority and who, despite

> their often lesser qualifications, are in a position to exert greater influence by virtue of their proximity and access to the Minister. In other words, the ministerial aides are seen to wield a level of influence over policy that is inversely proportional to their qualifications and ability.
>
> (Benoit 2006, p. 187)

Senior advisors also acted on behalf of Ministers. Former Executive Assistant Fred Drummie stated that ‘any decision taken by the Chief of Staff is the same as a decision taken by the Minister. The Chief of Staff is the Minister’s *alter ego* and that must be understood’ (quoted in Benoit 2006, p. 194). This was exhibited in the Sgro scandal in 2004 (discussed in chapter four), where political advisors for the Immigration Minister acted on the Minister’s behalf, even signing significant documentation such as visa approvals (Canada, Office of the Ethics Commissioner 2005, p. 22). Once the Minister had approved the issue of a temporary residence permit, the Chief of Staff or another political staffer would sign the ministerial authorisation. In addition, political staffers operated independently of the Minister in meeting and making representations to various stakeholders. However, Minister Sgro’s staff showed poor judgment, which led their Minister to be embroiled in controversy and prompted her resignation.

The increasing roles and influence of political staffers culminated in the Sponsorship Scandal (discussed in chapter four), stemming from events that started in the Chrétien regime that later engulfed the Martin government. The Public Accounts Committee investigating this scandal found that political staffers could and often would exert a substantial degree of influence on the development and administration of public policy in Canada. Revelations of corruption from the Sponsorship Scandal led to the defeat of the Liberal government.

In the Harper period (2006–2015), Jonathan Craft found that policy advisors were intimately involved in all aspects of policy advice, from provision (termed ‘buffering’), to circulation (‘bridging’) across substantive (‘shaping’) and procedural (‘moving’) dimensions of the advice (Craft 2016, p. 20). In the Harper government, there was both strong centralisation through the Prime Minister’s Office, as well as significant coordination between ministerial offices. The Prime Minister’s advisors worked across the administrative-technical and partisan-political dimensions to expedite policy development or remove identified roadblocks through Cabinet or Cabinet committee processes (Craft 2016, p. 109).

The level of coordination across ministerial offices was also well-solidified in this period, with chiefs of staff from different ministerial offices consulting each other to move policies forward. The interactions between ministerial offices were intended to ‘signal-check’ public service advice. Significantly, the signal checking was seen to be necessary as there was a suggestion that the public service may mispresent advice to political advisors. A former partisan director of policy stated, ‘sometimes messages get, I wouldn't say intentionally changed, but misinterpreted' (Craft 2016, p. 162).

Political advisors also frequently met with stakeholders outside government and used such interactions to contest and validate departmental policy advice (Craft 2016, p. 166). A chief of staff stated:

> … Getting policy advice from the outside was just a regular, regular thing, and the departments were doing that too. Sometimes we'd meet independently with those guys, other times we'd meet together, but it was ongoing, every day, every week.
>
> (quoted in Craft 2016, p. 167)

Political advisors also played a role in gate-keeping sources of policy advice to the Minister, in the sense of 'triaging'. Advisors would 'sift and sort' priority items for the Minister based on established strategic priorities, but not to the extent of 'funnelling' or filtering unwelcome or politically unfeasible policy advice (Craft 2016, pp. 167–68).

The role specialisation of political advisors in Canada is much higher than other Westminster jurisdictions. A snapshot of the government directory for the 2015 Harper Prime Minister's Office shows the following units: appointments, communication, issues management, policy, principal secretary (correspondence, photography and speech writing), strategic communications, tour and scheduling, stakeholder relations and outreach, and deputy chief of staff. The Prime Minister's chief of staff is charged with the administration of political staff, conveying the Prime Minister's directives and helping advance the government's agenda in both Houses of Parliament, including caucus relations, parliamentary affairs and issues management (Canada, Office of the Conflict of Interest and Ethics Commissioner 2017, p. 14). David Emerson, former Minister, described a chief of staff's role:

> The chief is always the person who is the gatekeeper, filtering the advice you're getting. But I would say a good chief is not the person who sits there scratching their head, basically coming up with advice to give the minister. The chief is the person who is much more a conductor, so making sure the different points of view from the political advisors are sifted and sorted and weighted appropriately, and so on, and making sure that we're not getting cross-threaded with the public service, and so on. I see the chief of staff role as obviously a wise political counsel, but also as somebody who is very much managerial in the performance of their role.
>
> (quoted in Craft 2016, p. 169)

The principal secretary is a senior role, and is effectively the co-chief of staff and the key strategist who takes a macro perspective on the government's policy and political agenda. The communications group deals with the day-to-day media activities, while the tour and scheduling branch plans and coordinates the Prime Minister's travel and events. The stakeholders and outreach branch meets with special interest groups, including lobbyists, while the correspondence unit deals with inbound communications (Marland 2016, pp. 217–8).

As the first Prime Minister to experience the intensity of social media, in addition to the 24/7 news cycle of dedicated news networks scrutinising government action, Harper introduced two new categories of political staff: issues management and strategic communications. These are specific categories that do not exist in other Westminster jurisdictions. The Harper PMO had about eight issues management staff that coordinated daily with other ministerial offices. They identified potentially negative stories, developed responsive political messaging and then passed that messaging either to Ministers to use in Question Period or to communications staff to push out to the media. This is a reactive role that deals with 'fire-fighting' and hosing down scandals on the front page of the news. Staff in this area 'detect and correct' by developing rapid political strategies to deal with negative stories or events (Esselment and Wilson 2017). This role is a combination of communications, political management and coordination, rather than a policy role. According to the former PMO issues management director, William Stairs, issues management was 'very much a 100 per cent partisan tool to get the government's communications out and make sure everyone is singing from the same song sheet' (quoted in Esselment and Wilson 2017, p. 231). Although issues management staff began at the PMO level, this staffing structure was soon emulated by other ministerial offices, and was retained by the subsequent Trudeau government. Although Harper was the Prime Minister who introduced issues management as a discrete unit, it is worth noting that the fire-fighting function has existed in the Canadian Prime Minister's Office since the 1990s and early 2000s under different monikers, such as 'parliamentary affairs'.

The strategic communications staff, on the other hand, are more proactive and seek to identify strategies to highlight government accomplishments through long-term agenda planning, branding and positioning (Esselment and Wilson 2017). All government activities and key external events are mapped out day by day on a communications planning calendar that allows the PMO to micro-manage the government (Marland 2016, p. 295). The strategic communications function is thus strongly centralised, with the PMO staff deciding on the message of the day based on themes such as 'support for small business' or 'being tough on crime'. The political staff would then schedule the Finance Minister or Attorney-General to make an announcement and coordinate such that other Ministers and MPs discuss this issue, and the political staffers pick the locations of the announcements to maximise political impact. A former manager of the PMO calendar stated:

> I used to explain it as the job of an air traffic controller. You can't have two major 747s in the same airspace at the same time. I couldn't have Jim Flaherty giving an economic speech while John Baird was doing an

> environment speech in the same Toronto media market, for example. So you have to decide which one takes precedence there. That comes down to the brand, the messaging, what's the message of the day that we're trying to push.
>
> (quoted in Marland 2016, p. 300)

Thus, contemporary Canadian political advisors have varied tasks across the whole spectrum of policy advice and coordination, media management, as well as liaising with various stakeholders internal and external to government. The Canadian system is characterised by the highest level of functional specialisation, which can be attributed to the larger number of political staff in Canada compared to all other jurisdictions. The roles of issues management and communications have firmly taken root in Canada. There is a very high level of centralisation in the Prime Minister's Office, with the PMO scheduling and directing Ministers on how to announce issues and deal with controversies. This is part of an overall element of centralisation of power in the Canadian system of governance compared to other Westminster jurisdictions. Due to the significant concentration of power over the past four decades, the Canadian Prime Minister is the central lever of power in the political system, (Savoie 1999). Canadian Prime Ministers cannot be removed by caucus, unlike Australia and the UK. A long-serving deputy minister remarked:

> You have no idea what kind of power the prime minister holds over ministers. He has in his hands the minister's car, his chauffeur, his office, his job, his ego, and so on. I have been in the public service for nearly thirty years in the Privy Council Office and line departments, and I can tell you that the grovel count in the great majority of ministers has always been quite high and, if anything, it keeps getting higher as the years go by.
>
> (quoted in Savoie 2003, p. 195)

The influence of the Prime Minister extends to both political advisors and the bowels of the public service. The Prime Minister is responsible for appointing political staffers and senior public servants, leading to both partisan advisors and the bureaucracy to at times be more loyal to the Prime Minister than their own Minister. The Canadian Prime Ministerial control over appointing staff can create tensions and distrust between the Ministers and their own staff. A former deputy minister stated:

> If you are in a department where the minister mistrusts the chief of staff because the chief of staff was given the mandate to control the minister and was appointed by the Prime Minister's Office, the whole thing could be dangerous. I experienced this type of situation and had to defend a minister against the chief of staff.
>
> (quoted in Plasse 1994, p. 27)

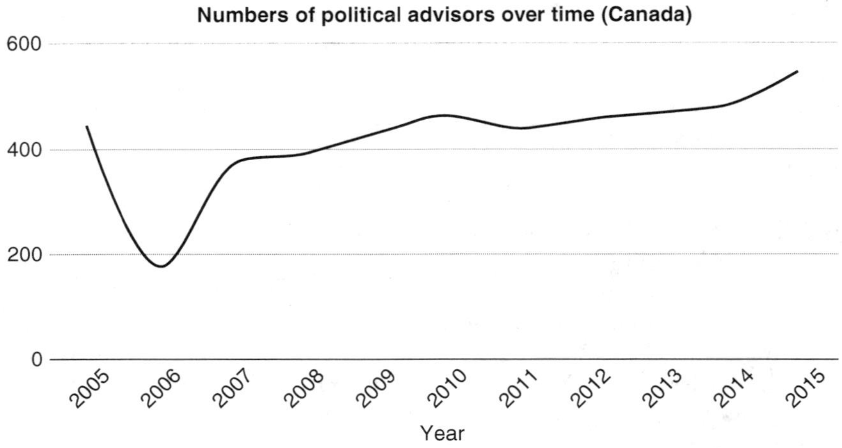

Figure 2.2 Number of political advisors in Canada from 2005–2015

The loyalty to the centre also applies to the senior bureaucracy. Deputy ministers (departmental heads) are appointed by the Prime Minister and may see their primary duty as being to the Prime Minister, rather than their own Minister. A deputy minister stated that where there is a potential conflict between a Minister and the Prime Minister, the deputy minister is bound to give primary allegiance to the Prime Minister (Osbaldeston 1989, p. 58). In fact, in some situations, the Prime Minister specifically installed strong deputy ministers 'to keep a new or inexperienced minister out of trouble' (Osbaldeston 1989, p. 59). This means that the bureaucracy may act against the interests of their Minister in favour of the Prime Minister. If a Minister 'goes rogue' against the Prime Minister's agenda, then the deputy minister will inform the Clerk of the Privy Council (equivalent to head of the Prime Minister's department) (Savoie 2003, p. 141). Nevertheless, it is rare for the Prime Minister to intervene in the day-to-day operations of a department (Bourgault 2006, pp. 280–282).

As can be seen in Figure 2.2, the number of political advisors in Canada has grown by 22 per cent over the ten years to 2015, from 447 in 2005 to 544 in 2015. At the beginning of the Harper government in 2006, there was a dip in the number of advisors; otherwise, there is a discernible upward trend. By contrast, the number of ministerial portfolios remained relatively stable at around 27, indicating that Ministers were relying on increasing numbers of political advisors.

In Canada, there is a two-tier system with Ministers of State providing support to Ministers. From 2005 to 2015, the number of Ministers of State has typically averaged around 14. As of June 2015, there was an average of 19 exempt staff per Minister, with an average of just over one staff member for each Minister of State. Documents provided to the author under the *Access to Information Act* reveal that, since 2012, some of these Ministers of State have been employing their own exempt staff: generally a chief of staff and director, with the possible addition of a press secretary or private secretary. The number of advisors in Canada far exceeds those in any other Westminster jurisdiction. Strikingly, the Prime Minister's Office has a far larger number of advisors than other Ministers, with about 80–100 advisors, showing a strong centralisation of power.

A recent 2016 court case about Senator Mike Duffy's parliamentary expenses (discussed in chapter four) exposed the extraordinary level of control that Harper's PMO staff wielded over Canadian Senators. Mr Justice Vaillancourt detailed how Nigel Wright, Harper's former Chief of Staff, directed a clearly compliant ('I am always ready to do exactly what is asked') Senator Stewart-Olsen to 'make this happen', that is, script the conclusion of an independent auditor's report (*R v Duffy* (2016) ONCJ 220, p. 238). The judge concluded that the Prime Minister's Chief of Staff was 'ordering senior members of the Senate around as if they were mere pawns on a chessboard', while those Senators were 'meekly acquiescing' to the Chief of Staff's orders and 'robotically marching forth to recite their provided scripted lines' (*R v Duffy* (2016) ONCJ 220, p. 246). Mr Justice Vaillancourt stated:

> If anyone was under the impression that this organization [the Prime Minister's office] was a benign group of bureaucrats taking care of the day to day tasks associated with the Prime Minister, they would be mistaken. The approximately one-hundred or so members of the PMO may be tasked to carry out the mundane matters of bureaucracy but the evidence in this trial shows that this group wields significant power in the corridors of Parliament Hill.
>
> (*R v Duffy* (2016) ONCJ 220, p. 222)

This shows the power of the Prime Minister's Office and the corresponding weakness of the Canadian Senate, whose unelected members acted on the direction of political advisors.

Australia

From federation in 1901 to the 1940s, there was close cooperation between politicians and public servants. The initial Secretaries of the Prime Minister's Department played the role of personal advisor to the Prime Ministers, rather than the traditional public service role (Walter 1986, pp. 76–110). After 1949, the close collaboration between politicians and public servants was reduced. Despite this, from 1949 to 1972, Ministers were largely content to rely on private secretaries from the public service departments. Appointments of ministerial advisors before 1972 were at relatively junior levels, with a private secretary of a middle level rank. Ministers tended to accept advice from their departments and rely on them to do work of a political nature.

In 1972, the Whitlam government (1972–1975) increased the number of ministerial advisors and permitted Ministers to appoint personal and partisan loyalists from outside the public service. This was attributed to the new Labor government's distrust of a public service with 23 years of serving under Liberal-Country governments. The public service was seen to be too inflexible and entrenched in its own ways to adapt to a strong Labor reform agenda.

The approach of appointing ministerial advisors external to the public service was a radical departure from the previous practice of utilising public servants as the main source of advice. Nevertheless, the roles of ministerial advisors during the Whitlam years were mainly administrative, with a lesser focus on advising the Minister on policy issues. This led the 1975 Royal Commission on Australian Government Administration to conclude that:

> [a]lthough the work of ministerial advisers varies considerably, most of it is concerned with the running of the office and liaison with departments; participation in the policy advising process has been essentially limited and restricted.
>
> (Australia, Royal Commission on Australian Government Administration 1976, p. 104)

This trend was continued in the Fraser government (1975–1983), where ministerial advisors largely tended to adopt administrative and non-partisan roles, although Fraser himself boosted the number of policy advisors within the Prime Minister's Department (Maley 2010).

Under subsequent governments, the roles of ministerial advisors expanded greatly. For instance, it was clear that the ministerial advisors in the Hawke government (1983–1991) were 'more policy-oriented and politically engaged' than their predecessors (Walter 1984, pp. 203, 216). Their roles were multifarious, and included policy advice, liaison with the public service, troubleshooting, general office administration, personally assisting the Minister, dealing with the press, speech-writing, political party work and handling electorate matters.

In line with the increased role of ministerial advisors, the Hawke and Keating governments also introduced more formal mechanisms to consolidate and institutionalise the position of ministerial advisors. Significantly, the Hawke government (1983–1991) introduced a legislative framework governing the employment of ministerial advisors, the *Members of Parliament (Staff) Act 1984* (Cth). Initially ministerial advisors were employed under the *Public Service Act 1922* (Cth) either by secondment from the public service or as exempt staff. The *Members of Parliament (Staff) Act* has symbolic significance as it was the first legislative recognition of the position of ministerial advisors. It meant that ministerial advisors were normalised as part of the institution of government, rather than just being staff employed as an exception to normal public service processes. The Act also meant that ministerial advisors were recognised as being substantively different from public servants. The institutionalisation and legislative recognition of the position of ministerial advisors in the Hawke/Keating government were accompanied by a large (63 per cent) increase in the number of advisors (Maley 2000b).

In the Keating government (1991–1996), ministerial advisors became an important part of the machinery of government as 'policy powerhouses' in their own right. They largely performed similar functions to those of the Hawke government era, but with a greater emphasis on steering policy by engaging departments in policy, generating ideas for policy-making, developing policy proposals, and implementing policy (Maley 2002, p. 76). During Keating's tenure, the role of ministerial advisors extended to overseeing policy implementation by departments and brokering policy positions with other Ministers' offices (Dunn 1995, p. 518). Previously ministerial advisors were more inwardly focussed on their own Minister and department.

More significantly, ministerial advisors had the role of acting as extensions of the Minister and directing the department about their interpretation of what the Minister wanted, and providing feedback from the Minister. Public servants would also utilise ministerial advisors as a sounding board for the Minister's likely reaction to proposals. A Senate Committee in 1993 asserted that ministerial advisors played a vital role in representing the Minister's interests in appropriate forums (Australia, Senate Select Committee on matters arising from Pay Television Tendering Processes 1993, pp. 15–16). A former Clerk of the Senate put it more strongly, arguing that ministerial advisors 'act as de facto assistant ministers and participate in government activities as such' (Evans 2002, p. 4). Maria Maley referred to this as advisors becoming 'surrogates' and making minor decisions in the Minister's name (Maley 2002, p. 123). In the Keating government period, some ministerial advisors were given 'almost complete delegation to run their program areas' (Maley 2002, p. 101–3). Maley noted the complications of a ministerial advisor acting as a 'surrogate':

> Acting as the minister's surrogate could involve fine judgments about when to involve the minister and when the adviser could act alone. How far could the adviser go in interpreting the minister's position and taking decisions without reference to the minister? There was an element of risk involved in these judgements which could leave advisers feeling exposed, particularly if their ministers were so busy that they were rarely available to them.
>
> (Maley 2002, p. 128)

In contemporary times, the roles of ministerial advisors continue to be broad-ranging. As Tony Nutt, a powerful senior ministerial advisor, noted:

> A ministerial advisor deals with the press. A ministerial advisor handles the politics. A ministerial advisor talks to the union. All of that happens every day of the week, everywhere in Australia all the time. Including frankly, the odd bit of, you know, ancient Spanish practices and a bit of bastardry on the way through. That's all the nature of politics.
>
> (quoted in Campbell 2013)

In 2012, at the Australian State level, a recent account of the duties and functions of a senior ministerial advisor was provided by a former Victorian Premier's Chief of Staff in proceedings before an administrative tribunal (*Herald and Weekly Times Pty Limited v Office of the Premier* [2012] VCAT 967 [22]). The Chief of Staff's duties included:

- research, evaluation and preparation of memoranda on major public policy matters for the Premier;
- advice to the Premier on political, party management, parliamentary management and public policy issues;
- dealing with a range of stakeholders, both with and without the Premier, and both with and without public servants;
- assisting the Premier by attending to many issues on the Premier's behalf, based on his instructions, in the development of responses to issues, management of issues or conduct of affairs;
- interacting with public servants at a senior level, both with and without the Premier, often within the Premier's private office;
- interacting with public servants and stakeholders via meetings, correspondence and telephone calls;
- dealing with a range of external contacts, including parliamentary colleagues, unions, community, business and ethnic organisations;
- parliamentary duties including dealing with questions to and speeches for the Premier and handling interactions between the Premier and other Members of Parliament;
- as Chief of Staff generally supervising, managing and dealing with responses to the large volume of correspondence received by the Office of the Premier;
- dealing with the media, as required, including input into press releases; and
- dealing with the Cabinet Office as the Chief of Staff of the Premier's Office.

This is a staggeringly long list of responsibilities overseen by the Premier's Chief of Staff that includes a large range of matters across the media, policy, administration and parliamentary domains. It is also apparent that the Chief of Staff operated with a high level of autonomy, and was authorised to attend meetings with the department and external stakeholders without the presence of the Premier, as well as to deal with issues on the Premier's behalf. This is the case at the federal level as well.

In general, there are five main categories of Australian ministerial advisors in contemporary times:

- *administrative and support staff*, who organise the appointment and diary scheduling, travel and correspondence of Ministers;
- *advisers to the Minister*, who assist with the Minister's portfolio policy issues, liaise directly and regularly with the public servants, key stakeholders and lobbyists on the substance of the policies, and provide advice to the Minister on the political perspective of how a policy could be negotiated, packaged and 'sold';
- *political staff*, who manage the Minister's responsibilities as a Member of Parliament, including maintaining relations with the political party, back bench colleagues and others;
- *media staff*, who manage the control and dissemination of information to the mass media, including television, newspapers, radio and social media; and
- *departmental liaison officers* (DLOs), who facilitate liaison between the Minister and department or agency on policy or administrative issues. DLOs are on placement from the public service and remain departmental officers employed under the *Public Service Act 1999* (Cth), but act under the Minister's direction for the duration of the employment (Tiernan 2007, pp. 19–20).

In April 2016, at the federal level, there were 335 advisors supporting 29 Ministers and 11 parliamentary secretaries across 41 portfolios. This equates to an average of 12 advisors per Minister or just over 8 advisors per portfolio. Annual data released through the Senate Estimates process shows that the number of ministerial advisors has increased by over 18 per cent in the 10 years from 2005 to 2015. From Figure 2.3 (see p. 42), we can see there was a sharp drop in 2008, which may be attributable to a Labor Party commitment in Opposition. Notwithstanding the temporary drop, the numbers soon climbed again. Historically, numbers peaked around 350 and appear to be stabilising at similar levels in 2016.

The large number of ministerial advisors has meant that layers of hierarchy have emerged within ministerial offices. In 2015, there were 16 bands of appointment, with 9 categorised as senior staff appointments, including the categories of chief of staff, principal advisor, senior advisor and senior media advisor. Other bands included media advisor, advisor, assistant advisor, executive assistant/office manager and secretary/administrative assistant.

The increase in numbers and broadening of roles of ministerial advisors in Australia indicate their increasing influence in the executive government. Australian ministerial advisors are influential in the following

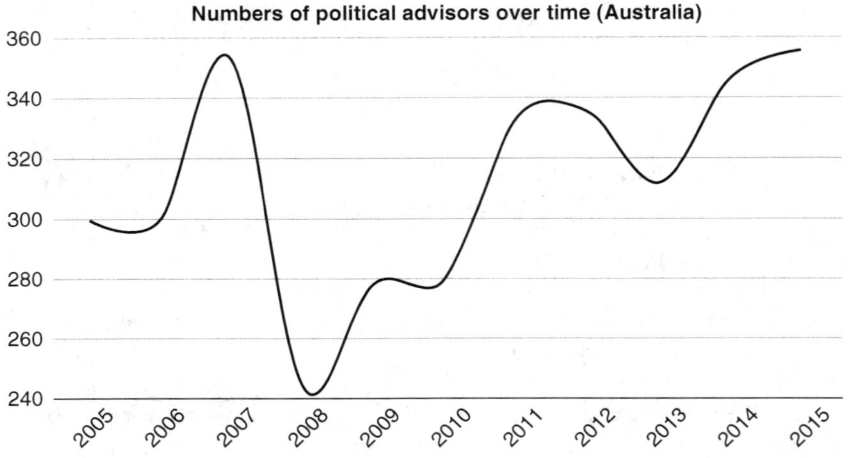

Figure 2.3 Number of political advisors in Australia from 2005–2015

ways: *functionally* in the roles they perform, *structurally* from the institutional arrangements in which they work and *implicitly* from the relationship they have with their Minister (Maley 2002, pp. 64, 106). For instance, some of the more recently developed roles – namely gate-keeping, filtering departmental advice, and brokering positions between departments – provide advisors with power and hierarchical superiority over the public service. Further, speaking on behalf of the Minister and filtering the advice that reaches the Minister effectively give them political power and allow them to influence the Minister's policy decisions.

Power in the Australian federal political system is centralised around the Prime Minister and a few senior Ministers, including the Deputy Prime Minister, Treasurer and Finance Minister. Ministerial advisors linked to these most senior Ministers have a lot of power (Rhodes and Tiernan 2014). At the State level, former Deputy Premier John Thwaites stated that the 'Prime Minister and [State] Premier are extraordinarily powerful, and they're supported by a media unit and a ministerial office that has significant power over all the Ministers and their offices' (quoted in Ng 2016, p. 28). Thwaites stated that:

> Often the ministerial advisors you find in the Prime Minister and Premier's office are as powerful or more powerful than some Ministers. The Head of the Media Unit, the Chief of Staff and maybe one or two advisors in the Prime Minister's and Premier's office are more powerful, have more influence on the decision-making in most cases than certainly junior Ministers and more than most Ministers.
>
> (quoted in Ng 2016, p. 29)

This was affirmed by former Treasurer Peter Costello, who asserted that senior ministerial advisors to very senior Ministers, such as the Prime Minister's Chief of Staff, have a lot of influence (quoted in Ng 2016, p. 29). Former Finance Minister Lindsay Tanner stated that ministerial advisors exercised strong influence at a day-to-day level that is derived from the Minister's authority (quoted in Ng 2016, p. 29). Tanner thought that media advisors in particular, especially those in the Prime Minister's office, exercised 'significant power, including over individual Ministers' (quoted in Ng 2016, p. 29).

Peta Credlin, former Chief of Staff to Prime Minister Tony Abbott, is a notable example of a formidable ministerial advisor who was widely regarded as one of the most powerful figures in Australian politics. She was rated as Australia's most powerful woman in the 2015 Australian Women's Weekly Power 100 List and was ranked as number one in Business Review Weekly's 2012 Spinners and Advisors Power Index. There were frequent media reports about Credlin giving directions to and berating Ministers and Members of Parliament. This included enforcing a ban on Ministers appearing before the Australian Broadcasting Corporation's Q&A programme. Credlin also reportedly sat in on Cabinet meetings and vetted Ministers' staff selection and media appearances, to their consternation. As a Liberal insider stated: 'She's tough, she's a player, she makes demands, she gives directions, she bawls people out' (Knott 2012). Credlin undoubtedly had a lot more power and influence than most Ministers.

The strong influence of ministerial advisors can be attributed to their physical proximity to the Minister and the resultant high level of access. Former Minister David Kemp stated that even since 1975, the Chief of Staff would usually have an office next to the Minister, as opposed to the public service, who were located in a different building, which meant that 'ministerial staff have a proximity to the Minister that the public service doesn't have' (quoted in Ng 2016, p. 29).

Tanner stated that the relationship between Ministers and their advisors was an intimate one:

> There is an intimacy in a ministerial office. People work ridiculous hours. You are living in each other's pockets. It is a relatively small area. You are under intense pressure. So the perceived power of ministerial advisors, some of it just arises from that intimacy. And by definition you have access, and you're talking about the weather or the football. So there's a trust or there's a bond. And there's a much more fertile ground for those kinds of exchanges than someone who's coming to see you every two days.
>
> (quoted in Ng 2016, p. 30)

At the State level, former Victorian Premier Steve Bracks (1994–2007) stated that as ministerial advisors are intimately involved with their Minister numerous times in a day, Ministers probably see their advisors more often than their partner (quoted in Ng 2016, p. 30). Former Victorian Premier John Brumby (2007–2010) contrasted the close relationship that tended to develop between a Minister and their advisors due to the high stress environment and long working hours of politics, with the more arm's length relationship between a Minister and public servants:

> Politics is a harsh business. And for the things you achieve, the successes, they rarely ever make the front page of the paper. But your failures certainly do. So your political staff tend to be also a strong source of personal support … in a sense they're your advisors, but they also become almost your friends. They are not just acquaintances. They're part of the extended family, almost. So you're close to them.
>
> And you're not close in that way to a public servant. And you shouldn't be. I think the separation of powers is very important. And I think public servants have to understand politics but they should never be political players. And they shouldn't be your best mates. In a sense, their job is to give you independent, impartial, apolitical advice without fear or favour. It's their job. It's not to curry friendship. So their roles are somewhat different.
>
> (quoted in Ng 2016, p. 30)

Along with a high level of access to their Minister, some ministerial advisors were given significant discretion to speak on their Minister's behalf to public servants, other Ministers, the party, and the media. For example, former Minister Lindsay Tanner gave his advisors a lot of discretion to speak on his behalf as he had a 'degree of trust' in them and their competence and capabilities (quoted in Ng 2016, p. 30). Senator Kim Carr stated that ministerial advisors have positions of trust and confidence, given that Ministers are unable to monitor their behaviour all of the time:

> These are positions of trust. They must enjoy your confidence. And they are effectively in the eyes of other people, speaking on your behalf.
>
> (quoted in Ng 2016, p. 31)

Carr confirmed that he gave his advisors considerable discretion to speak on his behalf in all regards, because it was impossible to second-guess everything that was said where he did not know the particular circumstances that had arisen. He stated:

> That relies on you having confidence in their judgment. If you don't have confidence in their judgment, there will be a parting of the ways. That is the inevitable consequence of losing confidence. That means that you have to be aware of what they're doing, and you can't always be. So I always encourage people to tell me how people were performing. If the

> advisor does not have the common sense to know an issue is above their pay grade, then they're in the wrong job.
>
> (quoted in Ng 2016, p. 31)

Thus, there is a close bond that develops between Ministers and their advisors due to the high-pressure political environment and long working hours involved in a Minister's office. This creates a relationship forged in fire – leading to intimacy, trust, and confidence between Ministers and their advisors. It is clear that ministerial advisors do exercise a great deal of influence due to their unprecedented level of access and proximity to Ministers compared to any other stakeholder in the political system. As a result, senior ministerial advisors to powerful Ministers have a greater influence than elected Ministers and Members of Parliaments. Influential advisors have the power to support, obstruct, or veto policy proposals, are more likely to get their way, are involved in key decisions and have access to the decision-makers (Maley 2011, p. 1478). In addition, senior ministerial advisors, such as chiefs of staff, operate with a high level of autonomy, and are authorised to attend meetings with the department and stakeholders without the presence of their Minister, as well as to deal with issues on the Minister's behalf. Consequently, in the last few decades, ministerial advisors have grown to become key institutional actors within the Australian executive.

New Zealand

Political advisors in New Zealand started to emerge in the mid-1980s, much later than the other Westminster jurisdictions (Eichbaum and Shaw 2010). Unlike many of the other jurisdictions, the development of the position of political advisors was on an ad hoc and incremental basis, rather than through explicit governmental impetus (Eichbaum and Shaw 2007b, p. 611). From the late 1980s to mid-1990s, Ministers chose whether or not to have a ministerial advisor on their staff, and some did not. For instance, one Minister reiterated his faith in the classical Westminster bureaucratic arrangements and stated:

> At no stage did I entertain any paranoias that seconded staff [from the public service] were anything other than fully motivated to assist me – whether in dealing with the public service or with the world beyond it.
>
> (quoted in Eichbaum and Shaw 2007a, p. 459)

In terms of prime-ministerial advisory support, advisors to the Prime Minister existed since 1970s, where Robert Muldoon (1975–1984) used his advisors as his 'eyes and ears' (Mulgan 2004). However, the Prime Minister's Department was seen to be too politicised, as the bureaucratic and political streams of advice were mixed (Palmer 2013). In 1990, Prime Minister Geoffrey Palmer (1989–1990) introduced central coordination reforms that led to the formation of the impartial Prime Minister's Department and political Prime Minister's Office, which provided two separate streams of advice to the Prime Minister (Hunn and Lang 1989; State Services Commission 2013, p. 17). The Prime Minister's Department provided impartial advice, while the political office provided personal support and media services, as well as advice of a political nature.

The position of political advisors solidified in New Zealand following a significant reconfiguration of New Zealand's constitutional system. Since the 1996 election, New Zealand moved from a first-past-the-post system to a mixed-member proportional electoral system. As a result, New Zealand has had coalition or minority governments for the last 20 consecutive years. In a situation of minority government, Ministers found that they needed more political advisors to broker and coordinate policy positions between parliamentary parties. In a 2005 survey, 93 per cent of Ministers agreed or strongly agreed that ministerial advisors facilitate relationships between coalition partners, while 87 per cent felt that political advisors smoothed the way between governments and their parliamentary support parties (Shaw and Eichbaum 2014, p. 594). As a former Minister explained, there are:

> more groups to talk with and keep happy and keep on board. The new system is all about compromise, the art of the possible, etc. In many ways it is much less capable of vigorous analysis [and] principled directions than the old [plurality] system. Maintaining the coalition (especially the leadership) is the sole purpose of government!
>
> (quoted in Shaw and Eichbaum 2014, p. 591)

By 2006, every ministerial office had a political advisor due to the mixed-member proportional electoral system, with a total of 161 advisors. As the numbers began to climb, the State Services Commissioner claimed that the increases in numbers of ministerial advisors 'raised fears in some quarters about the potential for politicisation of the Public Service', as there was a risk that public service advice may be supplanted by political advice and that ministerial advisors may assume an executive authority and give instructions to public servants (Wintringham 2002, p. 10).

Political advisors in New Zealand are explicitly acknowledged in the *Cabinet Manual 2017* (New Zealand, Cabinet Office, 2017), which is an authoritative guide to the uncodified constitutional system. The Manual notes the important role played by political advisors in supporting Ministers in their management of relationships with other political parties, and in negotiating support for policy and legislative initiatives (cl 3.25). The Manual also provides that a Minister may involve political advisors in policy development and other areas of work that might otherwise be performed within the Minister's department (cl 3.26).

A contemporary ministerial office in New Zealand is typically a small unit, with each Minister having on average about 5 or 6 advisors. The office is led by a chief of staff and senior private secretary, who have overall management responsibility for the office and for the support provided to the Minister. In a ministerial office, there are typically the following cast of characters:

- Portfolio private secretaries seconded from the department manage the flow of information and documentation between the Minister and the department, including briefings, policy papers and Cabinet papers;
- A ministerial advisor provides general policy and political support to the Minister by maintaining a strategic overview of portfolio activities, providing advice on policy issues and options, liaising with other advisors, Ministers and select committees, consulting with other political parties, groups and individuals, as well as managing the flow of answers to written and oral parliamentary questions and *Official Information Act* requests;
- The press secretary advises on public relations matters, prepares speeches and media releases, and liaises with the media and other media advisors; and
- Administrative staff carry out a wide range of administrative activities, including providing word processing and information management services.

Ministerial advisors are located with their Ministers in an Executive wing adjacent to Parliament, dubbed the 'Beehive'. Ministers and their advisors are thus physically separated from public servants, as in Australia but unlike the United Kingdom. If public servants are more physically distant from Ministers, this may mean that they have less influence on Ministers or face more communication difficulties compared to ministerial advisors. Nevertheless, as New Zealand is a small country and Wellington is a small city, there are fewer communication issues compared to Australia (Lodge et al 2013, p. 82). Interaction with the public service tended to be with ease and informality due to the 'small, somewhat incestuous community' (Matheson 1997, p. 158).

Ministerial advisors in New Zealand play a significant role in the policy process. A 2005 survey found that almost all ministerial advisors (93.8 per cent) regularly attended meetings with Ministers and officials, while 87.5 per cent read and commented on officials' advice before it reached the Minister's desk (Eichbaum and Shaw 2007a, p. 462). Ministerial advisors also acted as a sounding board for bureaucrats, with 90.6 per cent conveying or clarifying the Minister's wishes to officials on a frequent or very frequent basis. Half of advisors (50.1 per cent) met regularly with officials to develop public policy. In 2006, over half of advisors raised and debated new policy initiatives with their Minister on a frequent or very frequent basis. Hence advisors were involved in policy evaluation and coordination and, to a lesser extent, policy formation with both Ministers and the civil service. The contribution of ministerial advisors to the policy process was rated very positively by Ministers, with 93 per cent agreeing or strongly agreeing that ministerial advisors made a positive contribution to the policy process. Ministers were happy with the contestability of advice to counteract the monopoly of public service advice. There was, however, markedly less enthusiasm by the bureaucracy, with only half (52.2 per cent) of senior officials agreeing or strongly agreeing that the contribution of ministerial advisors was positive (Eichbaum and Shaw 2007b, p. 621; Shaw and Eichbaum 2014, p. 603).

Following the move to a mixed-member proportional electoral system and the effective institutionalisation of minority government, there has been an increase in liaison roles. For example, in managing the coalition between the Clark Labour government and the Greens (2005–2008), three new positions were added: a Government Relationship Manager and two Ministerial Liaison Senior Advisors. These advisors were based in the Prime Minister's Office, and were tasked with liaising between the Prime Minister's Office and the Greens Party, including negotiations about specific policy or legislative initiatives (New Zealand, Office of the Auditor-General 2016). In 2005, a survey found that 59.4 per cent of ministerial staff regularly assisted with coalition consultation or management (Eichbaum and Shaw 2007a, p. 461).

Besides coordinating between parliamentary parties, ministerial advisors in the Clark government (1999–2008) played a strong central coordinating function between different departments across government (Shaw and Eichbaum 2014, p. 606). Prime Minister Helen Clark utilised ministerial advisors as a mechanism of prime-ministerial coordination and oversight through a horizontal network of relationships between ministerial advisors. In 2005, over two thirds (68.7 per cent) of ministerial advisors met with members of the Prime Minister's staff regularly or very regularly, while 78.1 per cent regularly accompanied their Minister to meetings with other Ministers and met with other ministerial advisors. In addition, ministerial advisors also regularly liaised with external interest groups.

In the Key government period (2008–2016), ministerial staff exercised powers on behalf of Ministers, which raised issues about whether they were going beyond the appropriate boundaries of their role. In 2013, the Prime Minister's Chief of Staff, Wayne Eagleson, was found to have authorised the release of phone records and email metadata of certain Ministers and ministerial staff to a parliamentary committee inquiry without seeking consent from individual Ministers (New Zealand Privileges Committee 2013). In Eagleson's view, he had sufficient authority to authorise the release of the metadata because all Ministers involved had been made aware of the inquiry's terms of reference. Then Prime Minister John Key defended the actions of his Chief of Staff, stating that Eagleson acted 'absolutely professionally and quite correctly' (Johnson and Watkins 2013). Eagleson's actions show that senior ministerial advisors can and do exercise authority independent of their Ministers. Eagleson's authorisation on behalf of the Prime Minister affected

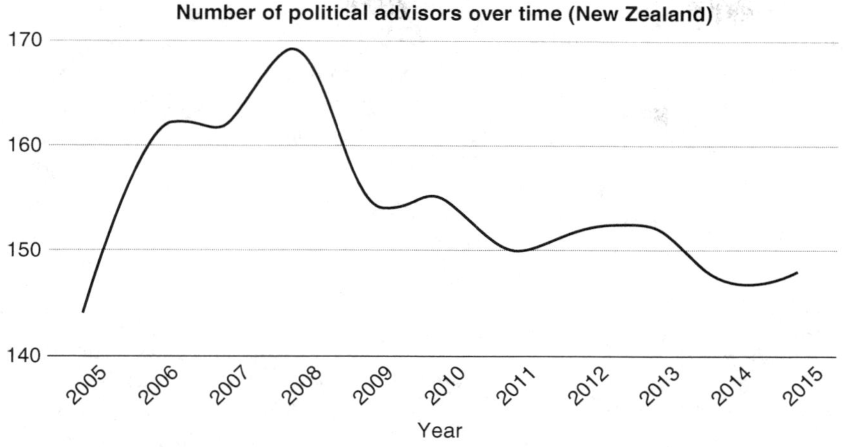

Figure 2.4 Number of political advisors in New Zealand from 2005–2015

the privacy of the communications of other Ministers and their staff, and Eagleson assumed that due to his central position in the Prime Minister's Office that he was able to make authorisations on behalf of all Ministers and ministerial staff. Thus, senior ministerial advisors, particularly those in the PMO, have strong independent authority and influence.

With the election of the Key government in 2008, the number of political advisors reached its zenith: there were 169 advisors, an increase from 144 advisors in 2005. The number has subsequently subsided to about 148 advisors in 2015. Generally the numbers of ministerial staff in New Zealand remain lower than all jurisdictions apart from the United Kingdom, with only a small (less than 3 per cent) growth in the number of advisors over the last ten years (2005–2015). Unlike the deep functional specialisation of political staff in Canada, some ministerial advisors in New Zealand undertake mixed functions due to the comparatively low numbers of advisors per Minister. In 2005, ministerial advisors who worked on policy reported that they undertook limited media functions, including writing speeches, working on press statements or government publications and engaging with office-holders from the Minister's party (Eichbaum and Shaw 2007a, p. 460). There are, however, press secretaries who solely undertake media functions.

It is clear that over time, political advisors in New Zealand have increased in influence. A 2005 survey showed that 59.8 per cent of senior officials agreed or strongly agreed that ministerial advisors were more influential than they once were (Eichbaum and Shaw 2007b, p. 621). This influence seems to have increased further with the advent of the Key government, where advisors started to sit in on Cabinet meetings, with the ability to contribute advice. Ministers attributed the rise of political advisors to the increasingly demanding nature of modern government, as well as a desire to politicise the machinery of executive government (Shaw and Eichbaum 2014, p. 591). Ministers also criticised the deficit in the capability of the public service to provide multi-faceted advice in a complex policy environment.

Analysis

Numbers of advisors

All jurisdictions started with a small handful of political staffers supporting each Minister, and have had an increasing number of political advisors over time, leading to institutionalisation of large ministerial offices with specialised advisors overseen by a chief of staff. The Canadian system of advisors is the most entrenched, dating from the 1950s, as well as the most numerous. Although the UK system developed in the 1960s, the UK has the smallest number of advisors, which can be attributed to the extremely high level of media and parliamentary scrutiny of these advisors, combined with a political cap of two advisors per Minister (as will be discussed in chapter five). This is followed by the Australian system dating from the 1970s, with a significant number of advisors. New Zealand also has a low number of advisors, with ad hoc development of the position of these advisors in the 1980s. In 2015, there were 544 advisors in Canada, 355 advisors in Australia, 148 advisors in New Zealand and 87 advisors in the United Kingdom.

There are common themes in the surge in the numbers of advisors in each jurisdiction. Political advisors rise to prominence where a new government is elected that has spent a long period in Opposition. These governments tend to distrust the civil service and doubt its ability to respond to their policy priorities. This happened with the Blair government in the United Kingdom, the Mulroney government in Canada, the Whitlam government in Australia and the Key government in New Zealand. Another instance where the numbers of advisors increase is where a minority government is elected. More advisors are needed to coordinate and broker positions between the different political parties. This is a recurring element of the New Zealand system following the move to mixed member proportional voting, and the Cameron government in the United Kingdom also found that minority government required an increased number of advisors, despite their pledge to keep the numbers of advisors low.

As can be seen in Table 2.1, ministerial offices in Australia and Canada are roughly similar in size, whereas ministerial offices in the United Kingdom and New Zealand are roughly equivalent in size. As such, the number of advisors that serve in each portfolio is also very different, with Ministers in New Zealand and the United Kingdom being the least supported with an average

Table 2.1 Average number of advisors per minister

	Canada	*New Zealand*	*United Kingdom*	*Australia*
Growth 2005–2015	22 per cent	3 per cent	32 per cent	18 per cent
Average Number per Minister (2015)	19	6	4	12

of about 4–6 advisors per Minister, while Australian and Canadian Ministers are very well-supported by political staff, with an average of between 12–19 advisors per Minister. The Canadian Prime Minister is the overall champion, with 80–100 advisors, showing the strong centralisation of political power in Canada.

Related to this, the level of centralisation of power in the Prime Minister varies dramatically across jurisdictions. The British system of governance is characterised by a weak centre compared to jurisdictions such as Australia and Canada – there is no Prime Minister's Department and thus no army of civil servants to support the Prime Minister (Yong and Hazell 2014, p. 14). Only a handful of special advisors support the British Prime Minister. Jonathan Powell, former Chief of Staff to Blair, stated:

> The guilty secret of our system, despite everything that is written in the newspapers, is that No. 10 Downing Street and the Prime Minister are remarkably unpowerful in our system. People talk about imperial prime ministerships but it certainly does not feel that way when you get into Downing Street. It is like the gold at the end of the rainbow: when you get there it is not actually there.
>
> (corrected transcript 2013)

On the other hand, there is a strong element of centralisation in the Canadian system compared to other Westminster jurisdictions. The Canadian Prime Minister is able to control both political advisors and the civil service across government as the Prime Minister appoints these positions (Benoit 2006, pp. 172–173). This may lead to both partisan advisors and the civil service to at times be more loyal to the Prime Minister than their own Minister.

The structure of ministerial offices has remained relatively consistent across jurisdictions, with advisors located within the Minister's private offices led by a chief of staff. The United Kingdom has been the most experimental, with David Cameron introducing extended ministerial offices, with a mix of civil servants and partisans within the same body. This can be said to be a move towards the more fluid European *cabinet* structure. However, this experiment was quickly abandoned as not many Ministers took the opportunity to restructure their offices in this way, perhaps indicating that the move to the European *cabinet* structure was not seen to be necessary.

Roles of advisors

Advisors across the Westminster jurisdictions all undertake remarkably similar functions that can be broadly divided into several categories:

- providing advice (on research, policy, media and strategy);
- consulting with stakeholders internal and external to government;
- administering the Minister's office; and
- acting on behalf of the Minister (Ng 2016, p. 26).

There is increasingly sophisticated academic literature that seeks to create a typology of the work of political advisors by categorising the functions that political advisors undertake. For instance, Bernadette Connaughton sets out a model that differentiates between four main roles of political advisors: expert, partisan, coordinator and minder (Connaughton 2010, pp. 351–2; Connaughton 2015). The expert is a highly qualified political outsider who initiates and contests policies and ideas, while the coordinator's role is procedural and includes monitoring and liaising with various groups to facilitate oversight and delivery of the Minister's agenda. On the political dimension, the partisan is appointed predominantly on the basis of political affiliation rather than specific expertise, and undertakes work of a politically partisan nature, such as representing their Minister in political negotiations. Another political role, the minder, protects the Minister by looking out for issues that may harm the Minister politically and in terms of reputation. An advisor may adopt one or more of these roles.

In addition, academics have focussed particularly on the policy roles of advisors. Maria Maley (2000a, 2015) identifies the policy work of partisan staff as occurring in three different arenas:

- *working with the department* through supervising, orienting and mobilising the department, and generating ideas, policy development and policy implementation;
- *working with other Ministers* through facilitating cabinet decision-making, resolving policy conflict and coordinating new policy; and
- *working with stakeholders* through *agenda-setting* by coming up with ideas and ensuring the ideas are lifted onto the Minister's agenda; *linking ideas, interests and opportunities*, including with broader agendas within government, and using their connections to bring stakeholders internal and external to government together to create policy outcomes, *mobilising* to push proposals forward and build political will within and outside of government, *bargaining* and negotiating between other advisors to seek consensus between different portfolios in government; and *delivering*, that is, bringing all four roles together.

Jonathan Craft (2016, pp. 25–43) expands on this and identifies both the substantive and procedural dimensions of a policy advisor's work through

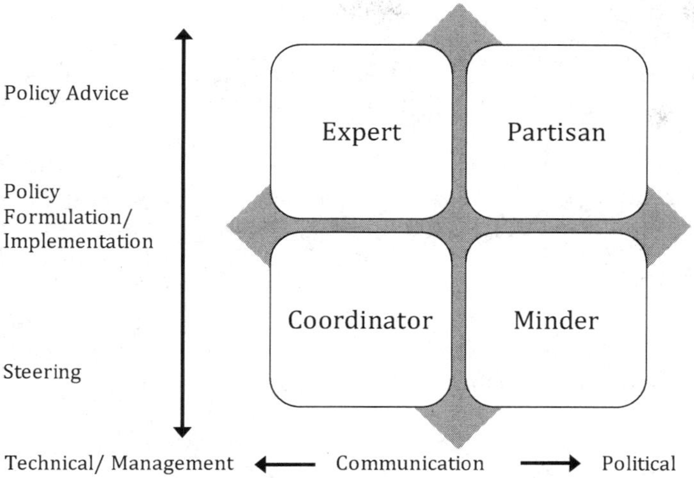

Figure 2.5 Configuration of advisor roles
Source: Adapted from Connaughton (2010).

the concepts of buffering, bridging, moving and shaping. Policy advisors 'buffered' by providing substantive comments on policy advice by departmental officials, and 'bridged' by procedurally integrating policy advice from departmental officials, other political advisors and stakeholders outside government (Craft 2016, pp. 88, 145). Political staffers also shaped policy by applying a political lens to policy and developing policy (Craft 2016, p. 207), and moved policy through coordination with the Minister and bureaucracy, as well as between ministerial offices. This strand of literature clearly illustrates the expansion of the roles of policy advisors as they are increasingly involved in all roles across the policy spectrum, from policy formation, to substantive policy advice, as well as procedurally coordinating policy though networking both horizontally and vertically across and beyond government.

These models provide a useful framework to analyse the distinctive work carried out by political advisors. As the position of advisors gradually solidified within the political system and their numbers grew, each jurisdiction showed a gradual expansion in the roles of advisors, as well as deeper role specialisation. Although advisors in all jurisdictions were initially limited to more procedural administrative roles, as time went on, they started adopting more substantive policy roles. As governments struggled to adapt to media demands following the 24/7 news cycle, media advisors became extremely important figures. In addition, the range of stakeholders that advisors interacted with increased over time, from merely dealing with their own Minister and department, to coordinating through horizontal networks across other ministerial offices and the Prime Minister's Office, as well as external stakeholders.

The larger number of political advisors has meant that ministerial offices have experienced a 'thickening', where layers of hierarchy have emerged within the organisation (Light 1995). The modern ministerial office is a sophisticated operation with advisors undertaking distinct and specialised roles. In the Canadian context, the roles are specialised to the greatest extent, with categories of advisors that explicitly look at short-term reactive matters (issues management), as well as staff that focus on long-term strategy (principal secretary and strategic communications). Other jurisdictions have tended to neglect the long-term dimension of political advice, with roles that focus more on short-term reactive issues or 'fire-fighting' or media presentation. In New Zealand, which has a low number of advisors, individual ministerial advisors may undertake mixed roles, from policy advice to engaging with the media.

Influence of advisors

It is clear that political advisors wield a great deal of power and influence in all jurisdictions.

Partly the influence arises from the roles they perform. The more recent roles of advisors in coordinating or 'bridging' between the Minister, the department and external stakeholders gives political advisors the power to act as gate-keepers to the Minister. They are able to filter departmental advice, as well as broker positions between departments, the political party and the media. This means that they are able to influence and steer the Minister's agenda, as well as shape, control and potentially block information from the bureaucracy that reaches the Minister.

Structurally, political advisors also exercise influence through their physical proximity to the Minister, being the staff that are situated within the Minister's office, as opposed to civil servants, who are sometimes in a different building. Political advisors work intimately with their Minister in a hothouse high-pressure environment, where the Minister may see their advisors more often than they see their spouses. This means that political advisors have a greater opportunity to discuss issues with the Minister and push their agenda, compared to civil servants or any other stakeholder in the political system, who see the Minister less regularly.

More intangibly, political advisors also wield influence due to the emotional support they provide to their Ministers. Ministers, as rulers of the country, are 'in great need of emotional support, because of the loneliness and dilemma of their situation and the pressures to which they are subjected' (Dror 1987, p. 193). Former Canadian Prime Minister Jean Chrétien lamented that, 'The press wants to get you. The opposition wants to get you. Even some of the bureaucrats want to get you' (quoted in Savoie 2003, p. 47). Within a hostile system, the emotional support of 'friends' to the Minister is one part of the equation that explains the entrenchment and proliferation of political advisors. Advisors provide 'hot inputs' in terms of advancing the Minister's career and improving the Minister's image in the media and through public relations. Hot advice tends to be more reactive, ideologically-based, crisis-driven, partisan and biased, focussed on electoral winning (Prasser 2006). On the other hand, civil servants are charged with 'cold inputs', that is, information-based, neutral advice with a strategic, public interest focus. This involves objective estimates and professional analysis that are not calibrated to the possible emotional reaction of the Minister. The rise of political advisors may in part be attributed to their function in the system of both politically and emotionally protecting their Minister, leading Ministers to form deep attachments to their advisors, compared to the cold, impartial bureaucracy. The modern ministerial advisory system has to thus be conditioned to handle the 'contradiction between providing emotional support and proffering cold inputs, both of which are needed for enhancing the performance of rulers' (Dror 1987, p. 194). In this context, the informal role of advisors in providing hot advice to protect their Minister and acting as an emotional sounding board leads to an intimate relationship of trust and confidence between Ministers and their advisors.

In addition to internal factors, external changes have also led to the entrenchment of political advisors in the Westminster system. The frantic 24/7 news cycle and the rise of social media means that Ministers have to feed a hungry media machine and respond almost instantly to crises and issues around the clock. Governments have desperately sought to portray themselves in a positive light, and have employed media advisors to try to put a positive 'spin' or gloss on government actions, activities and programmes. This led to the formation of centralised media management units, particularly in the United Kingdom, Australia and Canada, where governments sought to implement a coordinated media response (as will be discussed in chapter four). This gave media advisors in the Prime Minister's Office unprecedented power, as they were able to vet the speeches and announcements of all elected Ministers across government. In the United Kingdom, prominent media advisors such as Alistair Campbell have become household names.

In short, the influence that political advisors exercise is due to both internal and external factors. Internally, there is an intimacy that develops between Ministers and their staff, due to the close proximity in highly pressurised working conditions and emotional support that advisors provide to their Ministers. This privileged position gives political advisors great influence over their Minister's deliberations and decision-making. In addition, as political advisors are interposed between the Minister and public service, they have the ability to filter information that reaches the Minister. External factors have also led to the increased influence of political advisors. The 24/7 media cycle and centralisation of media management has solidified the position of media advisors. Thus, political advisors have now become a major force in the Westminster system of government.

References

Books and journal articles

Aucoin, P, and Savoie, D, 2009, 'The Politics-Administration Dichotomy: Democracy versus Bureaucracy' in O Dwivendi, T Mau and B Sheldrick (eds), *The Evolving Physiology of Government: Canadian Public Administration in Transition*, University of Ottawa Press, Ottawa, pp. 97–117.

Aucoin, P, 2010, 'Canada', in C Eichbaum and R Shaw (eds), *Partisan Appointees and Public Servants: An International Analysis of the Role of the Political Adviser*, Edward Elgar, Cheltenham, pp. 64–93.

Bakvis, H, 2000, 'Rebuilding Policy Capacity in an Era of Fiscal Dividend: A Report from Canada' *Governance*, vol. 13(1), pp. 71–103.

Balogh, T, 1959, 'The Apotheosis of the Dilettante' in H Thomas (ed), *The Establishment*, The New English Library, pp. 83–126.

Barber, M, 2007, *Instruction to Deliver*, Politico, London.

Blick, A, 2004, *People who live in the Dark*, Politico, London.

Castle, B, 1993, *Fighting All the Way*, Macmillan, London.

Churchill, W S, 1948, *The Second World War, Vol 1: The Gathering Storm*, Carsell & Co, London.

Craft, J, 2016, *Backrooms and Beyond: Partisan Advisers and the Politics of Policy Work in Canada*, University of Toronto Press, Toronto.

Connaughton, B, 2010, 'Glorified Gofers, Policy Experts or Good Generalists: A Classification of the roles of the Irish Ministerial Adviser', *Irish Political Studies*, vol. 25(3), pp. 347–369.

Connaughton, B, 2015, 'Navigating the Borderlines of Politics and Administration: Reflections on the Role of Ministerial Advisers', *International Journal of Public Administration*, vol. 38(1), pp. 37–45.

Dror, Y, 1987, 'Conclusions', in W Plowden (ed), *Advising the Rulers*, Basil Blackwell, Oxford, pp. 185–215.

Dunn, D D, 1995, 'Ministerial Staff in Australian Commonwealth Government', *Australian Journal of Public Administration*, vol. 54(4), pp. 507–519.

Eichbaum, C, and Shaw, R, 2007a, 'Ministerial Advisers and the Politics of Policy-Making: Bureaucratic Permanence and Popular Control', *Australian Journal of Public Administration*, vol. 66(4), pp. 453–467.

Eichbaum, C, and Shaw, R, 2007b, 'Ministerial Advisers, Politicization and the Retreat from Westminster: The Case of New Zealand', *Public Administration*, vol. 85(3), pp. 609–640.

Eichbaum, C, and Shaw, R, 2010, 'New Zealand', in C Eichbaum and R Shaw (eds), *Partisan Appointees and Public Servants: An International Analysis of the Role of the Political Adviser*, Edward Elgar, Cheltenham, pp. 114–147.

Esselment, A L, and Wilson, P, 2017, 'Campaigning from the Centre', in A Marland, T Giasson and A L Esselment (eds), *Permanent Campaigning in Canada*, University of British Columbia Press, Vancouver, pp. 222–240.

Fawcett, P, and Gay, O, 2010, 'United Kingdom' in C Eichbaum and R Shaw (eds), *Partisan Appointees and Public Servants: An International Analysis of the Role of the Political Adviser*, Edward Elgar, Cheltenham, pp. 24–63.

Fabian Society, 1947, *The Reform of the Higher Civil Service: A Report by a Special Committee for the Fabian Society*, Fabian Publications, London.

Fabian Society, 1964, *The Administrators: The Reform of the Civil Service*, Fabian Tract.
Jones, N, 2002, *The Control Freaks: How New Labour Gets its Way*, Politico, London.
Larson, P, 1999, 'The Canadian Experience' in S Agere (ed), *Redefining Management Roles: Improving the Functional Relationship between Ministers and Permanent Secretaries*, University of Toronto Press, Toronto, pp. 55–74.
Lenoski, G, 1977, 'Ministers' Staff and Leadership Politics' in T A Hockin (ed), *Apex of Power: The Prime Minister and Political Leadership in Canada*, 2nd edn, Prentice-Hall, Ontario, pp. 165–175.
Light, P C, 1995, *Thickening Government: Federal Hierarchy and the Diffusion of Accountability*, The Brookings Institution, Washington.
Lodge, G, Kalitowski, S, Pearce, N, and Muir, R, 2013, *Accountability and Responsiveness in the Senior Civil Service: Lessons from Overseas*, Institute for Public Policy Research, Cabinet Office, United Kingdom.
Maley, M, 2000a, 'Conceptualising Advisers' Policy Work: The Distinctive Policy Roles of Ministerial Advisers in the Keating Government, 1991–96', *Australian Journal of Political Science*, vol. 35(3), pp. 449–470.
Maley, M, 2000b, 'Too Many or Too Few? The Increase in Federal Ministerial Advisers 1972–1999', *Australian Journal of Public Administration*, vol. 59(4), 48–53.
Maley, M, 2002, 'Partisans at the Centre of Government: The Role of Ministerial Advisors in the Keating Government 1991–96', PhD Thesis, Australian National University, Canberra.
Maley, M, 2010, 'Australia', in C Eichbaum and R Shaw (eds), *Partisan Appointees and Public Servants: An International Analysis of the Role of the Political Adviser*, Edward Elgar, Cheltenham, pp. 94–113.
Maley, M, 2011, 'Strategic Links in a Cut-throat World: Rethinking the Role and Relationships of Australian Ministerial Staff', *Public Administration*, vol. 89(4) pp. 1469–1488.
Maley, M, 2015, 'The Policy Work of Australian Political Staff', *International Journal of Public Administration*, vol. 38(1), pp. 46–55.
Mallory, J R, 1967, 'The Minister's Office Staff: An Unreformed Part of the Public Service' *Canadian Public Administration*, vol. 10(1), pp. 25–34.
Marland, A, 2016, *Brand Command: Canadian Politics and Democracy in the Age of Message Control*, University of British Columbia Press, British Columbia.
Matheson, A, 1997, 'The Impact of Contracts on Public Management in New Zealand' in G Davis, B Sullivan and A Yeatman (eds), *The New Contractualism?*, MacMillan, Melbourne, pp. 164–179.
Milward, A S, 1980, *War, Economy and Society 1939–1945*, University of California Press, Berkeley and Los Angeles.
Mulgan, R, 2004, *Politics in New Zealand*, 3rd edn, Auckland University Press, Auckland.
Naughtie, J, 2002, *The Rivals: The Intimate Story of a Political Marriage*, Harper Collins Publishers, London.
Ng, YF, 2016, *Ministerial Advisers in Australia: The Modern Legal Context*, Federation Press, Sydney.
Osbaldeston, G F, 1989, *Keeping Deputy Ministers Accountable*, McGraw–Hill Ryerson, Toronto.
Palmer, G, 2013, *Reform: A Memoir*, Victoria University Press, Wellington.
Pimlott, B, 1993, *Harold Wilson*, Harper Collins Publishers Ltd, London.

Plasse, M, 1994, *Ministerial Chiefs of Staff in the Federal Government in 1990: Profiles, Recruitment, Duties, and Relations with Senior Public Servants*, Canadian Centre for Management Development, Ottawa.

Powell, J, 2010a, *The New Machiavelli: How to Wield Power in the Modern World*, Bodley Head, London.

Prasser, S, 2006, *Providing Advice to Government*, Papers on Parliament. Canberra, Senate.

Radwanski, G, 1978, *Trudeau*, Macmillan, Edinburgh.

Richards, D, 2007, *New Labour and the Civil Service: Reconstituting the Westminster Model*, Sussex Academic Press, Brighton.

Rhodes, RAW, and Tiernan, A, 2014, *The Gatekeepers: Lessons from Prime Ministers' Chiefs of Staff*, Melbourne University Press, Melbourne.

Savoie, D J, 1999, *Governing from the Centre: The Concentration of Power in Canadian Politics*, University of Toronto Press, Toronto.

Savoie, D J, 2003, *Breaking the Bargain: Public Servants, Ministers, and Parliament*, University of Toronto Press, Toronto.

Schacter, M P H, 1999, *Cabinet Decision-making in Canada: Lessons and Practices*, Institute on Governance, Ottawa.

Seldon, A, 2005, *Blair*, 2nd edn, Free Press, London.

Shaw, R, and Eichbaum, C, 2014, 'Ministers, Minders and the Core Executive: Why Ministers Appoint Political Advisers in Westminster Contexts', *Parliamentary Affairs*, vol. 67(3), pp. 584–616.

Tellier, P, 1968, 'Pour une réforme des cabinets de ministers fédéraux', *Canadian Public Administration*, vol. 11(4), pp. 414–427.

Tiernan, A, 2007, *Power Without Responsibility: Ministerial Staffers in Australian Governments from Whitlam to Howard*, UNSW Press, Sydney.

Walter, J, 1984, 'Ministerial Staff under Hawke', *Australian Journal of Public Administration*, vol. 43(3), p. 203.

Walter, J, 1986, *The Ministers' Minders: Personal Advisors in National Government*, Oxford University Publishing, Melbourne.

Wearing, J, 1977, 'President or Prime Minister' in T A Hockin, *Apex of Power: The Prime Minister and Political Leadership in Canada*, 2nd edn, Prentice-Hall, Ontario, pp. 326–343.

Wilson, H, 1976, *The Governance of Britain*, Harper and Row, New York.

Yong, B, and Hazell, R, 2014, *Special Advisers: Who They Are, What They Do and Why They Matter*, Hart Publishing, Oxford.

Zussman, David, 2009, *Political Advisers*, Paris, OECD.

Legislation, codes, case law, government and parliamentary reports

Australia, Members of Parliament (Staff) Act 1984 (Cth).

Australia, Public Service Act 1922 (Cth).

Australia, Royal Commission on Australian Government Administration, 1976, Report. Prepared by H C Coombs, AGPS, Canberra.

Australia, Senate Select Committee on matters arising from Pay Television Tendering Processes, 1993, First Report, Parliament of Australia.

Benoit, L, 2006, 'Ministerial Staff: The Life and Times of Parliament's Statutory Orphans', *Restoring Accountability Research Studies Volume 1: Parliament,*

Ministers and Deputy Ministers, Commission of Inquiry into the Sponsorship Program and Advertising Activities, Canadian Government Publishing, Ottawa, pp. 145–252.

Bourgault, J, 2006, 'The Deputy Minister's Role in the Government of Canada: His Responsibility and His Accountability', *Restoring Accountability Research Studies, Volume 2: The Public Service and Accountability*, Commission of Inquiry into the Sponsorship Program and Advertising Activities, Canadian Government Publishing, Ottawa, pp. 253–296.

Canada, Dorion Inquiry, 1965, *Special Public Inquiry 1964, Report of the Commissioner*, prepared by the Honourable Frederic Dorion, Chief Justice of the Superior Court for the Province of Quebec, Privy Council Office, Canada.

Canada, Office of the Conflict of Interest and Ethics Commissioner, Canada, 2017, The Wright Report, Ottawa. Available at: http://ciec-ccie.parl.gc.ca/Documents/English/Public%20Reports/Examination%20Reports/The%20Wright%20Report.pdf.

Canada, Office of the Ethics Commissioner, 2005, *The Sgro Inquiry: Many Shades of Grey*, Prepared by B J Shapiro, Office of the Ethics Commission, Ottawa.

Canada, *Public Service Employment Act 1967*.

Corrected Transcript of Oral Evidence taken before the Public Administration Select Committee, *Future of the Civil Service*, 16 April 2013, Jonathan Powell.

Evans, H, 2002, 'Submission to Senate Select Committee on a Certain Maritime Incident', *A Certain Maritime Incident*, 22 March 2002. Available at: www.aph.gov.au/~/media/wopapub/senate/committee/maritime_incident_ctte/report/e03_pdf.ashx.

Herald and Weekly Times Pty Limited v Office of the Premier, [2012] VCAT 967.

Hunn, D, and Lang, HG, 1989, *Review of the Prime Minister's Office and Cabinet Office*, State Services Commission, Wellington.

Maer, L, and Everett, M, *Civil Service Recruitment: Heads of Department and Extended Ministerial Offices* (2016) House of Commons Library, Briefing Paper Number CBP06697.

New Zealand, Cabinet Office, 2017, *Cabinet Manual 2017*, Department of Prime Minister and Cabinet, Wellington.

New Zealand, *Official Information Act 1982*.

New Zealand, State Services Commission, 2013, Performance Improvement Framework: Review of the Department of the Prime Minister and Cabinet (DPMC). Available at: www.ssc.govt.nz/sites/all/files/pif-dpmc-review-june2013.pdf.

New Zealand, Privileges Committee, 2013, Question of Privilege regarding use of Intrusive Powers within the Parliamentary Precinct: Interim Report of the Privileges Committee.

New Zealand, Office of the Auditor-General, 2016, Inquiry into Funding Arrangements for Green Party Liaison Roles, Wellington. Available at: www.oag.govt.nz/2006/greens/docs/greens.pdf.

Powell, J, 2010b, Witness Transcript, *The Iraq Inquiry*, 18 January 2010. Available at: www.iraqinquiry.org.uk/media/95166/2010-01-18-Transcript-Powell-S1.pdf.

R v Duffy (2016) ONCJ 220.

United Kingdom, Committee on the Civil Service, 1968, *The Civil Service, Vol 1: Report of the Committee 1966–68*, Prepared by Lord Fulton, HMSO, London, UK.

United Kingdom, Cabinet Office, 2016, Code of Conduct for Special Advisers.

United Kingdom, Cabinet Office, Ministerial Code (1997).

United Kingdom, Cabinet Office, 2016, Ministerial Code.

United Kingdom, Cabinet Office, 2016, Model Contract for Special Advisers.

United Kingdom, Committee on Standards in Public Life, 2002b, *Public Hearings*, 9 July.

United Kingdom, Committee on Standards in Public Life, 2003, *Defining the Boundaries within the Executive: Ministers, Special Advisers and the Permanent Civil Service*, Ninth Report, London.

United Kingdom, *Civil Service Order in Council*, 1991.

United Kingdom, *Civil Service Order in Council*, 1995.

United Kingdom, *Civil Service (Amendment) Order in Council*, 1997.

United Kingdom, Civil Service Commissioner, Civil Service Code *2010*.

United Kingdom, Code of Practice on Access to Government Information, 2nd edn 1997.

United Kingdom, Constitutional Reform and Governance Act 2010.

United Kingdom, Freedom of Information Act 2000.

United Kingdom, House of Commons, 1964, *Debates*, 10 November 1964, cols 811–812.

United Kingdom, House of Commons, 1976, *Debates*, 29 March 1976, cols 887–888.

United Kingdom, House of Commons, 2000, *Written Answers*, 24 July 2000, cols 442–443.

United Kingdom, House of Commons, 2002, *Written Answers*, 10 December 2002, col 281.

United Kingdom, House of Commons, Public Administration Select Committee. 2002. *Minutes of Evidence*, 28 February 2002.

United Kingdom, House of Lords Select Committee on the Constitution. 2010. *The Cabinet Office and the Centre of Government*, The Stationery Office Ltd, London.

United Kingdom, Liaison Committee, 2002, *Minutes of Evidence*, 17 July 2002.

United Kingdom, Select Committee on Public Administration, 2006, Minutes of Evidence, 9 March, Q 229.

Wintringham, M, 2002, *Annual Report of the State Services Commissioner 2002*, State Services Commission, Wellington.

Newspaper articles

Bishop, G, 1974, 'Labour's private army in Whitehall' *New Statesman*, 10 May.

Campbell, J, 2013, 'Tony Nutt told Police Minister Peter Ryan 'to put a Sock in it', *The Herald Sun* (online), 4 March. Available at: www.heraldsun.com.au/news/victoria/tony-nutt-told-police-minister-peter-ryan-to-put-a-sock-in-it/story-e6frf7kx-1226589560123.

Darlington, R, 1978, 'Why there should be more special advisors in Whitehall', The Times, 18 July.

Davis, J, 2010, 'PMO Budget Largely Stable since 1975', *Hill Times*, 8 February.

Hardman, I, 2016, 'May's Man of Influence', The Spectator (Australia), 16 July. Available at: https://spectator.com.au/2016/07/mays-man-of-influence/.

Johnston, K, and Watkins, T, 2013, 'Key Backs Top Adviser over Phone Records Scandal', Stuff (New Zealand) 2 August. Available at: www.stuff.co.nz/national/politics/8993280/Key-backs-top-adviser-over-phone-records-scandal.

Knott, M, 2012, 'The Power Index: Spinners, the Most Powerful is … Peta Credlin', Crikey, 23 February. Available at: www.crikey.com.au/2012/02/24/the-power-index-spinners-the-most-powerful-is-peta-credlin/.

Perrior, K, 2017, 'Working in No 10, I was staggered by the arrogance of Nick Timothy and Fiona Hill', *The Times*, 10 June. Available at: www.thetimes.co.uk/article/i-was-staggered-by-their-arrogance-h3rl7d7ds.

Routledge, P, 1998, 'Ed Balls: Brown's Young Egghead' Independent, 8 March. Available at: www.independent.co.uk/voices/profile-ed-balls-browns-young-egghead-1148933.html.

3 Advisors and the civil service

The emergence, entrenchment and institutionalisation of political advisors within the Westminster system has been gradual and prompted by the necessities of modern governance, as well as the desire of Ministers to have a trusted source of advice to bolster their position relative to the civil service. Predictably the interface between political advisors and the civil service has been characterised by friction. This chapter examines the interaction between political advisors and civil servants, as well as the relative power and influence of the civil service in each jurisdiction.

United Kingdom

Commentators have argued that the influence of the British civil service has waned with the rise of special advisers. For instance, Peter Hennessy argued that: 'the clout, as it were, of the permanent Civil Service advisors is much diminished compared to some of the special advisors' (UK, Committee on Standards in Public Life 2003, p. 44). A few factors have led to the decline of civil service influence. First, the civil service may be sidelined as a result of the increased power and influence of special advisors. Sir Christopher Foster (2005, p. 243) stated that 'the relationship of partnership between ministers and civil servants … has been replaced by close relationships between ministers and a new, unelected political class who are no longer just advisors'. Cabinet Office Minister, Francis Maude, likewise complained that: 'Too often in recent years the Service has been marginalised, either through the spread of special advisors or the over-use of expensive consultants' (UK, House of Commons, Public Administration Select Committee 2012, p. 5). Second, a major concern was that special advisors may go beyond their proper role. The *Code of Conduct for Special Advisors* (2016) sets out what special advisors can do on behalf of their Minister when working with civil servants:

- convey to officials Ministers' views, instructions and priorities, including on issues of presentation, taking into account priorities Ministers have set;
- request officials to prepare and provide information and data, including internal analysis and papers;

- hold meetings with officials to discuss the advice being put to Ministers; and
- review and comment on – but not suppress or supplant – advice being prepared for Ministers by civil servants (UK, Cabinet Office, 2016).

Advisors are hence able to give certain directions to civil servants, act as a sounding board for officials and evaluate civil service advice for their Minister. The limitation is that advisors should not suppress or supplant civil service advice, so that bureaucratic advice is not blocked or censored.

Despite the codification of roles, special advisors have been found to overstep these boundaries. In acting on behalf of the Minister as the Minister's *alter ego*, special advisors have made representations without the authority of the Minister that may not accurately reflect the Minister's view. This is an issue as other parties with less privileged access are often not able to verify the accuracy of the advisor's representations. Robin Mountfield, former Permanent Secretary, told the Wicks Committee that special advisors in the Number 10 policy unit:

> are conveying the views of the Prime Minister to civil servants, sometimes I suspect claiming prime-ministrative authority for views that they made up themselves, but acting in effect as surrogate Ministers to some extent. That seems to me to be going beyond the proper role.
>
> (UK, Committee on Standards in Public Life 2002a)

This was corroborated by Jack Straw, former Foreign Minister, who felt that there were too many staff from Number 10, including junior staff, who gave instructions to civil servants and claimed that they had the authority of the Prime Minister although this was not necessarily the case (Campbell and Stott 2007, p. 606).

Nevertheless, although special advisors have come to be a powerful force in the British governmental system, they have not supplanted the behemoth of the British civil service. For one, the number of special advisors is small (70–100) compared to the number of senior civil servants (4,000) (UK, Committee on Standards in Public Life 2000, p. 39). The deeply entrenched civil service is unlikely to be overpowered by the small number of special advisors, numbering far less than the other Westminster jurisdictions. Corroborating this account is the finding by the Public Administration Select Committee that it was a common view amongst current and former Ministers that their private offices were too weak to achieve their policy agenda (UK, House of Commons, Public Administration Select Committee 2013, p. 26). For instance, former Minister Nick Herbert thought that Ministers' private offices were not sufficiently strong, and felt as if he had less support as a Minister than in Opposition (UK, House of Commons Public Administration Select Committee 2013, p. 26).

The British civil service tradition has deep roots that originate from the 1854 Northcote–Trevelyan Report, which established an impartial civil service recruited and promoted on merit. The Haldane Report, which conceptualised the relationship between Ministers and civil servants as being indivisible (UK, Ministry of Reconstruction, 1918), created a 'model of informal uncodified partnership between the civil servant and the Minister'; hence affirming a model of departmental relations based on the concept of ministerial responsibility (Moran 2003, p. 126) (further discussed in chapter six). The Civil Service Commission, which existed in various forms since 1855, grew more powerful over time, and became a strong institutional protector of civil service independence and a bulwark against political pressure. Together, these deeply ingrained elements resulted in a powerful bureaucracy insulated from political imperatives.

In the 1970s, the British civil service exercised an all-pervasive control over Ministers through a complex network of information that was fed upwards in the hierarchy. Lord Annan, cultural historian and former wartime intelligence officer, described the alarmingly omniscient level of bureaucratic control of Ministers:

> The mandarins are the permanent secretaries who are at the head of each Ministry. The spies are the young civil servants who are the private secretaries to the Cabinet Ministers. Every meeting a minister has is attended by his private secretary, who logs it; every conversation he makes on the phone is recorded; every appointment he makes in Whitehall is monitored. If a Secretary of State starts to throw his weight around, or adopts a policy the civil servants regard as dangerous, the warning bells ring, and in an emergency the top civil servant of all, the Secretary to the Cabinet, will intervene with the Prime Minister. If a Minister brings a political adviser into his ministry and the adviser does not toe the line, the mandarins cut off his information: he will appear at a meeting and discover that his rivals possess certain important memoranda that mysteriously have never reached his desk. He therefore appears to be badly briefed and loses credibility. Each Tuesday morning before the mandarins meet in the Cabinet Offices … they are briefed by their spies to hear what is cooking. If you try to bend a Minister's ear in his office, what you say will be round the Civil Service within forty-eight hours: the only way is to catch him at dinner in the evening when his attendant nurse from the mental clinic, his private secretary, is no longer observing his patient.
>
> (quoted in Hennessy 1989, pp. 511–2)

As the British civil service is deeply ingrained within the political system, the bureaucracy is generally parochial and resistant to change. Robin Mountfield, former Cabinet Office Permanent Secretary, acknowledged that there was 'a need for the Civil Service to continue to open itself up. It is still, to some extent, a secret garden' (UK, Committee on Standards in Public Life 2003,

p. 18). Jonathan Powell, former Chief of Staff to Tony Blair, also remarked on the resistance of the civil service:

> The Civil Service is akin to a monastic order, where people still enter on leaving university and leave on retirement. Their attitudes change slowly and their powers of passive resistance are legendary … it is still too much a cradle to grave career.
>
> (Powell 2010, p. 74)

The Weberian notion of a powerful permanent civil service dominating the dilettantism of elected Ministers thus persists in the United Kingdom, despite the democratic legitimacy of elected Ministers (Weber 1987, p. 225). Former Cabinet Office Minister Francis Maude summed up the general attitude among civil servants that 'ministers come and ministers go. We are the permanent Civil Service. We have been here, and our forebears have been here, for 150 years, and the system will exist after ministers go' (UK, House of Commons, Public Administration Select Committee 2013, p. 23). Thus, the civil service tradition is deeply embedded in the British system of governance and generates strong resistance to reducing bureaucratic power or influence.

Even so, the British civil service was not immune from the Thatcherite reforms in the 1980s, which sought to increase civil service efficiency. Thatcher detested senior civil servants 'as a breed' and took to new public management (NPM) and privatisation with vigour (Hennessy 1989, p. 592). The Thatcher government significantly restructured the civil service by implementing a systematic separation between service delivery and policy functions within departments, which has produced a large array of 'executive agencies' whose civil service heads work to performance targets framed in contractual language, but which remain subject to the policy direction of Ministers (Daintith and Page 1999, pp. 37–45). There were also drastic cuts to civil service jobs, from 732,000 in 1979 to 500,000 in 1997 – a 33 per cent reduction. Academics have suggested that Thatcher may have reduced senior bureaucrats' 'willingness to make tough, detached criticisms of politicians' favourite schemes' (Wilson and Barker 1995, p. 137).

In addition, over the years, the institutional protections for civil service independence and impartiality have gradually eroded, although not to the extent of other Westminster jurisdictions. In 2004, Tony Blair proposed to place all permanent secretaries on four-year contracts with no presumption of renewal, a sentiment that was echoed by the succeeding Conservative government. After a decade, this proposal finally came to fruition under broad-scale civil service reforms led by then Cabinet Office Minister Francis Maude where, from July 2013, fixed five-year tenure periods were introduced for all permanent secretary appointments, with a possibility for renewal. One year later, eight permanent secretaries were on fixed term appointments, while nine permanent secretaries were in specialist roles where contractual arrangements were already in place (UK, Civil Service Reform 2014, p. 36). The tenure terms are not to match with election periods, however, to avoid politicisation of the civil service. Maude's civil service reforms were accompanied by a severe reduction of the size of the civil service by a fifth, with 90,000 civil service jobs slashed between 2010 and 2015 (Mason 2015).

Another major structural change was the enactment of the *Constitutional Reform and Governance Act 2010*, which finally put civil service employment on a statutory basis. Prior to this, civil service employment was a prerogative matter. The relatively new civil service legislation in the United Kingdom has already resulted in substantive changes. For example, in 2013, the Civil Service Commission utilised its statutory powers under sections 10 and 11 of the *Constitutional Reform and Governance Act 2010* to set out recruitment principles that had the effect of blocking a proposal for Ministers to choose their permanent secretaries from a shortlist of candidates (Maer and Evertt 2016). The Commission did this to protect civil service impartiality, and only relented in 2014 to allow the Prime Minister to choose permanent secretaries from a list of appointable candidates selected by the Commission (Civil Service Commission 2015). Even with this change, the independence of civil service appointments is well-protected as the Commission still maintains strong control of the appointments process. This can be contrasted to Australia, where Ministers are able to make patronage appointments of departmental secretaries, who are on fixed-term contracts. As former permanent secretary Robin Young declared, the British civil service was the 'least politicised civil service probably in the whole world' (UK, Select Committee on Public Administration 2006).

Canada

The glory days of the Canadian civil service were in 1935–1957, when it was regarded as one of the best in the world, with a few legendary mandarins exerting strong influence on the Liberal government (Granatstein 1982, p. 277). The civil service in this period was small and modestly paid, but had the belief that public service was a 'civic virtue, a vocation' (Savoie 2003, p. 63). In this period, politicians and bureaucrats operated in distinct spheres, shielded by governmental secrecy in a cloistered world like a 'small village, where everyone knew everyone else, recognized their own place in the general scheme, and knew how to get things done without fuss' (Savoie 2003, p. 65).

Despite a minor hiccup with the election of the Diefenbaker Conservative government, the influence of the civil service continued unabated under successive Liberal administrations into the 1970s. Senior civil servants reached the apex of their power under the Liberal premierships of Louis St Laurent and Lester Pearson, where policy was initiated within a department or co-ordinated between departments, rather than Cabinet, and only when senior civil servants had a firm proposal did it come to the attention of the Minister, who then presented it to Cabinet (Schindeler 1977, p. 27). As Cabinet did not have much opportunity to evaluate the merits of the proposal before it was presented, Cabinet usually confirmed the recommendation. Senator Maurice Lamontagne, who was a Cabinet member from 1963 to 1965, called the senior civil service 'the Establishment' and stated that when 'it was united behind or against a certain policy, its advice was accepted by Cabinet' and recalled an instance where a Minister had to resign for reaching a decision without consulting his civil servants (quoted in Schindeler 1977, p. 27). The number of public servants more than doubled from 120,577 in 1946 to 282,788 in 1977 (Dwivedi and Gow 1999, p. 90).

By the 1970s, politicians and their advisors of all political stripes shared the sentiment that permanent public servants were running governments and their 'apparent deference to politicians was pure pretence' (Savoie 2003, p. 7). As public policy became increasingly complex, politicians became more dependent on the expert bureaucracy. Some politicians began to see the public service as 'a kind of entrenched aristocracy within a democracy' (Savoie 2003, p. 22). Strident criticisms abounded. Former Prime Minister Pierre Trudeau felt that senior officials ran their departments like 'personal fiefdoms and all too often left outsiders, including ministers, on the outside looking in' (quoted in Savoie 2003, p. 89). Likewise, a senior Minister complained that:

> Something is basically wrong with our system of government. We are the only ones elected to make decisions. But … [w]e move into government offices with no support. Everything in these offices belongs to the permanent government. We are only visitors, barely trusted enough not to break the furniture.
>
> (quoted in Savoie 2003, p. 124)

In the Trudeau government (1968–1979, 1980–1984), senior public servants remained extremely influential. For instance, senior finance officers had the role of full participants in cabinet committees and spoke on behalf of their Minister as active participants (Campbell 1987, p. 139). However, the rosy situation for the bureaucracy was about to be disrupted. The Glassco Royal Commission into the public service criticised both the personnel and financial management of the Canadian public service, arguing that the 'ponderous system, virtually unchanged in thirty years … no longer did the job' (Canada, Royal Commission on Government Organizations 1962, p. 91). Ministers widely considered the bureaucracy to be bloated, costly and inefficient. As such, in the 1984 election campaign, Conservative leader Brian Mulroney famously declared that senior public servants who did not understand that they were subordinates of Ministers would be 'given pink slips and running shoes' (quoted in Savoie 2003, p. 9). The Conservatives were deeply concerned about a strong 'red' Liberal influence on the public service. Previously prominent deputy ministers (departmental heads) had left the bureaucracy for politics, and they were always on the Liberal side (Aucoin 2010, p. 67). This included Lester Pearson, who became Prime Minister in 1963.

Upon the election of the Mulroney government, a few deputy ministers left, while 32 were transferred within the first two years. As a result, within two years, virtually all deputy ministers were replaced (Manion 1991, p. 363). The Mulroney government also embarked on a strong privatisation agenda, announcing that it would cut the Canadian public service by 15,000, while the Chrétien government announced that it would cut 50,000 positions (Savoie 2003, p. 101). In reality, the cuts made by Mulroney were far smaller, with 4,000 fewer public servants since he started, although the government claimed a greater victory through creative accounting (Savoie 1999, p. 267). Nevertheless, the number of public servants was cut by 25 per cent by the Chrétien period, from 234,000 in 1988 to 184,000 in 1998 (Roberts 2002, p. 30).

These changes unsettled the entrenched bureaucracy. A former deputy minister stated:

> You can't forget that the Mulroney government is the first government that had to dismiss deputy ministers. I think that this kind of situation created a mentality of fear among deputy ministers and among people who were less secure in their positions because they felt constantly threatened. I would say that today many deputy ministers are 'straw men' and that there are fewer deputy ministers who assume energetic leadership than before.
>
> (quoted in Plasse 1994, p. 56)

Senior officials complained that the bureaucracy was 'in trouble, demoralized, losing confidence in its leaders and themselves, unsure of their roles and their futures, overburdened with work, and chafing under perceived unfair criticism' (Manion 1990, pp. 10–11). In addition, the concurrent transition to a stronger private office in the Mulroney period (described in the previous chapter) created some friction with the Canadian civil service. Bernard Roy, former Prime Minister's Chief of Staff, explained:

> At first, there were difficulties at times, clashes, tensions, problems. I know that at the time, certain deputy ministers [departmental heads] resented the fact that some chiefs of staff, in addition to their political duties, were effectively taking over responsibilities that belonged to them. But I think that in these cases, there were also personality conflicts. There may have been cases of chiefs of staff who took on more than we wanted, who invaded the deputy minister's turf because their minister asked more of them, possibly due to a lack of confidence in the deputy minister.
>
> (Plasse 1994, p. 53)

Benoit explained that these young advisors, who often lacked professional qualifications in the ministries they served, had access and proximity to their Ministers that exceeded that of the public service:

> Confidants, advisors, comrades-in-arms in the political battles to get and retain power, these politically passionate staffers were the ones that were there at the Minister's side come the day's end, the ones who shared in the everyday frustrations, pressures, strategies, crises and victories that were the lifeblood of Parliament, and not surprisingly, the mandarins eyed them with not a little resentment and suspicion.
>
> (Benoit 2006, p. 157)

This unparalleled access allowed political staffers to prioritise and funnel information that reached the Minister. The funnelling effect, however, may lead to Ministers missing important issues or developing policy without sufficient advice. Public servants were concerned that information from the bureaucracy was being filtered by political staff and did not eventually reach the Minister. A senior bureaucrat expressed this concern:

> The Minister's staff gets to interpret the information and content that the bureaucrats provide ... Information filters up and back down and you wonder if it ever gets seen by the Minister. Stupid Ministers tend to have stupid staff and because they don't want to be threatened (by the expertise of the public servants), major policy ends up being developed in an intellectual vacuum.
>
> (quoted in Benoit 2006, p. 199)

Further, political staff gave directions to departmental officials in a 'subtle, reasonably pervasive' way and, in many instances, this was seen to be 'a practical necessity' (Benoit 2006, p. 237). Although the Privy Council Office and Treasury guidelines and the code of conduct stipulated that interactions between advisors the public service were supposed to be through the deputy minister, this was 'honoured more in the breach than in the practice' for expediency and efficiency (Benoit 2006, p. 195). Political staffers may seek to bypass the bureaucratic hierarchy and go straight to junior public servants for information. A deputy minister complained that his chief of staff blocked information from reaching the Minister and bypassed him in getting details from lower level departmental staff:

> On one occasion a key document that I forwarded to the minister was intercepted by the chief political aide and not even seen by the minister. The minister's staff went directly to my staff for information. I have gone to meetings where the minister's staff and my staff had documents I had not yet seen. How could I carry out my accountability obligations to my minister when there was someone operating between me and my minister?
>
> (quoted in Osbaldeston 1989, p. 40)

Privy Council guidance now more clearly sets out the boundaries of the relationship between political advisors and public servants, including prohibiting advisors from directing public servants on their responsibilities, operational matters or the management of departmental resources (Canada, Privy Council 2015, E3).

In spite of the incursions into the role of the public service, Benoit found that in the day-to-day government business, the bureaucracy was 'fairly resilient to attempts by rogue political staff to circumvent the rules of regulatory and sound financial management' (Benoit 2006, p. 237). Bernard Roy, former Prime Minister's Chief of Staff, thought that despite the cut in the numbers of public servants during the Mulroney government, the public service gained ground over time and had more authority and power in the system (Plasse 1994, p. 54). This was because deputy ministers control the giant behemoth of the bureaucracy and they 'know which lever to pull to make things happen' (Savoie 2003, p. 137). Cooperation with the public service was required to get things on the political agenda. A deputy minister stated:

> If the chief of staff and the deputy minister disagree, the deputy minister will call upon colleagues and they will 'kill' the issue. It will then get lost in the system and it will take six months before resurfacing: it's the same 'old boys' network' that operates everywhere.
>
> (quoted in Plasse 1994, p. 74)

There is a strong informal network between senior officials from departments and central agencies that lubricates the policy process. A deputy minister stated:

> The informal network should not be sneezed at as the old boys' network; it is the arterial system, it is the heart and blood of the system, and it is what makes the system work.
>
> (quoted in Osbaldeston 1989, p. 71)

Thus, senior officials in Canada still have the advantages of networks to manoeuvre within the system.

The Prime Minister has the power to appoint and dismiss deputy ministers and associate deputy ministers, the two highest ranks in the bureaucracy. As deputy ministers are appointed on open-ended terms and serve at the pleasure of the Prime Minister, this means that they do not enjoy security of tenure and can be dismissed following a change of government. By and large, appointments of deputy ministers are from within the ranks of the federal public service, with only very few exceptions (Aucoin 2010, p. 66). Although appointed politically, deputy ministers generally consider themselves to be part of the professional public service and non-politicisation of the public service is considered to be a constitutional convention in Canada (*Osborne v Canada* (1991) 2 SCR 69; Simpson 1988). Appointment of public servants below the ranks of deputy minister and assistant deputy minister is overseen by an independent Public Service Commission.

With the rise of political advisors, public servants found their advice to be increasingly contested and their access to Ministers reduced, with increased layers of hierarchy interposed between them and their Minister. A survey of Canadian public servants found that officials interacted more frequently with ministerial staff than with Ministers (Bourgault and Dunn 2012). There was also rude behaviour by political staffers at the PMO. In one recent account, a public servant in the Privy Council's Office (PCO) (equivalent to Prime Minister's Department) stated that Harper's director of communications made life difficult, reminiscent of *The Thick of It*:

> It didn't matter who he hurt, who he pissed off, this man had ultimate control. Grown men at PCO were scared shitless of him. And PMO was scared shitless of him. In meetings, he would just take 'em down. Grown men had tears in their eyes. If you're dealing with someone who has got the prime minister's ear, what are you going to do?
>
> (quoted in Marland 2016, p. 205)

Academics have found that in recent times, senior public servants have become more responsive to the political wishes of the Prime Minister's coterie of advisors (Aucoin and Savoie 2009, p. 110). Despite this, the recent consensus by commentators is that there is 'little evidence that political advisors have supplanted the core advisor role of the public service, systematically thwarted the access of departmental officials to ministers, or undermined important civil service norms' (Boston and Nethercote 2012, p. 202, Craft 2016, p. 246). Craft found that officials thought they were able to provide 'free and frank' advice to Ministers and push back and clarify issues in situations where tensions and conflict emerged, knowing that if Ministers did not accept their advice, that was fine, as long as they were still able to provide it (Craft 2016, p. 246). There were also more productive aspects to the relationship between public servants and political staffers. For instance, public servants would often use advisors as a sounding board to test whether Ministers would be receptive to policy ideas. An advisor stated, 'so there is a big element of face-saving and signal-checking throughout the system because no one wants to be on the wrong side of the ultimate decision, right?' (Craft 2016, pp. 110–111). Thus, public servants in Canada have, by and large, managed to hold their ground.

Australia

The 1950s and 1960s were seen to be the 'heyday of the mandarin' (Weller 2001, p. 22). In this period, the position of the departmental secretaries was strong. Under the *Public Service Act 1922* (Cth), they had tenured positions that could not be terminated unilaterally, with limited exceptions.

The public service clearly still plays a significant role in the operation of the Australian executive in contemporary times. Senator Kim Carr noted that when the relationship between the department and the Minister is good, the public service 'can play a critical role because they, like ministerial advisors, play that role of collection and evaluation of information' (quoted in Ng 2016, p. 32). Former Minister Lindsay Tanner thought that departmental secretaries had a lot of power, particularly the Secretary of the Prime Minister's Department (quoted in Ng 2016, p. 32). Tanner noted that Ian Watt, former Secretary of the Prime Minister's Department, had considerable power because his:

> aggregate knowledge of what is going on, who's doing what and what has happened in the past will invariably be much larger than any Member of Parliament and any Minister. And in any political process, power flows from knowledge.
>
> (quoted in Ng 2016, p. 32)

Nevertheless, not all Ministers enjoyed positive relationships with their department. A former senior Liberal Minister stated that although he had a good relationship with his department, other Ministers had antagonistic relationships with their departments:

> I think some people battle their departments. They come in and they get into an adversarial role. And I think that is distinctly unhelpful. I rarely ever question the motives of senior public servants. My department worked extraordinarily well with me.
>
> (quoted in Ng 2016, p. 32)

Concomitant with the increased reliance on ministerial advisors is the reduction in the influence of the public service. As expected, the introduction of an additional layer of advice between the Minister and public service in the Whitlam years (1972–1975) created some tension between the public service and ministerial advisors. An advisor to Whitlam stated that:

> Tension between Whitlam's staff and the entrenched bureaucracy was the defining feature of the Whitlam government's operations. The public service was run by an aristocratic cabal of venerable men who lunched regularly at the Commonwealth Club and regarded the new Labor Government with suspicion. Steeped in old-school values, they had no time for ministerial advisers.
>
> (Williams 2013, pp. 112–113)

However, over the years, with the rise of ministerial advisors as a major source of advice, the public service found in many instances that it assumed a subsidiary status. John Cain, former Victorian Premier, expressed concern about:

> the acknowledged and apprehended influence of the private stream of advice [of ministerial advisers] at the expense of the traditional public service, which retains the corporate memory and experience to show government how to implement things.
>
> (quoted in Ng 2016, p. 33)

For instance, former Prime Minister Kevin Rudd would ignore his department for months at a time and essentially froze the Secretary of his department out (Kelly 2014, pp. 69–84). Consequently, ministerial advisors became his primary source of advice. Depending on the Minister and how the ministerial advisors interacted with the bureaucracy, the public service could be completely sidelined and undermined as a source of information. There are several reasons for this.

First of all, the very existence of the Australian ministerial advisor system is expressly intended to reduce the influence of the public service. Former Minister David Kemp, who was responsible for implementing the ministerial advisor system for the Coalition government as former Prime Minister Malcolm Fraser's Chief of Staff, said that the intent of the ministerial staff system was to counter the impact of the 'imperial public service' that was not elected and had 'an excessive influence on government and was not under the control of the elected government'. Kemp argued that 'the evolution of the ministerial staff system in my view is an expression of the desire of the elected government to exercise greater control over the institutions of government' (quoted in Ng 2016, p. 33). Likewise Senator Kim Carr contended that 'the original intention of the advisor in some quarters was to provide the Minister with a counterweight to the department' (quoted in Ng 2016, p. 34). This shows that the motivation for introducing the ministerial advisor system was to directly counteract the influence of the public service on the Minister, which was perceived to be too strong.

Former Treasurer Peter Costello stated that public servants were not part of the day-to-day decision-making because of their lack of proximity to the centre of power:

> Public servants can have influence on particular issues, but they're not really part of the day-to-day decision-making. I think if you want to be part of the day-to-day decision-making, you have to be there. You have to be part of Cabinet. You have to be in the Parliament building when crises are occurring. Even though they are just down the hill, the fact they're not there means they are not really at the centre of decision-making.
>
> (quoted in Ng 2016, p. 34)

Costello noted that it was partly a geographic issue, but partly because 'the public service wants to be there forever. So they really want to keep themselves out of the day-to-day controversies' (quoted in Ng 2016, p. 34). Thus, in order for the bureaucracy to serve governments of different political persuasions, they may seek not to be embroiled in the controversies and may not desire to exert any influence in that arena.

The degree of interaction of Ministers with ministerial advisors exceeded the Ministers' interaction with the public service, which is another indicator of the waning influence of the public service compared to ministerial advisors. For example, former Minister Lindsay Tanner explained that as a Minister, he had at least one advisor with him even if he was not in his ministerial office in Parliament House, which meant that 'they were always present' (quoted in Ng 2016, pp. 34–5). This was less so for the public servants although Tanner stated that he would normally have several interactions per day with public servants (quoted in Ng 2016, p. 35).

Further, there have been changes in the governance and legislative framework of the public service that have reduced employment security of departmental secretaries. The Efficiency Taskforce for the Royal Commission on Australian Government Administration recommended that senior officials be deprived of guaranteed tenure and instead be hired on a contract basis or competence system (Caiden 1975, p. 201). By 1994, the tenure of all secretaries was removed and they were all employed on fixed term contracts for up to five years. The *Public Service Act 1999* (Cth) provides that the Governor-General may give written notice to terminate the appointment of a Secretary on the recommendation of the Prime Minister.

This meant that secretaries found their positions to be far more tenuous, particularly where there was a change of government. This was illustrated by the 'night of the long knives' in 1996, where the newly elected Howard government terminated the contracts of six departmental secretaries immediately after the government was sworn in. This meant that a third of departmental secretaries were terminated before they could provide their services to the new government. This happened again in 2013 with the Abbott government terminating the employment of three departmental secretaries on the day they were sworn into government, with a few others pressured to resign.

Another example that illustrates the precarious position of departmental secretaries was the sacking of Paul Barratt, former Secretary of the Department of Defence, without any suggestion of incompetence or misconduct (*Barratt v Howard* (2000) 96 FCR 428, 430, 448–9). Barratt previously worked for a number of Ministers, but failed to gain the confidence of John Moore, the Defence Minister, and was in conflict with Moore's Chief of Staff. After several months of unresolved tension between Barratt and Moore, the Secretary of the Prime Minister's Department recommended that Barratt be replaced. Barratt's employment was terminated after he rejected an offer of a diplomatic post to New Zealand.

Barratt challenged his termination in the Federal Court, and the matter was appealed to the Full Federal Court (*Barratt v Howard* (1999) 165 ALR 605; *Barratt v Howard* (2000) 96 FCR 428, 444). The Full Federal Court held that Ministers had to comply with procedural fairness in terminating the employment of secretaries under the *Public Service Act 1922* (Cth), including providing a reason for the termination. It is likely that procedural fairness would also be required under the current public service legislation as the *Barratt* case was explicitly cited as a guidance note in the *Public Service Act* (Australia, *Public Service Act 1999* (Cth) s 59). However, despite the requirement of procedural fairness, the Court in *Barratt* held that the power to terminate a fixed term employment contract was not limited to 'fundamental fault or culpable conduct or where there is unsuitability or unfitness for office' (p. 449). Further, the Court held that although the termination had to be on a positive ground or grounds related to the objects of the Act which were not 'capricious or whimsical', the reasons provided did not have to be proven to be well-founded (pp. 450–452). Thus, the reason given, namely that the Minister had lost trust and confidence in the Secretary, was held to be sufficient, without any need to prove that the reason was objectively well-founded. This means that as long as a reason for termination is given that is not completely arbitrary, the courts will accept this reason, whether or not it is well-founded. Although this is appropriate given the nature of judicial review, which is concerned about the procedure rather than the merits of a decision, it shows the tenuous nature of the employment of Australian senior public servants.

The Barratt sacking confirms that Australian departmental secretaries are in a vulnerable position of being able to be removed if the Minister is not satisfied with their performance. Although the Minister has to negotiate with the Prime Minister and the Prime Minister's Office to remove their secretary through a centralised process, removal of secretaries is easier than in the past.

At a broad level, the removal of tenure for departmental secretaries was an attempt by politicians to exert control over the bureaucracy and to provide incentives for the top government officials to be responsive to the needs of the government of the day, rather than a plan to introduce patronage into the public service, where the friends of politicians are elevated to high positions. For Ministers to properly govern, it is important to have secretaries who are sympathetic and thus responsive to the government.

However, an excessive focus on responsiveness through politically loyal senior executives may ultimately undermine efficiency and service delivery, as there is a loss of institutional knowledge when secretaries are replaced. It is also arguable that the politicisation of the appointments of secretaries has resulted in the reluctance by secretaries to provide 'frank and fearless' advice. In addition, although such a system is not primarily intended to install a system of patronage, this may nevertheless be the result of politicising the top layer of the public service.

Concurrently, there has been an increase of contractual positions across the public service relative to permanent positions. In 2016, 11.5 per cent of Australian public servants were employed in non-ongoing or contract positions, which was an increase of 10.3 per cent from the previous year (Australian Public Service Commission 2016, p. 9). Thus, a significant group of public servants do not have the traditional job security normally afforded to their position. These employees may be reliant on the opinions of senior public servants, ministerial advisors and Ministers to get their employment renewed. This could reduce their willingness to provide frank and impartial advice.

Therefore, the emergence and increase of influence of Australian ministerial advisors has fundamentally altered the relationship between Ministers and the public service, such that the influence of public servants has generally declined. Further structural change has eroded the security and arguably the independence of the public service as a whole, particularly at the senior levels.

New Zealand

New Zealand moved from a patronage public service to a neutral one with the enactment of the *Public Service Act* in 1912, which introduced a professional, politically neutral career public service. The number of public servants grew swiftly under the first Labour government, which was intent on implementing a welfare state, and continued to increase in the post-war decade of prosperity. In 1962, the *State Services Act* gave permanent heads of departments the power to elect a 'higher appointments board' who would pick the new permanent heads. This effectively meant that senior public servants could grant each other lifetime tenure within an insular system. The appointments board was dubbed the 'College of Cardinals' after the powerful and secretive Vatican body that appoints the pope. In this period of economic prosperity, public servants enjoyed secure jobs, good salaries and protected appointments.

As the post-war economic boom subsided, sentiments towards the public service turned hostile. The Labour government under Prime Minister Norman Kirk (1972–1974) was suspicious that the public service would be unreceptive and unable to adapt to Labour ideas. Kirk complained that 'the virus of empire-building lies dormant in every vein' of the bureaucracy and that he was sick of the views of public servants 'paid to serve being expressed as if they were elected to govern' (quoted in New Zealand, State Services Commission 2013, p. 19). The subsequent Muldoon government (1975–1984) imposed a freeze on new staff.

This was only the tip of the iceberg. Public servants in New Zealand faced significant upheaval in the 'new public management' (NPM) movement in the 1980s and 1990s. New Zealand took the new public management mantra to heart and has 'gone the farthest along the entrepreneurial path' (Osborne and Gaebler 1993, p. 30). As part of NPM, successive governments undertook significant reforms to the structure and operations of the public service to separate ownership and purchase responsibilities, establish a division between policy and service delivery and create competition between service providers (Scott 1997, p. 158). As a result, a core public service was retained that delivered policy advice and essential public functions, but many functions were contracted out or performed by state-owned enterprises. Ministers were conceived of as political principals responsible for 'purchasing' outputs from administrative agents.

In part, the motivation for the large-scale reforms was to remedy the complaint that permanent heads of departments behaved like they 'really ran the country', while the Ministers were the 'amateur public face of government' (Norman 2003, p. 11). The number of public servants was drastically cut by one third, from 84,000 in 1984 to 30,000 in 2000 (Wanna 2005, p. 175). The culling of public servants was due to criticisms of a bloated, inefficient bureaucracy with a monopoly on policy implementation and advice (New Zealand, The Treasury 1987, ch. 2). In 1983, the then Opposition Leader complained that 'departments were run by their civil servants rather than their Ministers' (quoted in Roberts 1987, p. 100).

As part of the NPM reforms, the *State Sector Act 1988* removed the tenure of senior public servants, placed Chief Executives (departmental heads) on five-year contracts and made them responsible for the employment of their employees. The *State Sector Act* replaced what Richard Norman called a 'hierarchical structure and a clan-like focus on lifetime employment', with 'delegation of flexibility and discretion to chief executives and opening up of public service roles to external competition' and 'external focus and differentiation of public sector tasks': in short, a change from 'hierarchy and clan solutions' to 'market and network solutions' (Norman 2008, p. 34).

As a result of the increased accountability of Chief Executives, senior public servants in New Zealand have a greater public profile and media presence compared to Whitehall. Chief Executives are expected to appear in the media to explain government policy and its implementation, and to give public explanations when there has been an administrative deficiency in their department.

Appointments to the public service were impartial and not subject to patronage. After the insular appointments board was abolished, the appointment of senior public servants became strictly on a merit basis with the State Services Commissioner running a robust and independent process in consultation with Ministers. Hence there is less politicisation of the public service compared to Australia. The NPM fervour has since died down and the pendulum has swung the other way, with the State Services Authority expressing concerns about fragmentation and lack of central coordination due to the proliferation of agencies (New Zealand, State Services Commission 2001, p. 28).

Despite the extreme shocks to the bureaucracy, initially the public service remained relatively sanguine about the rise of political advisors. In a 2005 survey, more than half (57.9 per cent) of senior officials rated the advent of ministerial advisors as a positive development overall, while 72.7 per cent indicated that their personal relations with advisors were generally positive (Eichbaum and Shaw 2008, p. 349). Public servants expressed a quiet confidence in their ability to ensure that they were not marginalised in the policy process (Eichbaum and Shaw 2007, p. 635).

Nevertheless, there was still evident friction in the interactions between advisors and officials. A significant proportion (22.4 per cent) of public servants agreed or strongly agreed that advisors obstructed officials' access to their Minister, while almost a third (30.1 per cent) agreed or strongly agreed that advisors were a risk to the neutrality of the public service. Further, nearly half (49.4 per cent) reported that ministerial advisors impeded their work or the department (Eichbaum and Shaw 2007, p. 626). A public servant stated that they had:

> experienced instances where ministerial advisers have actively criticised [departmental] staff to undermine their ability to give advice. I have had instances where advisers have asked to review policy papers and seek changes before being submitted to ministers. I have had examples where advisers have over-ridden ministerial decisions.
>
> (quoted in Eichbaum and Shaw 2007, p. 626)

It is evident that a significant proportion of public servants perceive that ministerial advisors do impede their work and ability to advise Ministers. In 2005, 35.8 per cent of officials thought that advisors actively discourage the provision of free and frank advice by officials, while 26.2 per cent believed that advisors do in practice exert too much control over the policy agenda (Eichbaum and Shaw 2008, pp. 348–349).

The election of the Key government (2008–2016) was a major turning point in the interactions between Ministers and public servants. From 2009, there were rumblings of discontent from the public service indicating a more strained relationship between the bureaucracy and political advisors. In 2009, the Public Service Association asked the Auditor General to investigate the government's use of political advisors in government departments, arguing that 'use of the advisors suggests the Government does not trust public servants' and calling the advisors 'spies in government departments'. Further, the National Secretary of the Public Service Association, Erin Polaczuk, asserted that the public service was increasingly under pressure:

> We have members [public servants] expressing opinions like they have to match the advice they give to ministerial expectations rather than to the best advice … It sounds as though they feel there is a lot more political meddling by Ministers at the moment into the work that they are doing … It is not as free and frank as it needs to be.
>
> (Radio National 2015)

These strident comments show an increased level of hostility between the public service and ministerial staff. Further, in recent times, the public service felt hindered from providing frank and fearless advice to Ministers. A survey showed that, in 2017, more than half of public servants felt they were less likely to provide free and frank advice compared to the past (Eichbaum 2017).

Ministerial staff under the Key government had broader roles and were more interventionist than their predecessors. For example, the Inspector-General of Intelligence and Security found that under previous governments, the relationship between the New Zealand secret service and the Prime Minister was conducted almost exclusively between the Prime Minister and the Director of the Service, with very little involvement by officials or advisors. After the change of government to Prime Minister Key, however, contact between the Service and the Prime Minister's Office became more diffuse and Service staff engaged directly with political advisors in the Prime Minister's private office.

As will be discussed in chapter four, there has also been evidence of politicisation of the New Zealand public service following investigations of the *Dirty Politics* revelations (Hager 2014). In 2014, the Inspector-General found that a senior civil servant compromised the principle of political neutrality by releasing information under the *Official Information Act* (OIA) to blogger Cameron Slater, while blocking similar requests from the mainstream media, following the Prime Minister's Office leaking confidential information to the same blogger (New Zealand, Office of the Inspector-General of Intelligence and Security 2014). The Ombudsman also found that there was pressure exerted by political staff on the public service in relation to OIA requests and some agencies were vulnerable to inappropriate interference by ministerial offices (New Zealand, Office of the Ombudsman 2015). This may indicate that the balance in public service advice in New Zealand has shifted from 'neutral competence' towards 'responsive competence'.

Analysis

It is clear that there has been tension in the relationship between political advisors and civil servants in all Westminster jurisdictions, as civil servants were forced to adapt to a new world order where they no longer had the monopoly on providing advice to Ministers. As political advisors grew in numbers, power and influence, civil servants faced the challenge of having an additional advisory layer interposed between them and the Minister. Some civil servants felt disempowered by the existence of political advisors as their advice was sidelined, while others used political advisors more positively as a springboard to test and gauge the Minister's response to their ideas.

David Zussman conceives of three main models of how political advisors interact with Ministers and the civil service: collaborative, gatekeeper and triangulated (Zussman 2009, p. 14). The collaborative model involves a cooperative relationship between civil servants and political advisors, with advice being jointly tendered to the Minister in a collaborative fashion. The gatekeeper envisages political advisors as funnels or filters who interpose themselves between the Minister and the civil service and potentially blocking officials from accessing Ministers. The triangulated model involves

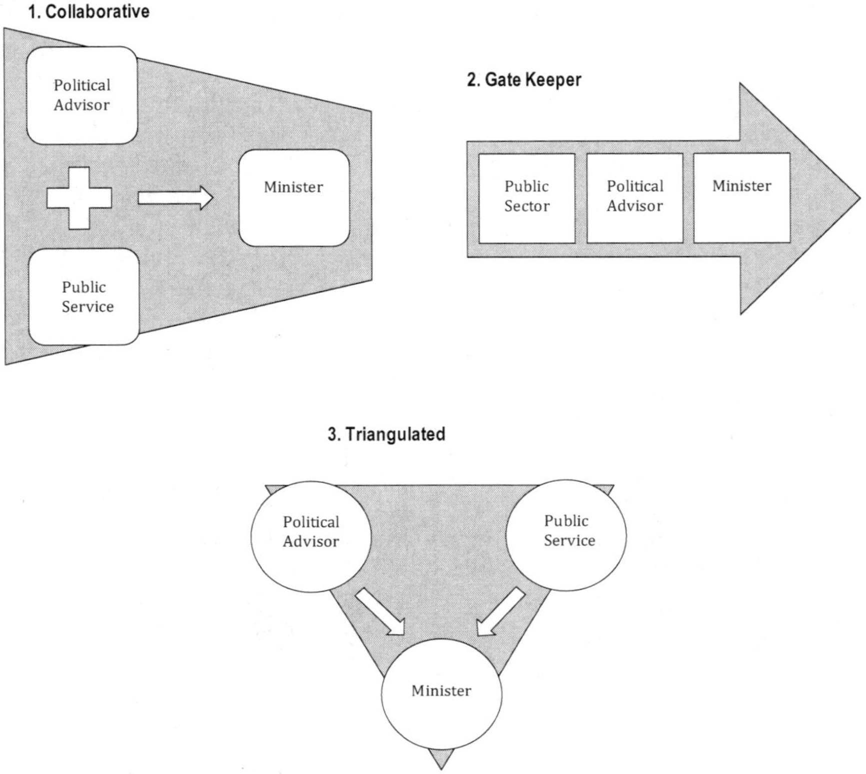

Figure 3.1 Three models of political advisors and the machinery of government
Source: Adapted from Zussman (2009).

civil servants and political advisors independently and separately providing advice to the Minister.

If the political advisor functions in a collaborative manner or in a triangulated way, acting as a separate channel to provide advice to the Minister and generally not interfering with civil service advice, the relationship between the political advisors and civil service is more likely to be harmonious. However, where political advisors act as a funnel or gatekeeper by censoring or blocking information that reaches the Minister, tension might build up within the ranks of the civil service and the quality of the advice may also be negatively impacted.

In acting as a funnel or gatekeeper, political advisors are able to act as a 'bridge' between the Minister and civil servants in a positive and negative sense (Craft 2013, p. 214). Positive bridging can increase the availability or circulation of policy advice by leveraging from various internal and external sources within the policy advisory system. On the other hand, negative bridging can restrict or exclude policy advice by filtering, blocking or screening advisory inputs before reaching the Minister. As James Walter argued, where advice is funnelled, this may result in 'narrowing the options only to those predetermined by an ideological agenda rather than seriously "testing reality"' (Walter 2006, p. 26).

Another major issue is that civil servants have complained that political advisors have interfered with bureaucratic advice and decision-making. We will see in chapter four that this behaviour has led to controversies. The interference with the bureaucracy could stem from advisors being ignorant about the appropriate boundaries of their role in relation to the civil service. As such, written guidance should be issued to delineate the boundaries between political advisors and civil servants. For instance, there is a legislated requirement for guidelines on the interactions between ministerial advisors and public servants in the Australian State of Western Australia. The *Public Sector Management Act 1994* (WA) provides that a Minister must make arrangements in writing governing the dealings and communications between the department and ministerial office, and between ministerial advisors and public servants (s 74). It also prohibits ministerial advisors from directing a public servant to perform their departmental duties unless they have departmental approval to do so. This is a good way to provide clarity about the scope of power and appropriate interactions between ministerial advisors and civil servants. As we will see in chapter five, Codes of Conduct in the United Kingdom, Canada, Australia and New Zealand also delineate the appropriate boundaries of interaction between advisors and the civil service. This should be coupled with training for political advisors that provides them with guidance and advice on how to deal with the civil service. Ministers and chiefs of staff in ministerial offices should also exercise greater managerial competence over the actions of their staff and rein in any improper behaviour towards civil servants, whether in terms intrusion into civil service decision-making or rude behaviour.

External forces have also rocked the stable foundations of the Westminster civil service. The new public management (NPM) movement that swept through many democracies from the mid-1980s has destabilised and weakened the civil service, and concomitantly led to the entrenchment of the position of political advisors. Ministers considered the civil service to be bloated, cumbersome, sluggish, resistant to change and operating in its own self-interest. Reformers were adherents of public choice theory, which postulated that the bureaucracy would perpetually seek to increase its power, budget and grip over politicians (Niskanen 1971). The panacea to these ills was seen to be the importation of private sector management methods into the public sector. New public management is thus premised on a reconceptualisation of the way governments should be managed, with an increased focus on reducing costs, managing programmes more efficiently and public service managers being more accountable for the results.

The new public management movement had its genesis in New Zealand in the late 1970s and spread to Australia and the United Kingdom in the 1980s. Canada experimented the least, with the focus being on cutting the civil service and decentralisation, rather than the significant restructuring that happened in New Zealand and the United Kingdom (Savoie 2003, p. 61). The mechanisms of NPM include internal managerial changes, such as the implementation of key performance indicators, accompanied by large-scale institutional reorganisation, such as privatisation and outsourcing of governmental operations. Under NPM, the neat dichotomy of Ministers and civil servants was disrupted by the creation of statutory agencies and contracted out services, as well as the introduction of political advisors into the system.

The level of destabilisation of the civil service has varied across the Westminster jurisdictions. Although all jurisdictions have felt the impact of the new public management movement, the United Kingdom civil service has shown the most successful resistance to the loss of power, with senior mandarins largely maintaining their grip on recruitment processes at a senior level. At the other end of the spectrum, senior public servants in Australia are in a far more tenuous position, being on short-term contracts that can be easily terminated by Ministers. In all jurisdictions, civil servants have complained that their access to Ministers has reduced with the advent of political advisors, and that advisors have sought to block their advice. While the star of political advisors has risen, the influence of the civil service has correspondingly waned.

References

Books and journal articles

Aucoin, P, 2010, 'Canada', in C Eichbaum and R Shaw (eds), *Partisan Appointees and Public Servants: An International Analysis of the Role of the Political Adviser*, Edward Elgar, Cheltenham, pp. 64–93.

Aucoin, P, and D Savoie, 2009, 'The Politics-Administration Dichotomy: Democracy versus Bureaucracy?' in O P Dwivedi, B M Sheldrick and T A Mau (eds), *The Evolving Physiology of Government: Canadian Public Administration in Transition*, University of Ottawa Press, Ottawa, pp. 97–117.

Boston, J, and Nethercote, J R, 2012, 'Reflections on "New Political Governance" in Westminster Systems', *Governance*, vol. 25(2), pp. 201–207.

Bourgault, J, and Dunn, C, 2012, 'Deputy Ministers and Policy Advice in Times of a Conservative Government in Canada', Paper presented at International Political Science Association Annual Conference, 8–12 July, Madrid.

Campbell, A, and Stott, R, (eds), 2007, *The Blair Years: Extracts from the Alastair Campbell Diaries*, Hutchinson, London.

Campbell, C, 1987, 'Canada' in W Plowden (ed), *Advising the Rulers*, Basil Blackwell, Oxford, pp. 124–146.

Craft, J, 2013, 'Appointed Political Staffs and the Diversification of Policy Advisory Sources: Theory and Evidence from Canada', *Policy and Society*, vol. 32, pp. 211–223.

Craft, J, 2016, *Backrooms and Beyond: Partisan Advisers and the Politics of Policy Work in Canada*, University of Toronto Press, Toronto.

Crossman, R, 1975, *The Diaries of a Cabinet Minister*, vol. 1, Hamilton and Cape, London.

Daintith, T, and Page, A, 1999, *The Executive in the Constitution: Structure, Autonomy, and Internal Control*, Oxford University Press, Oxford.

Dwivedi, O P and Gow, J J, 1999, *From Bureaucracy to Public Management: The Administrative Culture of the Government of Canada*, Broadview Press, Toronto.

Eichbaum, C and Shaw, R, 2007, 'Ministerial Advisers, Politicization and the Retreat from Westminster: The Case of New Zealand', *Public Administration*, vol. 85(3), pp. 609–640.

Eichbaum, C and Shaw, R, 2008, 'Revisiting Politicization: Political Advisers and Public Servants in Westminster Systems', *Governance*, vol. 21(3), pp. 337–363.

Foster, C, 2005, *British Government in Crisis*, Hart Publishing, Oxford.

Granatstein, J L, 1982, *The Ottawa Men: The Civil Service Mandarins, 1935–37*, University of Toronto Press, Toronto.

Hager, N, 2014, *Dirty Politics: How Attack Politics is Poisoning New Zealand's Political Environment*, Craig Potton Publishing, Nelson.

Hennessy, P, 1989, *Whitehall*, Fontana Press, London.

Hockin, T A, 1975, *Government in Canada*, Weidenfield and Nicholson, London.

Kelly, P, 2014, *Triumph and Demise: The Broken Promise of a Labor Generation*, Melbourne University Publishing, Melbourne.

Manion, J L, 1990, 'Notes for a Presentation to the Dalhousie Conference on Career Public Service' 5 October, Canadian Centre for Management Development, Ottawa.

Manion, J L, 1991, 'Career Public Service in Canada: Reflections and Predictions', *International Journal of Administrative Studies*, vol. 57(3), p. 363.

Marland, A, 2016, *Brand Command: Canadian Politics and Democracy in the Age of Message Control*, University of British Columbia Press, British Columbia.

Moran, M, 2003, *The British Regulatory State: High Modernism and Hyper-innovation*, Oxford University Press, Oxford.

Ng, YF, 2016, *Ministerial Advisers in Australia: The Modern Legal Context*, Federation Press, Sydney.

Niskanen, W, 1971, *Bureaucracy and Representative Government*, Aldine-Atherton, Chicago.

Norman, R, 2003, *Obedient Servants? Management Freedoms and Accountabilities in the New Zealand Public Sector*, Victoria University Press, Wellington.

Norman, R, 2008, 'At the Centre or in Control? Central Agencies in Search of New Identities', *Policy Quarterly*, vol. 4(2), pp. 33–38.

Osbaldeston, G F, 1989, *Keeping Deputy Ministers Accountable*, McGraw–Hill Ryerson, Toronto.

Osborne, D, and Gaebler, T, 1993, *Reinventing Government*, Plume, New York.

Plasse, M, 1994, *Ministerial Chiefs of Staff in the Federal Government in 1990: Profiles, Recruitment, Duties, and Relations with Senior Public Servants*, Canadian Centre for Management Development, Ottawa.

Powell, J, 2010, *The New Machiavelli: How to Wield Power in the Modern World*, Bodley Head, London.

Roberts, A, 2002, 'A Fragile State: Federal Public Administration in the Twentieth Century' in C Dunn (ed), *The Handbook of Canadian Public Administration*, Oxford University Press, Toronto, pp. 18–36.

Roberts, J, 1987, 'Ministers, the Cabinet and Public Servants' in J Boston, J Martin and M Holland (eds), *The Fourth Labour Government: Radical Politics in New Zealand*, Oxford University Press, Auckland, pp. 89–110.

Savoie, D J, 1999, *Governing from the Centre: The Concentration of Power in Canadian Politics*, University of Toronto Press, Toronto.

Savoie, D J, 2003, *Breaking the Bargain: Public Servants, Ministers, and Parliament*, University of Toronto Press, Toronto.

Schindeler, F, 1977, 'The Prime Minister and the Cabinet: History and Development' in T A Hockin (ed), *Apex of Power: The Prime Minister and Political Leadership in Canada*, 2nd edn, Prentice-Hall, Ontario, pp. 22–47.

Scott, G, 1997, 'The New Institutional Economics and Reshaping the State in New Zealand' in G Davis, B Sullivan and A Yeatman, *The New Contractualism?* (Melbourne, MacMillan): pp. 154–163.

Simpson, J, 1988, *Spoils of Power*, University of Toronto Press, Toronto.

Walter, J, 2006, 'Ministers, Minders and Public Servants: Changing Parameters of Responsibility in Australia' *Australian Journal of Public Administration*, vol. 65(3), pp. 22–27.

Wanna, J, 2005, 'New Zealand's Westminster Trajectory: Archetypal Transplant to Maverick Outlier' in H Patapan, J Wanna and P Weller (eds), *Westminster Legacies: Democracy and Responsible Government in Asia and the Pacific*, UNSW Press, Sydney, pp. 153–185.

Weber, M, 1987, (1947), *The Theory of Social and Economic Organisation*, Trans. Henderson, E M and Parson, T, Free Press, New York.

Weller, P, 2001, *Australia's Mandarins: The Frank and the Fearless?*, Allen & Unwin, Crows Nest.

Williams, E, 2013, 'Inside the Prime Minister's Office' in T Bramston (ed), *The Whitlam Legacy*, Federation Press, Sydney, pp. 112–119.

Wilson, G K, and A Barker, 1995, 'The End of the Whitehall Model?', *West European Politics*, vol. 18(4), pp. 130–149.

Zussman, D, (2009), *Political Advisers*, OECD, Paris.

Legislation, codes, case law, government and parliamentary reports

Australia, Public Sector Management Act 1994 (WA).

Australia, Public Service Act 1922 (Cth).

Australia, Public Service Act 1999 (Cth).

Australian Public Service Commission, 2016, State of the Service Report 2015–2016.

Barratt v Howard (1999) 165 ALR 605.

Barratt v Howard (2000) 96 FCR 428.

Benoit, L, 2006, 'Ministerial Staff: The Life and Times of Parliament's Statutory Orphans', *Restoring Accountability Research Studies Volume 1: Parliament, Ministers and Deputy Ministers*, Commission of Inquiry into the Sponsorship Program and Advertising Activities, Canadian Government Publishing, Ottawa, pp. 145–252.

Caiden, G E, 1975, *Towards a More Efficient Government Administration, First Report*, Royal Commission on Australian Government Administration, Task Force on Efficiency, AGPS, Canberra.

Canada, Dorion Inquiry, 1965. Special Public Inquiry 1964, Report of the Commissioner, prepared by tshe Honourable Frederic Dorion, Chief Justice of the Superior Court for the Province of Quebec, Privy Council Office, Canada.

Canada, Conflict of Interest and Post-Employment Code for Public Office Holders (2006).

Canada, Privy Council, 2015, *Open and Accountable Government*, Privy Council Office.

Canada, Royal Commission on Government Organization, 1962, *Final Report*, The Glassco Commission, Queen's Printer, Ottawa.

New Zealand, Official Information Act 1982.

New Zealand, Public Service Act 1912.

New Zealand, State Sector Act 1988.

New Zealand, Office of the Inspector-General of Intelligence and Security, 2014, Report into the Release of Information by the New Zealand Security Intelligence Service in July and August 2011, Public Report, Prepared by C Gwyn, Inspector-General of Intelligence and Security.

New Zealand, Office of the Ombudsman, 2015, Not a Game of Hide and Seek: Report on an Investigation into Central Government Agencies for the Purpose of Compliance with the OIA, prepared by Dame B Waken, Chief Ombudsman.

New Zealand, State Services Commission, 2001, Report of the Advisory Group on the Review of the Centre, Report prepared by Ministerial Advisory Group, State Services Commission, Wellington.

New Zealand, State Services Commission, 2013. 100 Years of Public Service, A Centenary Celebration of New Zealand's State Services Commission.

New Zealand, The Treasury, 1987, Government Management: Brief to the Incoming Government, Volume 1, GPO, Wellington.

Osborne v Canada (1991) 2 SCR 69.

R v Duffy (2016) ONCJ 220.

United Kingdom, Cabinet Office, 2016, Code of Conduct for Special Advisers.

United Kingdom, Civil Service Commission, 2015, Recruitment Principles. Available at: http://civilservicecommission.independent.gov.uk/wp-content/uploads/2017/01/RECRUITMENT-PRINCIPLES-April-2015-as-of-January-2017.pdf.

United Kingdom, Civil Service Reform, 2014, Civil Service Reform Plan Progress Report.

United Kingdom, Committee on Standards in Public Life, 2000, Reinforcing Standards: Review of the First Report of the Committee on Standards of Public Life.

United Kingdom, Committee on Standards in Public Life 2002a, Public Hearings, 27 June.

United Kingdom, Committee on Standards in Public Life 2002b, Public Hearings, 9 July.

United Kingdom, Committee on Standards in Public Life, 2003, Defining the Boundaries within the Executive: Ministers, Special Advisers and the Permanent Civil Service.

United Kingdom, Constitutional Reform and Governance Act 2010.

United Kingdom, House of Commons, Public Administration Select Committee, 2002, Minutes of Evidence, 1 November 2001.

United Kingdom, House of Commons, Public Administration Select Committee, 2012, Special Advisors in the Thick of It. Sixth Report of Session 2012–2013, The Stationery Office Ltd, London.

United Kingdom, House of Commons, Public Administration Select Committee, 2013, Truth to Power: How Civil Service Reform Can Succeed, Vol 1, Eighth Report of Session 2013–2014, The Stationery Office Ltd, London.

United Kingdom, Ministry of Reconstruction, 1918, Report of the Machinery of Government Committee, Prepared by Viscount R Haldane, Machinery of Government Committee, HMSO, London.

Newspaper articles

Eichbaum, C, 2017, 'Chris Eichbaum: Free and Frank Advice Fast Disappearing', The Dominion Post, 8 August. Available at: www.stuff.co.nz/national/politics/95499693/chris-eichbaum--free-and-frank-advice-fast-disappearing.

Mason, Rowena, 2017, 'Francis Maude to Step Down as MP after Three Decades in Parliament', The Guardian, 2 Feburary. Available at: www.theguardian.com/politics/2015/feb/01/francis-maude-step-down-mp-cabinet-office-horsham-general-election.

Radio National New Zealand, 2015, 'Public Service Neutrality under Threat?' *Insight Program*, radio transcript, Radio National New Zealand, 6 December. Available at: www.radionz.co.nz/national/programmes/insight/audio/201781443/insight-for-6-december-2015-politics-and-public-servants.

4 Scandals and controversies

The integration of political advisors into the Westminster system of government has not gone without a hitch. There have been tensions due to the highly partisan behaviour of advisors which causes them to exceed the appropriate boundaries of their role. Further, in a frenetic and largely media-driven environment, the way in which political advisors have utilised the media has created problems. This chapter examines the scandals and controversies that have engulfed political advisors in the Westminster jurisdictions over the years. It categorises the commonalities between the various scandals and elucidates the causes of these scandals.

United Kingdom

Between 1997 and 2013, there have been at least 26 public allegations of special advisor misconduct in the United Kingdom (Lock 2013). The trend is towards increasing accusations of misbehaviour in recent times. All but one of the scandals involved misbehaviour by media advisors, while one third of the scandals involved the Prime Minister's Office. The scandals broadly fall into two main categories:

- **Exceeding authority**: Special advisors acting beyond their remit; or
- **Media issues**: Special advisors leaking information to the media, including factionally within government and against the Opposition.

Exceeding authority

In 2011, Adam Smith, special advisor to Culture Secretary Jeremy Hunt, provided a stream of commercially confidential information to a News Corporation lobbyist during News Corporation's bid to take full control of BSkyB. This included information about the content of the Minister's future statements to Parliament, as well as an intention to share confidential reports assessing News Corporation's bid. Smith also repeatedly suggested that his Minister wanted the bid to succeed. In a space of 13 months during the passage of the bid, the lobbyist made a staggering 191 phone calls, wrote 158 emails and sent 799 texts to Hunt's office. Smith, in turn, texted the lobbyist 257 times in that period. Minister Hunt was given quasi-judicial oversight of the bid and the takeover process was to be fair and impartial, without favouritism.

When Smith's extensive correspondence with the lobbyist came to light in a public inquiry, Smith resigned, saying he acted without the authority of his Minister and that he had allowed the impression to be created that the relationship between News Corporation and the Department for Culture, Media and Sport was too close. The Minister refused to resign, stating that he was unaware of 'the volume and tone' of Smith's contacts with News Corporation. He claimed that his special advisor had 'overstepped the mark unintentionally'. Thus, a special advisor acted outside his remit in a quasi-judicial inquiry. Following this event, the Cabinet Secretary and Head of the Civil Service issued supplementary guidance on the handling of quasi-judicial decisions by Ministers (UK, House of Commons, Public Administration Select Committee 2012, para 27).

There have also been issues with a person acting beyond his remit by masquerading as a special advisor. Adam Werritty, a personal friend of Defence Minister Liam Fox, distributed misleading business cards calling himself an advisor to Liam Fox bearing Parliament's portcullis logo and accompanied Fox on official business trips, although Werritty held no official position as a special advisor. Werritty arranged meetings between lobbyists and the Minister. This led to Minister Fox's resignation, as he was implicated in requesting donors to channel money through Werritty's company. Due to Fox's requests, Werritty's activities were funded by companies and individuals that potentially stood to benefit from government decisions, including defence lobbyists.

Media issues

British special advisors have been involved in leaking information to the media and seeking to fabricate issues against their political opponents, whether factional opponents within their own party or opposing parties. In terms of leaking to the media, an infamous event occurred after the terrorist attacks on September 11 2001. Jo Moore, special advisor to the Transport Minister, sent an email to her department, stating that 'it's now a very good day to get out anything we want to bury'. She then suggested, 'Councillors' expenses?' (Sparrow 2001). The email was leaked by civil servants, causing public uproar over her cavalier attitude in looking to capitalise on a tragedy. Moore also attempted to manage civil servants by asking departmental press officers to brief against the Transport Commissioner for London, which they refused to do. Later Moore wanted to bury bad news on rail performance indicators on the day of Princess Margaret's funeral. This was again leaked by civil servants, who were clearly hostile to her as she allegedly engaged in bullying behaviour. After much media furore, Moore resigned from her position. The permanent secretary Richard Mottram pronounced that: 'We're all f**ked. I'm f**ked. You're f**ked. The whole department's f**ked. It's been the biggest cock-up ever and we're all completely f**ked' (Brogan 2002). This dire prediction did come true. The acrimonious battle contributed to the resignation of Transport Minister, Steve Byers, due to miscommunication about the resignations of his staff, payoffs to these staff being aired in the media and allegations that the Minister had misled Parliament. In the end, the entire department was abolished and the permanent secretary was transferred to another department. The Public Administration Select Committee concluded following its inquiry that:

> Ms Moore took on a series of executive and, in effect, managerial tasks without reference to proper procedures. In addition, a number of civil servants abandoned professional standards by leaking information and misinformation in a way intended to undermine Ms Moore. Management found itself unable to prevent a catastrophic taking of sides at senior level in the department.
>
> (UK, House of Commons, Public Administration Select Committee 2003, p. 5)

Thus, Moore acted beyond her remit in instructing officials to leak material and also interfered with the operation of the bureaucracy. Furthermore, she acted in an underhanded manner in trying to bury bad news. Clearly there were ongoing schisms between Moore and the civil servants that played out publicly through leaks to the media, resulting in a complete omnishambles: a flood of senior resignations and the eventual collapse of the department.

In 2009, Damian McBride, former advisor to Prime Minister Gordon Brown, was forced to resign following leaked emails about his plans to run a smear campaign by publishing fabricated rumours against senior Conservative MPs on a private blog. McBride's memoirs showed that he leaked information to the press often, including negative stories about other Ministers. For instance, McBride once rebuked a Minister speaking about tax publicly in the media, 'telling the papers as a No. 10 source that Ivan should concentrate on his day job or he might soon find himself without one' (McBride 2013, p. 415). When the Minister told McBride that he was not intimidated, McBride leaked a story to *News of the World* about the Minister pestering a young civil servant who used to work in his private office: 'It was so obviously a hatchet job from me that many MPs and commentators immediately called it as such and it was one of the major factors that led to me being forced to step away from my press briefing role after the October reshuffle' (McBride 2013, p. 415). Despite being dismissed in disgrace in 2009, McBride later managed to find his way back into being a special advisor for the Labour shadow defence secretary.

McBride's modus operandi of personal attacks was not an isolated incident. Fiona Cunningham (now Hill), advisor to then Home Minister,

Theresa May, was forced to resign in 2014 after a Downing Street inquiry found she had briefed against Education Minister Michael Gove in a dispute between the two Ministers over Islamic extremism in schools. Hill was later appointed as Prime Minister May's Chief of Staff. Likewise, Dominic Cummings and Henry De Zoete, special advisors to the Education Minister, were accused of using an anonymous Twitter account @toryeducation to personally attack political opponents and journalists in 2013. Cummings was previously accused of bullying and intimidating a senior civil servant, who claimed that exchanges with Cummings were 'more reminiscent of an episode of "The Thick of It" than a reflection of acceptable behaviour of employees of the Department of Education'. The claim was settled for £25,000 so it would not go to a tribunal. Goves' special advisors were also criticised by the Information Commissioner in 2011 for using private email accounts to hide information from civil servants and avoid scrutiny under freedom of information legislation (UK, Information Commissioner's Office 2012). Following prolonged controversy, Cummings and De Zoete stepped down as special advisors in 2013 and 2014 respectively. Cummings later became the campaign director of the victorious Brexit campaign.

There has also been uproar about the appointment of controversial media advisors. Former Prime Minister's David Cameron's chief media advisor, Andy Coulson, initially blocked Dominic Cummings' appointment as being too high risk. Paradoxically Coulson himself was forced to resign in 2010 amid allegations that he was involved in phone hacking while editor of *News of the World*. Coulson was later found by the court to have sanctioned phone hacking by his journalists. It was a widespread practice in the paper to intercept voicemail messages of thousands of people, including politicians, the royal family and even a murdered schoolgirl, to generate news. As a result, Coulson was jailed for 18 months for conspiracy to intercept communications. Due to the scandal, the tabloid paper was shut down.

Although Coulson's misconduct occurred before he became a special advisor, questions can be raised about the appointment and vetting process for special advisors. When he was Opposition Leader, Cameron appointed Coulson in 2007 amid investigations into the phone hacking issue. Although Cameron was cautioned against appointing Coulson when he became Prime Minister in 2010, he nevertheless made the appointment. Following Coulson's resignation, Cameron apologised for employing him.

Canada

There have been significant controversies and scandals throughout Canadian history involving political advisors. The controversies can be classified into three main categories:

- **Interference with the bureaucracy**: Political advisors interfering with bureaucratic decision-making;

- **Exceeding authority**: Political advisors acting beyond their remit; or
- **Miscommunication**: Failure of communication between political advisors and their Ministers or the bureaucracy.

Interference with the bureaucracy

The most well-known event in Canada that sparked strong regulation of political advisors through the *Federal Accountability Act* was the Sponsorship Scandal. This scandal occurred in the wake of a Canadian federal government desperate to maintain Canadian unity in the face of possible secession of Quebec. Sponsorship funds were set aside to promote federal unity. However, an Auditor-General's report revealed that up to $100 million of the $250 million programme had been paid to advertising agencies with close links to the Liberal Party, although they had performed little or no work (Canada, Auditor-General 2003, ch. 3). The Gomery Commission found that the Minister and political advisors had been directly involved in the sponsorship selection, which amounted to inappropriate 'political encroachment into the administrative domain' (Canada, Commission of Inquiry into the Sponsorship Program and Advertising Activities 2005, p. 427).

At the centre of this scandal was Jean Pelletier, then Prime Minister's Chief of Staff, who regularly gave instructions and directions to a mid-ranking public servant without the presence of the deputy minister (departmental head). The instructions included which agencies should be funded and to what amount, expressed as 'suggestions' that the bureaucrats took to be directives. As Benoit stated, there was a 'wink-nod relationship that allows the ministerial staff to protest their adherence to the letter of the "no direction" guideline, while "sinning in their hearts" against the spirit of the protocol' (Benoit 2006, p. 192).

The Gomery Commission investigating the incident found that the Prime Minister, Jean Chrétien, was responsible for the actions of his Chief of Staff, to whom he had delegated the responsibility for the sponsorship programme. In addition, then Minister of Public Works, Alfonso Gagliano, was directly involved in decisions to provide funding to events and projects for partisan purposes. These actions circumvented the normal departmental procedures, safeguards and controls, leading to a lack of transparency on how the sponsorship programme was directed and funded.

In addition, it was found that a lobbyist and owner of an advertising firm, Jacques Corriveau, had organised kickbacks to the Quebec wing of the Liberal Party of Canada on commissions paid to communications agencies, in exchange for securing sponsorship contracts for these agencies due to his political influence. This was a form of illegal campaign financing. As a result, advertising agencies who contributed to the financing of the Liberal Party reaped great profits. This sparked concerns that there was a link between the financial contributions and the expectation that government contracts be awarded, which led to a perception of corruption.

The influence of money in politics has had deep roots in Canadian history. The spectacular Rivard affair in 1964 involved political advisors embroiled in a heady mix of drugs and political donations. The Executive Assistants to the Immigration and Justice Ministers used intimidation and bribery to block the extradition to the United States of notorious underworld figure and convicted heroin smuggler, Lucien Rivard, who had close ties to the Quebec wing of the Liberal Party. As a parliamentarian alleged, the 'tentacles of [an] international cartel dealing in narcotics extended into the very offices of two ministers of the federal government' (Canada, House of Commons, 1964, p. 10383).

Mr Justice Frederic Dorian was appointed to conduct an inquiry into the Rivard affair. Dorian J found that Raymond Denis, Executive Assistant to the Minister for Citizenship and Immigration, offered the prosecutor, Pierre Lamontagne, a $20,000 bribe if he did not oppose Rivard's application for bail, stating that the Liberal Party would receive a substantial amount of financial recompense for Rivard's release (Canada, Dorion Inquiry 1965). In addition, Dorian J found that the Executive Assistant to the Minister for Justice, André Letendre, also intervened in the case to try to pressure the prosecutor, Lamontagne, to secure bail for Rivard; conduct condemned by Mr Justice Dorian as 'reprehensible'. This scandal prompted the resignation of the Minister of Justice Guy Favreau and the conviction of Executive Assistant Raymond Denis for attempting to obstruct justice. Denis spent two years in jail.

In the meantime, Rivard himself escaped from jail by climbing a wall with a garden hose, which he borrowed to flood a skating rink on a frosty spring evening. Rivard managed to flee authorities for four months before being captured again. Rivard was finally extradited to the United States, where he was convicted of drug smuggling and sentenced to 20 years in jail.

At the provincial level, advisors have been accused of behaving improperly in interfering with public service activities for partisan purposes, document destruction and the mass deletion of email records relevant to controversial incidents to avoid scrutiny. The two most senior political advisors in Ontario, the Premier's Chief of Staff and Deputy Chief of Staff, were charged by the police with criminal offences for their alleged deletion of thousands of computer files related to the Ontario gas plant scandals. The Liberals decided to cancel two gas plants before the 2011 election, paying $1.1 billion in compensation. The parliamentary committee investigating the incident received documents from the government, but there were no documents from political advisors. In 2013, the Ontario Privacy Commissioner investigated the incident and found that all emails from the ministerial offices relating to the gas plant scandal had been deleted (Ontario, Office of the Information and Privacy Commissioner 2013). The Commissioner concluded that the indiscriminate deletion of all emails sent and received by senior political advisors violated the *Archives and Recordkeeping Act* and the records retention schedule for ministers' offices developed by the Ontario Archives, and undermined the purposes of the *Freedom of Information and Protection of Privacy Act*. The Commissioner stated: 'It truly strains credulity to think that absolutely no records responsive to the Estimates Committee motion and the Speaker's ruling were retained' (Ontario, Office of the Information and Privacy Commissioner 2013, p. 1).

The Premier's senior advisors, David Livingston and Laura Miller, were alleged to have arranged for Miller's partner to be paid $10,000 from the Liberal caucus taxpayer-funded budget to get 20 hard drives in the Premier's Office wiped clean. The week before the gas plant emails were deleted, senior public servants warned Livingston that he had to preserve those documents (Blatchford 2017). The trial was ongoing at the time of writing, with Livingston and Miller being charged for breach of trust, mischief in relation to data and unauthorised use of a computer. The scandal contributed to the resignation of Premier Dalton McGuinty. The succeeding Premier, Kathleen Wynne, used the Liberal majority to shut down hearings of a parliamentary committee into the deleted documents before the staffers could be called to face questions about the wiping of the hard drives. This illustrates the weakness of the parliamentary accountability framework in Canada, even where alleged criminal activity has occurred. The matter will be fully ventilated in judicial proceedings.

In British Columbia, the Information and Privacy Commissioner uncovered practices of ministerial staff triple deleting emails, where an email is moved to the computer system's 'deleted' folder, expunged from the folder itself and then manually erased from a 14-day backup system (British Columbia, Office of the Information and Privacy Commissioner 2015, p. 13). These practices were designed to evade freedom of information laws. The Premier's Deputy Chief of Staff, Michele Cadario, routinely deleted emails in this fashion. In 2015, the Commissioner found that a staffer in the transportation ministry, George Gretes, had intentionally deleted emails and records connected to the Highway of Tears, a stretch of road notorious for cases of missing and murdered women, and lied under oath about the deletions (British Columbia, Office of the Information and Privacy Commissioner 2015, pp. 5–6). Gretes resigned from his position and was charged in court. He pleaded guilty to lying to the Commissioner and was fined $2,500. The whistle-blower in this case, Tim Duncan, who was a political advisor who left government, said that political staff 'are mainly concerned about protecting their Ministers and the Liberal party at any cost' (Shaw 2016).

The practice of deleting emails to avoid freedom of information laws had an earlier genesis in the 'quick wins' ethnic outreach scandal in British Columbia in 2013. This involved a partisan campaign to woo ethnic voters, including issuing official apologies for historical wrongs, through a mix of partisan and provincial government activities and resources. The Premier's Deputy Minister, John Dyble, investigated the incident and found that several government officials breached the public service code of conduct and that government resources were misused for political purposes (British Columbia,

Office of the Premier 2013). The outreach strategy involved both party and government officials conducting their work through private emails to avoid freedom of information requests and to hide inappropriate partisan activities. Deputy Chief of Staff to the Premier, Kim Haakstad, orchestrated this plan in a meeting with public servants and political staff to brainstorm the partisan content of the plan. This meant that the political advisor was improperly involving public servants in partisan activities. Haakstad resigned when the scandal was unveiled. The scandal also prompted the resignations of public servants and a cabinet minister and led to criminal charges for breach of trust against government communications director, Brian Bonney.

The interference in freedom of information requests is not confined to the Canadian provincial level. At the federal level, the Information Commissioner found that former Director of Parliamentary Affairs at the Department of Public Works and Government Services, Sébastien Togneri, interfered in a departmental decision to release a government report under the *Access to Information Act* (Canada, Office of the Information Commissioner of Canada 2011, p. 15) (to be discussed in chapter five). The Commissioner concluded that ministerial staff exerted pressure on and gave instructions to departmental employees as to what to release or suppress, while the public servants in turn failed to fulfil their legislative duties due to a culture of pleasing the Minister's office.

Exceeding authority

There are significant instances of improper behaviour by advisors who acted independently without the authorisation of their Minister. An instance of improper behaviour by an advisor was in the Sgro affair, where a political advisor acted independently beyond his remit and without the Minister's knowledge. Then Immigration Minister Judy Sgro was accused of granting temporary visas and work permits to those who supported her re-election campaign in 2004. The Ethics Commissioner, Brian Shapiro, investigated the matter. He interviewed Minister Sgro, as well as her senior policy advisor and later acting Chief of Staff, Ihor Wons, and examined several ministerial staff under oath: Katherine Abbott, Leigh Lampert and Ian Laird. All participants were cooperative.

It turned out that senior policy advisor Ihor Wons had orchestrated the approval of the work visa for Alina Balaican, who volunteered for the Minister's re-election campaign, despite Wons' assurance to the Prime Minister's office that there were no volunteers with open visa files. In addition, Wons sought to intervene to assist another person, Harjit Singh, who provided free food to the Minister's office, writing, 'We owe this guy – a look at the fax he sent you today – to see if it changes where we're going on this file. After we make the final decision we should call him with the end result'. However, following discussions with the department and the Solicitor-General's office, Singh was eventually deported. Before the federal election, Wons also met with the owners of two strip clubs to discuss whether the Minister might be able to assist them in bringing additional strippers into Canada. However, no assistance was given following the meetings, and no extra strippers entered Canada. Wons was acting independently in all instances and the Minister did not meet these people personally although she did approve Balaican's visa. Nevertheless, Wons' advocacy was not always successful, showing the independence of the bureaucracy in their ultimate decision-making.

The Commissioner stated that although the Minister had a policy of being circumspect in issuing visas in the election period, ministerial staff felt pressured by the electoral environment to assist people to obtain visas. The Commissioner found that there seemed to be some indirect connection between working as a volunteer on the Minister's campaign and a benefit that might accrue to relatives, friends or organisations. Although the Immigration Minister clearly has wide discretionary powers under law to approve visas, ministerial staff did not take enough care to protect their Minister by separating campaign matters from departmental business and excluding volunteers with open immigration files from the campaign office. The Commissioner found that the actions of ministerial staff placed their Minister in a position of conflict of interest (Canada, Office of the Ethics Commissioner 2005).

Another instance of an advisor acting beyond their remit was in the Senator Duffy expenses scandal. In the context of growing public concern about Senators fraudulently claiming their expenses in 2013, Nigel Wright, Prime Minister Harper's Chief of Staff, wrote a personal cheque of $90,000 to repay Senator Mike Duffy's housing expenses. Duffy had imprudently claimed these expenses and the Prime Minister's Office was seeking to bury these politically embarrassing claims. Duffy resigned from the Conservative caucus following these revelations, while Wright resigned from his position as Chief of Staff. Prime Minister Harper stated that he was not aware of his staff's actions and Wright corroborated this. This was despite an email from Wright stating 'we are good to go from the PM' on the payment.

After the Senate hired an external auditing firm, Deloitte, to review residence claims of three senators, including Duffy, the Prime Minister's Office exerted significant pressure on Duffy to repay his claims, including by threatening his position as a Senator. There were ongoing negotiations with Duffy and his lawyer to reach an agreement with the Prime Minister's Office in which Duffy would accept some responsibility for his expenses, believed at that point to be $32,000. During those negotiations, Duffy demanded a number of things, including that he would be withdrawn from the external audit process and that the government would repay his parliamentary expenses and cover his legal fees.

The chair of the Conservative fund, Senator Irving Gerstein, had agreed they would cover Duffy's expenses from the party fund. But when the true outstanding expense amount of $90,000 was revealed, Gerstein retracted and said the party would not cover the expenses. At that point, Wright decided to personally intervene using his own money to cover the outstanding expenses, as they previously agreed that Duffy would not be out of pocket. Duffy agreed to follow what he later describes as a PMO-drafted plan to cover up the source of the $90,000 payback to the Senate, including a story that he borrowed the money from the Royal Bank of Canada. Duffy stated: 'On February 21st, after all of the threats and intimidation, I reluctantly agreed to go along with this dirty scheme'. In an emotional speech in Parliament, Duffy urged Senators to 'restrain the unaccountable power of the PMO. That's what this Senate is about, sober second thought, not taking dictation from kids in short pants down the hall' (Canada, Senate 2013, p. 56).

Duffy was investigated by the Canadian police and exonerated from charges of fraud, breach of trust and bribery. Wright appeared in court to testify about the money he gave to Duffy, stating that he gave the money in the public interest. The legal proceedings threw light on the power and inappropriate machinations of the Prime Minister's office.

Mr Justice Charles Vaillancourt took four hours to read his verdict. He issued a scathing critique of the way Harper's office was run and of the actions of the Prime Minister's staff to try and make the scandal go away. 'The precision and planning of this exercise would make any military commander proud,' he said. 'In the context of a democratic society, the plotting as revealed in the emails can only be described as unacceptable' (*R v Duffy* (2016) ONCJ 220, p. 247). The judge stated that the methods employed by the Prime Minister's Office to achieve a successful outcome to calm the political storm of Senator Duffy's expenses 'seemed to have known no bounds' (p. 222), and suggested that the PMO's actions were 'driven by deceit, manipulations and carried out in a clandestine manner' (p. 307).

Thus, in this case, a political staffer was personally involved in a financial transaction that led to a perception of conflict of interest in providing his own personal funds to bury a political scandal. The Chief of Staff also gave explicit directions to senior Senators, which were meekly followed, and sought to interfere with an independent auditor's report. The Ethics Commissioner investigated Wright's actions and found that Wright contravened the conflict of interest legislation in furthering Duffy's private financial interests as a public office-holder and influencing a Senator to repay Duffy's expenses out of the Conservative Party fund (Canada, Office of the Conflict of Interest and Ethics Commissioner 2017). In 2015, Prime Minister Harper blamed Wright for the damage done to his office's reputation, stating 'There's no person on my staff that I believe deceived me or acted unethically or irresponsibly … Other than Mr Wright' (Battersby 2015). Harper lost the 2015 election.

Miscommunication

A number of administrative blunders made by political advisors have had serious repercussions. The Arar affair illustrates the devastating consequences of a communication failure between a political advisor and Minister. Maher Arar, a Canadian citizen, was arrested by American officials in New York as a suspected terrorist, and removed against his will to Syria, his country of birth, where he was imprisoned for a year. In prison, Arar was interrogated, tortured, beaten with a cable, forced to wear the same clothes he had urinated in for two and a half months, and held in a rat-infested cell the size of a grave. In the weeks leading up to Arar's return to Canada, unnamed officials leaked material to the media, including misinformation portraying Arar as a terrorist. Arar suffered deep psychological and economic harm from his experiences.

The government commissioned Mr Justice Dennis O'Connor to conduct an inquiry into Arar's detention and torture. Mr Justice O'Connor found Arar to be completely innocent of any offences and stated that Arar posed no threat to national security (Canada, Commission of Inquiry into the Actions of Canadian Officials 2006). The inquiry raised serious concerns about the actions of Canadian officials, which may have delayed the return of Arar to Canada, including a lack of communication between agencies and governmental reports that downplayed the torture. In one instance, a public servant told a senior policy officer at the Minister's office, Robert Fry, that they were operating on the working assumption that Arar was being tortured in Syria. However, the political advisor did not inform the Minister about this assumption and the Minister's briefing materials did not include information about possible torture. Thus, there was a failure by a political advisor to communicate to his Minister public service concerns about torture at the early stages of the incident. Further, there were damaging leaks emanating from either the public service or ministerial office seeking to undermine Arar's reputation. Mr Justice O'Connor condemned the officials who leaked material to the media, causing severe damage to Arar's reputation. The inquiry was unable to locate the source of the leaks.

The Harper government formally apologised to Arar and paid him \$10.5 million in compensation. The Commissioner of the Canadian police also apologised to Arar, and resigned after admitting to giving false information about Arar to a House of Commons committee.

In the Al-Mashat affair, Mohammed Al-Mashat, a former Iraqi ambassador to Washington and prominent media spokesperson in Iraq with ties to the Iraqi dictatorship, was granted highly expedited permission to immigrate to Canada under the retirement class visa. This sparked controversy as Al-Mashat was a vigorous supporter of the Iraqi invasion of Kuwait. Joe Clark, then Minister for External Affairs, claimed that he could not be held responsible for this sensitive decision as he was not aware of the permit granted to Al-Mashat, and refused to resign over the matter.

In 1991, the House of Commons Standing Committee on External Affairs and International Trade investigated this matter (Canada, House of Commons, Standing Committee on External Affairs and Trade 1991). The government blamed the administrative blunder on the Chief of Staff, David Daubney, and a senior public servant, Raymond Chrétien. Chrétien was responsible for expediting the process, while Daubney failed to inform his

Minister of the matter. Daubney claimed the public service failed to highlight the matter with a marker which was the signal that the item was worthy of special attention, although the public servant who delivered the files did verbally mention to Daubney that an important item was on the way. It turned out Daubney had actually read the memo but subsequently lost it and failed to bring it to the Minister's attention. Thus, there was a breakdown in communication where sensitive information was provided by the bureaucracy and failed to reach the Minister due to the negligence of a political staffer.

There were more minor administrative errors as well. For example, a political advisor resigned when she forgot a binder full of documents labelled 'secret' on Canada's nuclear strategy at a television station for a week. Natural Resources Minister Lisa Raitt offered to resign, but the Prime Minister refused to accept her resignation, stating that the breach was not as a result of the Minister's actions. The advisor's resignation was seen to be sufficient.

Australia

Australian ministerial advisors have been embroiled in a number of controversies that can be classified into three main categories:

- *Media issues*: Ministerial advisors behaving improperly or unethically in leaking information;
- *Interference with the bureaucracy*: Ministerial advisors interfering with bureaucratic processes or decision-making; or
- *Parliamentary issues*: Ministerial advisors being banned from appearing before parliamentary committees.

Media issues

Tony Hodges, ministerial advisor to then Prime Minister Julia Gillard, leaked information to protesters from the Aboriginal Tent Embassy about the location of the then Opposition Leader, Tony Abbott. This led to the Australia Day riot in 2012, where 200 protesters surrounded a restaurant in Canberra, angered by reports that the Opposition Leader had said it was time to pull the Aboriginal Tent Embassy down. Gillard had what the international media described as a 'Cinderella' moment: she had to be unceremoniously evacuated from the restaurant by a security guard, losing her shoe along the way. Gillard later stated: 'Mr Hodges in taking these actions acted alone and his actions were not authorised. Clearly they are viewed by me as unacceptable'. Following public revelation of his behaviour, the advisor resigned.

Similarly, in 2017, David De Garis, senior media advisor to Employment Minister Michaelia Cash, leaked to the media information about controversial police raids on the Australian Workers' Union (AWU). The raid was ordered by the Registered Organisations Commission, which was investigating a $100,000 donation from the AWU to activist organisation

GetUp. This investigation was said to be politically motivated to discredit Opposition Leader Bill Shorten, who was the head of AWU at the time of the donation. Cash had previously repeatedly told a Senate Committee that her ministerial office had no involvement in tipping off the media about the police raid. Her advisor later confessed that he had leaked this information to the press. Cash retracted her statements and the advisor resigned from his position. Cash refused to resign, claiming that she was unaware of the actions of her staffer.

Interference with the bureaucracy

Ministerial advisors have interfered with Freedom of Information processes at the Australian State level. In 2012, almost half of Victorian Ministers were reported to use senior ministerial staff to decide what should be released through FOI requests, rather than departmental FOI officers (Tomazin 2012). The New South Wales Ombudsman also found that Ministers' offices were reviewing new and contentious FOI applications and draft determinations, which caused a delay in processing applications (New South Wales Ombudsman 2009, p. 38). These actions may politicise the FOI decision-making processes, such that public servants are unable to properly fulfil their statutory duties. Interference with FOI processes is also part of a broader information control strategy by governments, to actively block the dissemination of information that will be detrimental to its interests.

Parliamentary issues

The Australian political system retains some elements of its British roots. It is a constitutional monarchy with two Houses of Parliament. Significantly, the introduction of proportional representation in 1949 has made it probable that the Upper House will not be controlled by the government. To illustrate, in the period of more than 40 years from the Whitlam Government (1972–1975) to the present, the government has only controlled the Senate for approximately seven years. Thus, the trend is for the Senate to be more independent of government as it lacks a government majority.

Despite the independent Senate, there have been significant issues relating to ministerial advisors appearing before parliamentary committees, as highlighted by scandals such as the 'Children Overboard' incident at the Commonwealth level and the 'Hotel Windsor' incident at the Victorian State level. In the 'Children Overboard' incident in 2001, the then Immigration Minister reported that an asylum seeker boat was exceptional: the passengers had thrown their own children overboard. The Prime Minister said publicly, 'I don't want people like that in Australia. Genuine refugees don't do that … They hang on to their children.' Within a few days, several public servants found out that the children overboard story was false. This information was sent to a ministerial advisor at the Department of Defence. Nonetheless,

Ministers continued to make public statements about asylum seekers throwing children overboard as part of an election campaign.

When pressed for evidence of children being thrown overboard, the press secretary of the then Defence Minister asked a public servant in the Department of Defence to email two photographs to him. The photos were actually of two brave navy sailors who rescued two terrified asylum seekers and their children in the open sea when their boat sank. The press secretary was informed soon after this incident that the photos were not of the children overboard incident, but of the rescue operation.

Nevertheless, the Ministers released these photographs to the media as evidence of children being thrown overboard. Even after being made aware that the photos were misleading and there was no evidence that children had been thrown overboard, the Ministers did not correct the public record and continued to assert that children had been thrown overboard.

After the election, a Senate Committee was formed to investigate the 'Children Overboard' incident. The Defence Minister refused to appear before the Senate Committee on the basis that he had immunity from being compelled to appear before the other House of Parliament. In addition, the government refused to allow ministerial advisors to appear before the Committee. The Senate Committee was highly critical of this, stating that '[s]uch bans and refusals are anathema to accountability' (Australia, Senate Select Committee for an Inquiry into a Certain Maritime Incident 2002, p. xxxiv).

At the State level, in 2010, Peta Duke, media advisor to the Victorian Minister for Planning, accidentally sent an email to a journalist at the Australian Broadcasting Corporation, instead of to her manager. The email contained the Minister's media plan, which stated that the Minister's office intended to run a sham public consultation for the $260 million redevelopment of the iconic Hotel Windsor. In an interview, the Minister denied any knowledge of the media plan or strategy. The Minister said that 'Ms Duke used inappropriate language and poetic licence in a speculative document'.

A Legislative Council Committee created an inquiry into the Hotel Windsor redevelopment planning process. The Victorian Attorney-General refused to allow ministerial advisors to appear before the parliamentary committee. The committee concluded that its investigations were 'significantly hindered as a result of the Attorney-General's interference' (Victoria, Legislative Council Standing Committee on Finance and Public Administration 2010, p. 18).

These two incidents highlight a method that Australian Ministers have used to effectively evade their responsibility to Parliament. First, they refuse to appear before Upper House committees on the basis that they have an immunity from being summoned by the other House of Parliament. They then blame ministerial advisors for certain actions or inactions and distance themselves from the actions of their advisors. Following this, they forbid their advisors from appearing before parliamentary committees and making other public appearances. In this way, both the Ministers and ministerial advisors do not appear before Upper House committees. This causes parliamentary investigations to reach a dead end and undermines the doctrine of ministerial responsibility.

In these controversial incidents, ministerial advisors were alleged to be mere emanations of their Minister and it was contended that advisors were only accountable to their Minister personally, while the Ministers are accountable to Parliament. It has been claimed that ministerial advisors are thus not required to appear before parliamentary committees. However, the argument that ministerial advisors should not appear before parliamentary committees subverts the very objective of responsible government. An essential aspect of responsible government is to ensure executive accountability to Parliament (Mill 1861, p. 104; *Egan v Willis* (1998) 195 CLR 424, pp. 451–2, 475). If both Ministers and ministerial advisors do not appear before parliamentary committees, Ministers are able to effectively escape scrutiny for their actions and deny responsibility for controversial events or policies. Thus, all facets of accountability are undermined, from explanatory accountability, where the Minister explains their actions, to the Minister accepting any sanction for their behaviour, and undertaking remedial action to rectify the issues. This is a failure at a systemic level, where Ministers are able to utilise ministerial advisors to avoid their own responsibility to Parliament.

Although Parliament has the power to punish ministerial advisors (or any other individuals) who do not appear before its committees for contempt, including imprisoning such advisors, Parliament has shown great restraint in using this power (Ng 2016). This is justified as it is generally not fair for Parliament to adopt a heavy-handed approach, because it is too harsh to imprison advisors who are acting on the direction of their Minister. Further, Parliament is not bound by the rules of evidence and does not need to provide for due process and procedural fairness. A better solution is to have guidelines on the appearance of political advisors before parliamentary committees, akin to the UK Osmotherly Rules, that are ideally negotiated between Parliament and the executive.

New Zealand

New Zealand has emerged relatively unscathed and has escaped the large-scale scandals that have engulfed other Westminster jurisdictions. More recently, however, a controversy has come to light involving the murky world of media relations and interference with the bureaucracy.

In the book *Dirty Politics* by Nicky Hager (2014), it was alleged that Jason Ede, senior advisor to Prime Minister John Key, was intimately involved in working with a right-wing blogger, Cameron Slater, to launch negative attack campaigns on Opposition Labour Members, including personal and sexual smears. These activities were exposed by Hager, an investigative journalist, who published a book that was released just before the New Zealand 2014 election. Despite the scandal being unveiled, Key managed to win the election.

The shady activities of Key's advisor, Ede, included entering Labour's computer system to access Labour online membership records and political donations data with a view to leaking personal details to try to scare off Labour's donors and activists (Hager 2014, p. 34). Ede also allegedly manipulated *Official Information Act* (OIA) processes repeatedly to provide normally classified documents to the blogger to damage political opponents. Following the revelations in the book, Ede resigned in disgrace.

In 2014, the Inspector-General of Intelligence and Security conducted an investigation into allegations in the Hager book that NZ Secret Service documents were declassified in order to be used for political purposes. By this stage, Ede had permanently deleted all emails, including those sent from his personal accounts. The Inspector-General found that the PMO's Deputy Chief of Staff, Phil de Joux, provided a description of secret service documents to Ede, and insinuated that there could be OIA request for those documents (New Zealand, Office of the Inspector-General of Intelligence and Security 2014). Ede then gave that information to a blogger, Cameron Slater, discussed the OIA request with Slater and provided Slater with draft blog posts on the issue. The Inspector-General thus confirmed that a PMO staffer was intimately involved in disclosing secret service information to a blogger for political purposes. The leaking of information was not a one-off issue. As the Prime Minister's Chief of Staff in fronting a parliamentary committee in 2013 about an investigation into a leak ruefully said: 'In terms of other leaks, it's perhaps unfortunate to say, but that's a reality of working in this building, there are leaks from time to time.'

More troubling is the fact that the political neutrality of the public service was compromised due to the pressure by ministerial advisors. Following the blogger Cameron Slater making an OIA request based on information leaked by the PMO, the Inspector-General found that the Director of the NZ Security Intelligence Service made serious errors of judgment in dealing with the OIA request by the blogger. The Director almost immediately gave his preliminary view that information should be granted under the OIA to the blogger, resulting in the response being finalised within the next 24 hours. At the same time, similar requests by the mainstream media were refused. This resulted in Slater effectively receiving an exclusive news story. To compound this, the documents disclosed under OIA contained inaccurate and incomplete information about the Leader of the Opposition. As a result, the Inspector-General found that the Director compromised the principle of political neutrality (New Zealand, Office of the Inspector-General of Intelligence and Security 2014, p. 69).

The Ombudsman also initiated an inquiry about alleged breaches of the OIA Act. The Ombudsman found that a few ministerial advisors were attempting to limit the scope of requests for official information or change an agency's proposed decision for unwarranted reasons. Nevertheless, the Ombudsman found that such attempts were rejected by agency officials and the final decisions made by the agency were compliant with the OIA (New Zealand, Office of the Ombudsman 2015, pp. 115–6).

The Ombudsman's investigations showed that there was inappropriate pressure by ministerial staff on public service officials in relation to OIA requests. Public servants feared their agency would agree to the demands made by the Minister's office because it needed to maintain a good relationship, or had other policy decisions to get through their Minister and they needed to choose 'which battle to fight'. Further, the Ombudsman also found that many public servants 'described bitter, confrontational discussions with Ministers and their political advisors about certain OIA requests' (p. 117). The Ombudsman voiced the concern that:

> [I]f it is applied incorrectly by Ministers and their officials, the principle [of 'no surprises'] may be misused to defeat the proper operation of the OIA by providing an opportunity for improper pressure or political manipulation to influence either the substantive decision or the timing of the delivery of the agency's response to the requester. This can have the effect of enabling accountability to be avoided or reduced, or opportunities for meaningful participation to be missed. One experienced Minister identified that the real issue about the role of the ministerial/political advisor is where they stray and take over the role of the Minister: There will be times where they may be the eyes of the Minister, and on occasion they speak on behalf of the Minister, but they cannot make decisions as if they are the Minister.
>
> (p. 120)

The Ombudsman concluded that some agencies' practices could leave them vulnerable to interference by Ministers' offices in the preparation of OIA responses that may be in contravention of the law and public expectations (p. 5).

There has thus been improper pressure and political manipulation of the OIA Act. Nevertheless, the Ombudsman did find that ultimately public servants were still able to exercise independence in making their decisions and exercised their powers appropriately. In more recent times, however, there has been more cause for concern. A 2017 survey found that interference by ministerial staff in departmental OIA decision-making was rife (Eichbaum 2017). Thus, the increased roles of ministerial advisors who act on behalf of their Minister and increased inappropriate pressure exerted on the bureaucracy is a trend that needs to be carefully monitored to avoid further controversies.

Therefore, although New Zealand has thus far escaped the large-scale scandals that have plagued other countries, there is no room for complacency. The revelations about advisors to the Prime Minister seeking a back-door channel to defame their political opponents show that party factionalism may lead to unethical and improper behaviour. Excessive interference with the advice of public servants and abuse of the OIA system may also lead to politicisation of the public service.

Classification of scandals

The controversies in the Westminster jurisdictions are summarised in Table 4.1. Although the scandals in the Westminster jurisdictions vary greatly in terms of significance and effect, there are a few common themes across the jurisdictions. These include media issues, political advisors interfering with the bureaucracy and exceeding their authority, as well as issues of miscommunication between political advisors and the Minister or the civil service.

Media issues

With the advent of the 24/7 news cycle, media issues involving political advisors have become pervasive, particularly in the United Kingdom. There is a consistent trend of advisors leaking confidential information to the media for political purposes.

Almost all of the major controversies in the UK involve issues with the media. As the Public Administration Select Committee stated, although media advisors only form a small proportion of the total number of advisors:

> the challenges [media advisors] pose to the effective management of the public service and the potential damage to the reputation of the Government are out of all proportion to that number and to their contribution.
>
> (UK, House of Commons, Public Administration Select Committee 2003, p. 17)

Table 4.1 Scandals

	Canada	*New Zealand*	*United Kingdom*	*Australia*
Lobbying	✓		✓	
Interference with bureaucracy	✓	✓	✓	✓
Illegal activity	✓			
Inappropriate use of funds	✓			
Conflict of interest	✓	✓	✓	
Document destruction	✓			
Exceeding authority	✓	✓	✓	✓
Withholding documents from the Minister	✓			✓
Leaks		✓	✓	✓
Parliamentary issues	✓			✓

Leaking also occurred by the civil service in the Jo Moore incident, where the bureaucracy sought to undermine the special advisor who was accused of bullying behaviour. Leaking is not confined to the United Kingdom. In Australia, Tony Hodges, ministerial advisor to the Prime Minister, leaked the location of the Opposition leader, leading to the Australia Day riot. An Australian ministerial advisor to the Employment Minister also tipped off the media about police raids of the offices of the Australian Workers' Union. In New Zealand, the Prime Minister's Chief of Staff confirmed to a parliamentary committee that leaking was a practice that did happen (New Zealand Privileges Committee 2013).

Leaking is not a recent phenomenon. The process of politicians and public servants leaking documents was established in Australia well before the late 1960s (Schultz 1998, p. 184). In the 1970s Wilson period in the United Kingdom, Harold Wilson himself acknowledged that there were issues with special advisors leaking information to the media through unauthorised disclosures. He stated that this was being dealt with in a 'typically British way … [working] out the problems as we go along'. More recently, former special advisor Charlie Whelan claimed that 'most Labour MPs I know are thoroughly fed up with the unattributable briefings emanating from No. 10 against people they don't like' (Whelan 2000). Ironically Whelan himself was forced to resign over allegations that he leaked information against former Trade Secretary Peter Mandelson, exposing the fact that Mandelson had received a secret loan of £373,000 from Paymaster General Geoffrey Robinson to help buy his London home.

The continued prevalence of leaking may be attributable to the fact that special advisors who leaked to the media were dismissed in the short term, but their careers did not suffer in the long run. For instance, Dominic Cummings resigned but then resurfaced as the campaign director of the Brexit movement, while Fiona Hill was forced to resign but was then later elevated to the lofty post of Prime Minister's Chief of Staff. Even the most egregious example, Damien McBride, managed to get another position as a special advisor.

In addition, media advisors can form unnaturally close relationships with the media, which can cloud their judgement. Notorious special advisor Damian McBride's relationship with the press was close at a personal level, such that he saw his role as to feed information from the Prime Minister's Office to journalists:

> I regarded my function in No. 10 simply as providing the hacks with a service, and imagined myself to be the person 'embedded' in No. 10 on their behalf. To that extent, I regarded the journalists I worked with every day as akin to colleagues, even when they were giving Gordon and the government an enormous kicking. And like any colleagues, the more we got to know each other, the more those relationships extended outside of work. I attended stag-dos, weddings, Arsenal matches, Bruce Springsteen

> concerts, karaoke sessions, double dates, birthday parties and Christmas lunches with journalists, and why the hell not? That was our spare time and, as far as I was concerned, it only ever made it easier for us both to do our jobs
>
> (McBride 2013, p. 283)

As we will see in chapter five, the UK Code of Conduct for special advisors now regulates against leaking and personal attacks. However, leaking has continued unabated despite the new provisions. For example, former Prime Minister David Cameron was asked by Cabinet Secretary Gus O'Donnell to restrain special advisors in the Department for Communities and Local Government who had briefed against the Chair of the Electoral Commission. In the Leveson Inquiry into media practices, David Cameron explained that 'briefing against people, doing people down' was a phenomenon that had plagued both sides of politics in recent years, which he decried as 'dreadful' and 'deeply regrettable' (quoted in Information Commissioner's Office 2012, p. 1212).

Another media issue that has surfaced in recent years is the use of social media and private blogs to discredit the Opposition. In New Zealand, a staffer in the Prime Minister's Office orchestrated the leak of secret service information to a private blogger to smear the Opposition (New Zealand, Office of the Inspector-General of Intelligence and Security 2014). In the UK, media advisor Damien McBride had to resign following revelations that he plotted to set up a private blog to fabricate sexual rumours against the Opposition (McBride 2013). In addition, two special advisors, Dominic Cummings and Henry De Zoete, used an anonymous Twitter account to attack the Opposition. The unregulated domain of social media and private blogs means that information posted does not have to be accurate, and is not vetted in any way through traditional journalists or the mainstream media. Using private or social media is also a way to spread defamatory material anonymously.

Advisors overstepping their roles

Political advisors have been embroiled in controversy where they have exceeded the proper boundaries of their role and acted without the knowledge of their Minister. In New Zealand, 20 per cent of Ministers agreed that ministerial advisors sometimes exceed their authority (Shaw and Eichbaum 2014). This has led to controversy in Canada, where Nigel Wright acted without the knowledge of the Prime Minister in personally repaying Senator Mike Duffy's expenses, putting himself in a position of conflict of interest. Ihor Wons likewise acted without the express knowledge of his Minister in seeking to push for visa approvals for volunteers in the Minister's election campaign. In the United Kingdom, Adam Smith acted beyond his remit in communicating extensively with a lobbyist although his Minister was acting in a quasi-judicial role, leading to a perception of conflict of interest. Adam

Werritty also acted beyond his authority in masquerading as a special advisor to Liam Fox, although the Minister did authorise his actions. In the 'Hotel Windsor' incident at the Victorian State level in Australia, the Minister was able to deny knowledge of a controversial incident, claiming that his advisor acted independently in writing an incriminating email. It is problematic when political advisors act as independent agents without their Minister's authorisation, particularly without a parallel increase of legal or political accountability. This is also an issue of managerial competence within a ministerial office, where Ministers need to ensure that political advisors do not overstep their boundaries.

Another issue is that Ministers can strategically use political advisors to 'do their dirty work for them' or become scapegoats for certain issues. Former Australian Minister Lindsay Tanner was of the opinion that ministerial advisors generally acted with the authority of their Minister, but it often suited Ministers to 'allow ministerial staff to take flack for political issues': 'it's like a shock absorber; people are yelling at somebody other than them, which is always a good thing' (quoted in Ng 2016, pp. 97–8). This could mean that in some instances where political advisors allegedly exceeded their authority, they are in reality acting with the Minister's instructions, but are seeking to protect their Minister and take the fall for them.

Categorisation of advisors' roles

I will adopt Connaughton's model to discuss the various aspects of advisors' roles that have caused controversies. It will be recalled that Connaughton's model differentiates between four main roles of political advisors: expert, partisan, coordinator and minder (Connaughton 2010 pp. 351–2; Connaughton 2015). The expert is a highly qualified political outsider who initiates and contests policies and ideas, while the coordinator's role is procedural and includes monitoring and liaising with various groups to facilitate oversight and delivery of the Minister's agenda. On the political dimension, the partisan is appointed predominantly on the basis of political affiliation rather than specific expertise and undertakes work of a politically partisan nature, such as representing their Minister in political negotiations, while the minder protects the Minister by looking out for issues that may harm the Minister politically and reputationally.

An expert specialist engaged in the substance of policy issues rarely causes any controversy. For example, the British war experience of bringing in economic giants such as Keynes to boost advisory capacity raised no eyebrows and undoubtedly brought significant expertise to government in a crucial period.

The partisan's role is uncontentious in the sense that it is the task of a political advisor to provide a political gloss over policy advice or, in Craft's terminology, engage in 'buffering' or 'shaping' (Craft 2015, pp. 146–149). Nevertheless, a partisan may cause issues in two respects. The first is that a

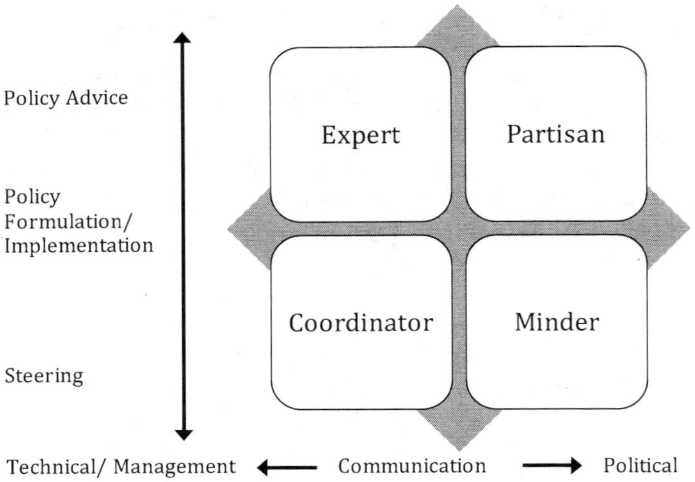

Figure 4.1 Configuration of advisor roles
Source: Adapted from Connaughton (2010).

partisan who represents the Minister may overstep the boundaries and claim the Minister's authority without having it. Another problem lies in the fact that advisor appointments are made predominantly on the basis of partisan affiliation, rather than merit, which may lead to the recruitment of incompetent advisors.

A minder who guards the Minister's interest at all costs may cause significant issues. The minder who overzealously protects the Minister's factional position may engage in activities that conflict with the best interests of the government as a whole. This was exemplified by the tense Blair/Brown leadership era, where Brown's special advisors continually tried to undermine anyone associated with the Blair camp through damaging leaks to the media.

The coordinator role, i.e. liaising with various internal and external stakeholders on behalf of their Minister, may cause issues depending on the method of interaction. The main internal stakeholder that political advisors deal with is the civil service. Political advisors can interact with civil servants in a few different ways: collaborative, gatekeeper or triangulated (Zussman 2009, pp. 14–15). As noted in chapter three, if a political advisor functions in a collaborative manner in working together with civil servants to tender advice jointly to the Minister, or in a triangulated way, with public servants and political advisors independently supplying advice to Ministers, issues are less likely to arise. However, where coordinators act as a funnel or gatekeeper, and block information from reaching the Minister, this strains the relationship between political advisors and the civil service and may negatively impact on the quality of the advice. In general, external stakeholders such as lobby groups have less privileged access to Ministers due to their lack of locational proximity to the Minister. Thus, it is likely that political advisors will adopt the gatekeeper role in relation to them. If political advisors block or filter advice, vital information may not reach the Minister.

Interference with the bureaucracy

Related to advisors' overstepping their roles, although political staff are not to exercise executive power, they have interfered with public service decision-making for partisan reasons. A prominent example is the Canadian Sponsorship Scandal, where political staff took control of decisions about who to allocate funding to, although this was supposed to be the province of the impartial public service. The illicit payments and kickback funds were allocated to donors to the Liberal Party, as well as their supporters in advertising agencies. Public servants meekly acceded to the veiled requests of political staffers. The Canadian 'Rivard affair' also shows the extreme measures that a political advisor took to assist a drug smuggler who was also a Liberal party donor to get out of jail, including trying to intimidate the prosecutor of the Rivard case. These two incidents show the influence of money in politics, where political advisors sought to reward those who had opened up their purse strings and shown their party largesse in the past.

Political staff have also sought to interfere with public service decision-making in freedom of information and media requests, which is a consistent theme across the jurisdictions. In New Zealand, the Inspector-General of Intelligence and Security found that a political advisor in the Prime Minister's Office orchestrated the release of sensitive secret service documents to a private blogger and the civil service bowed to the pressure to expedite the release of OIA information to the blogger. A 2017 survey in New Zealand found that ministerial staff involvement in processing OIA requests have become endemic throughout the public service, with advisors examining all OIA requests and interfering with departmental decision-making by pressuring departments to redact or withdraw items (Eichbaum 2017). Likewise, in Canada a political staffer, Sébastian Togneri, was found to have interfered in FOI requests (to be discussed in chapter five). Further, a Canadian senior bureaucrat revealed to a parliamentary committee that there was significant interference with departmental media decisions, with 22 per cent of decisions altered (Canada, House of Commons, Standing Committee on Access to Information, Privacy and Ethics 2010). In 2014, the Canadian Information Commissioner concluded that there was systemic interference by ministerial staff into departmental processing of Access to Information files. Even worse, at the provincial level in Canada, political advisors have been mass deleting their emails to evade FOI requirements. Similar allegations of interference have been made at the

Australian State level in Victoria and New South Wales. The consistency of interference in FOI decision-making across jurisdictions may be part of a broader information control strategy, to protect the government against the disclosure of embarrassing material.

Miscommunication

Administrative blunders such as miscommunication between political advisors and the Minister or the bureaucracy are also a common problem. In the notorious 'Children Overboard' incident in Australia, Ministers claimed that their advisors did not tell them that the photos of children being thrown overboard were false and therefore escaped the blame for spreading a lie in a fear-mongering election campaign about asylum-seekers. In Canada, the Arar case is an example of a serious administrative blunder by a political advisor that led to the prolonging of the overseas torture of a Canadian citizen. The political advisor failed to pass on important information from the civil service to the Minister relating to Arar's torture. In the Al-Mashat incident, the political advisor lost a memo from a civil servant and failed to bring information to the attention of his Minister about the risks of expediting the visa of Al-Mashat, who had ties to the Iraqi dictatorship.

If these events are viewed with a less benign lens, it can be argued that political staff acting as gatekeepers may try to shield their Minister from blame by delaying or withholding controversial communications to ensure the Minister's 'political safety'. A former staffer in Canadian Prime Minister Jean Chrétien's office stated that there was a cultural norm within the Prime Minister's office of putting as little as possible in writing, to avoid the potential trouble of incriminating emails or memos surfacing later (Thomas 2009, p. 34). The Ontario and British Columbia Privacy Commissioners' recent investigations reinforced this notion, as they found at the provincial level that ministerial offices operated on a culture of 'verbal government' where not much was committed to writing (Ontario, Office of the Information and Privacy Commissioner 2013, p. 29; British Columbia, Office of the Information and Privacy Commissioner 2015, p. 3).

Causes of scandals

These controversies illustrate a number of problems with advisors within a Westminster context. The media/politics interface poses great problems in modern Westminster democracies and leads to issues relating to information management. The faction/opposition interface is another major cause of advisor misbehaviour, primarily caused by excessively partisan behaviour by political advisors. Further problems stem from the appointment of some incompetent political advisors by patronage, alongside the influence of money in politics. Finally, the lack of legal, political or managerial regulation may have caused certain scandals.

The politics/media interface

The politics/media interface has become incredibly important in modern democracies, where the immediacy, ubiquitousness and continuous nature of the 24-hour media cycle dramatically increase the pressure on governments to respond to issues almost instantaneously, without much time for reflection (Blumler and Kavanagh 1999, p. 209). This change has been attributed to the:

> proliferation of traditional and new media outlets, an abundance of news sources and forms, 24 hours news services and cycles, intensified professionalization of political communication, increased competitive pressures on the media, popularization of political journalism and discourse, diversification and fragmentation of media, and an enhanced ability for citizens to include messages about politics in their media diet in the forms, at the times, and to the extent they prefer.
>
> (Swanson 2003, pp. 11–12)

In an era of saturated and diverse media streams, the government has to compete with soap operas and reality television shows to pierce through public consciousness. As Terence Daintith wryly remarked, the 'fact that public policies need to compete in the media market with soap powders for a share of consumer attention is an arresting symbol of the privatization of our society' (Daintith 2001, p. 617).

The Westminster liberal democracies examined in this book have free presses that are not controlled by government. Hence, in a situation of relentless media bombardment and critique, as well as competition for air-time, governments have become increasingly anxious to control the flow, timing and depiction of its policies, performance and reputation in the media. This process of careful media management and control is known as 'spin', that is, the deliberate attempt to depict a subject in the best possible light. However, the blurred boundary between 'policy exposition' and 'party propaganda' means that there might be unscrupulous but sanctioned uses of spin, such as presenting issues in a strictly speaking truthful but deliberately misleading way, or presenting in a way that might lack objectivity and impartiality (Yeung 2006). Mike Granatt, the UK Head of the Government Information and Communication Service, suggested that spin 'grew out of the American system where when an event happened, those who were representing others as spokesmen, rushed out to give the particular gloss to the event that their principal wanted' (UK, Public Administration Select Committee 2000, Q 89). For example, in Washington, during the reign of President Ronald Reagan, after the President's 'rare and hazardous' press conferences, 'spin patrols' went out among journalists immediately to straighten out what the President had said. Colin Seymour-Ure argues, however, that the purpose and practice of spin is not new and was known as 'propagandising' in the 1940s and 'news management' by the 1970s (Seymore-Ure 2003, p. 150).

Whether or not spin is a new concept, it is undeniable that political communication within government is a growth industry, with increased numbers, organisation and professionalisation of staff involved in the control and dissemination of information in government, including media and Freedom of Information officers within government departments, in conjunction with the growth of the number of partisan media advisors. Even at an early stage of the evolution of political advisors in the 1970s, there has been the position of press secretary. However, particularly with the advent of the 24-hour news cycle, successive governments have been more and more obsessed about controlling the media and have spent more money and energy in media monitoring and invested in disseminating positive information. The change in the relationship between government and the media has been analogised as the government being in a state of a 'permanent campaign' (UK, Committee on Standards in Public Life 2003, p. 19), which comprises a 'complex mixture of politically sophisticated people, communication techniques and organisations' where the unifying factor is the 'continuous and voracious quest for public approval' (Heclo 2000, p. 16).

In a traditional Westminster model of secrecy, information can be seen as a precious government resource. As such, governments have sought to control the dissemination of information through centralised media management utilising partisan media advisors and political advisors who obstruct freedom of information requests. Media management seeks to paint the government in the best light through the selective release of positive information, while FOI interference represents an attempt to block the flow of negative or controversial government-held information to the public. In the United Kingdom, Australia, New Zealand and Canada, we have seen political advisors deliberately interfere with FOI decision-making processes for partisan reasons, sometimes compromising the impartiality of civil servants in the process.

There is also increasing centralisation of government media management in various jurisdictions. Although politicians have always aimed to give a positive gloss to their actions, the politicisation of government information services is a newer phenomenon, as can be seen in the Blair government in the United Kingdom, which employed Alastair Campbell, a highly partisan special advisor, to lead its press operations with the power to direct civil servants (1997–2007). This was also evident in Australia, where the Hawke and Keating governments' National Media Liaison Service was led by a ministerial advisor (1983–1996), followed by the Howard government's centralised media management (1996–2007). In Canada, particularly in the Harper period (2006–2015), centralised government media management in the Prime Minister's Office has become firmly entrenched. Like a well-oiled machine, the Prime Minister's Office crafts the message and orchestrates media announcements by various Ministers for maximum impact for the government, by hosing down any potential negative coverage of government or seeking to promote the government's longer-term policy agenda. There is 'strict message control and image management' to achieve disciplined and centralised government communications (Marland 2016, p. 3). Departmental communications staff were required to prepare 'message event proposals' for the PMO to a neurotic level of detail, including specifying the 'desired news headline, key messages, media lines, strategic objectives, desired sound bite, ideal speaking backdrop, ideal event photograph, tone, attire, rollout materials, and strategic considerations' (Marland 2016, p. 304). No departmental announcements could be made without vetting by the PMO.

Government media management techniques include derogatory briefings against political opponents within or outside of government, the selective distribution of media releases, denying 'troublesome' journalists access to politicians or government officials, selective 'leaks', and 'exclusives' to favoured journalists or media outlets (Burton 2007 p. 188). For example, the Blair government was accused of using public information as currency in a 'system of favouritism, selective release and partisan spinning', with media advisors presenting a 'partial and distorted version of events' with little relationship to actual briefings and relying on off-the-record sources or even deliberate misrepresentation (Phillis 2004, p. 25). Rodney Tiffen has stated that debate about government information services 'is particularly marked by hypocrisy: each opposition rails against the iniquities of the government's bloated and misused propaganda machine, then promptly adopts similar practices after assuming power itself' (Tiffen 1989, p. 88).

Despite the government's attempts to maintain an iron grip over the release of information to the media through strong internal executive controls, the media/politics interface remains largely unregulated, partly due to the imperative of having a free press and the complicity between politicians and journalists in disseminating anonymous political information. Politicians and advisors tend to contact journalists to provide derogatory and unattributed briefings to the media against their factional or political opponents to further their own political interests. As seen above, there is a consistent trend of advisors leaking confidential information to the media for political purposes, which has created controversy in the United Kingdom, Australia and New Zealand. Leaks can be distinguished from background briefings, which are semi-institutionalised and intended to provide background information or the rationale behind a decision or action (Tiffen 1989, p. 97). Leaks on the other hand are officially disallowed and undermine central coordination, as they may be based on a personal vendetta divorced from the interests of government as a whole. Thus, the media/politics interface is characterised by a combination of tight central governmental control of media management, misbehaviour by political advisors in interfering with freedom of information requests and rogue individual leaks by political advisors, leading to a series of discrete scandals.

The faction/opposition interface

An element that has become increasingly prominent in the Westminster system is the faction-versus-opposition interface, where political advisors have a primary loyalty to a particular person or group, which might be their Minister alone, at the expense of the government as a whole, or their faction within their political party, at the expense of their Minister. The opposition can be factional opponents within their own party or the political opposition.

It is clear that factional behaviour is a principal cause of many of the controversies that have surfaced across Westminster jurisdictions. In New Zealand, a political advisor was alleged to have entered the Opposition party computer system to access membership records and donations data to leak information to a private blogger. Further, British special advisors have engaged in political behaviour by participating in factional warfare or zealously pursuing the interests of their Minister at the expense of the government as a whole, as exemplified by the bitter Brown/Blair infighting.

Overly partisan behaviour

Although special advisors are technically not supposed to indulge in party politics, attack individuals or enter into the party-political fray in an aggressive, personalised fashion as part of their official role, this is not the reality (UK, Committee on Standards in Public Life 2002). Factional behaviour is linked to some advisors' ambitions to eventually enter politics. Former parliamentarian Nigel Lawson stated that 'the job tends to attract bright youngsters who are contemplating a career in politics' (Lawson 1992, p. 263). Most did not 'disguise their ambitions and see their jobs as training for future ministerial careers' (Bishop 1974). Thus, advisors may prioritise their party faction over government interests to achieve their personal political ambitions.

Damian McBride is a notorious example of a British special advisor who leaked against members of his own party for his Minister's advancement. He prioritised the interests of his Minister over the broader interests of the government. McBride also stated that 'ambitious MPs or political advisors who want to destroy their rivals' provided him with confidential information and dirty secrets to be leaked (McBride 2013, p. 387). With the advisor doing the dirty work, the Minister could turn a blind eye while reaping the benefits of the leaks:

> [Gordon Brown] would sometimes say to me: 'How did you get this stuff?' after I'd tell him some crucial piece of intelligence about what the Tories were planning, obtained in return for a good splash, and I'd just say: 'Don't ask.'… and did those ends justify the means? … Keeping Gordon in No. 11 and getting him into No. 11 was my job, from where – in my mind – he could do what was best for Labour and the country.
>
> (McBride 2013, p. 193)

McBride's comments showed that he was very willing to protect his Minister at all costs, without any regard for whether his behaviour was ethical or appropriate. Leaks were used as a weapon to undermine others.

In Australia, there were instances where ministerial advisors prioritised their factions against the interests of the Ministers they were supposed to serve and consequently leaked confidential governmental information to their faction leaders. This occurred at the State level in the Victorian Cain government during union disputes against the government, where the Labor Party supported the Builders Labourers Federation and Nurses Union against the Labor government. Several ministerial advisors were more closely aligned to their party factions than their Minister. Former Premier John Cain explained that:

> We had instances of advisers who saw the Party's faction's interests as being in their hands. They should keep the Minister and the Department ideologically pure and the faction informed and satisfied.
>
> (quoted in Ng 2016, p. 50)

Cain noted that 'in some instances, the factions demanded of the Minister that their person "on staff" play a watchdog role':

> There were some advisers who kept their faction leaders informed about the progress of [the disputes]. This was an example of factional allegiance that may well be in conflict with the adviser's duty to his Minister and the Government. This demonstrated that they really did not understand what Government was about.
>
> (quoted in Ng 2016, p. 50)

Thus, a conflict of interest may occur between the advisor and the Minister where the advisors have a primary loyalty to a political faction. This is exacerbated where the political advisor harbours personal ambitions to be pre-selected as a parliamentary candidate by their political parties. In extreme cases, advisors can act to undermine their Minister for their own personal advancement within the political party.

Further, some advisors may prioritise their Minister's interests above the public interest or broader governmental interests. As a former permanent secretary noted, '[Special advisors] are defenders of their Minister that brought them in. They do all they can to bolster their minister; they don't really have allegiance to the government' (Yong and Hazell 2014, p. 136). This was particularly evident in the divisive period of leadership challenges in the Blair/Brown era where rival factions were seen to be 'the enemy'. McBride explicitly acknowledged that he regularly leaked information to the media against his own political party for the sake of the advancement of his Minister, Gordon Brown:

> So is leaking against your own government justified? I would strongly argue that done in the way I did it, it never did much harm, and it certainly did Gordon a lot of good. Which raises what I'm about to say to

> even greater heights of hypocrisy: me leaking against every other department was fine, but anyone leaking against the Treasury was asking to be put against a wall and shot.
>
> (McBride 2013, pp. 194–195)

It is clear that McBride had no qualms about leaking against members of his own party for his Minister's advancement. He prioritised the interests of his Minister over the broader interests of the government.

Appointments by patronage

Another issue within the faction/opposition interface is that the appointments process for political advisors tends to be from closed party-political networks. A former British Labour PMO advisor explained the UK appointment process:

> If [minister X] wanted to recruit someone who was a complete opponent of the Government to be a special advisor, then we were going to make it very, very difficult for him to do that … [Candidates] weren't vetted for competence in any way. They were only vetted for political danger … You don't want to have someone who has got a track record as a real troublemaker.
>
> (quoted in Yong and Hazell 2014, p. 58)

Similarly, in Canada political staffers are often recruited from the youth wing of political parties and university political clubs ('Growing Grits' and 'Tiny Tories') on the basis of political loyalty and partisanship (Benoit 2006, p. 166). Campaign loyalists are often hired, as well as defeated political candidates, children and relatives of politicians, friends and financial supporters (Benoit 2006, p. 166–167). Some well-connected political families 'can almost boast a dynasty', with a commentator observing 'I can't ever remember a Liberal government when there hasn't been a (Winnipeg) Richardson working on the Hill' (quoted in Benoit 2006, p. 167). A chief of staff stated:

> It is a small world here in Ottawa, a network. When you are looking to recruit someone, you ask yourself: 'Who would be appropriate for this position,' and once that is answered, there is the second question: 'What do you know about this person?' In short, it is a referral system, or a network. The minister often finds his or her chief of staff through another minister or someone else who is part of the network.
>
> (quoted in Plasse 1994, p. 28)

Benoit claimed in 2006 that there was a significant proportion of incompetent political staff, with the ratio of 'good' to 'bad' ministerial staff being about 50:50 or at best 60:40 (Benoit 2006, p. 179). A former bureaucrat stated,

'There are some very good individuals; others are venal, incompetent and dishonest' (Benoit 2006, p. 179).

The Canadian Prime Minister's office vets staff appointments to guard against Ministers appointing unsatisfactory advisors and to ensure that the appointments are politically appropriate (Benoit 2006, p. 172). However, some appointments were blocked vindictively, such as where Harper's office vetoed Graham Fox from being chief of staff to Minister Peter MacKay, due to Fox's previous criticism of Harper (Martin 2006). Although the central vetting process does not guarantee competence or prevent the hiring of political cronies, 'it does nonetheless assure the PMO that the cronies that are hired will be *their cronies*' (Benoit 2006, p. 173).

An appointment process based mainly on patronage opens up a risk of the appointment of people for roles they may not be suited to or who may lack the competence for the job. Ultimately this can lead to the appointment of young, inexperienced party apparatchiks who lack the skills to advise on how to run the country. For example, in Australia, there have been notorious examples of Ministers hiring their children or mistresses as advisors (Ng, 2016). This may lead to advisors exceeding their authority, interfering with bureaucratic decision-making or miscommunicating with the Minister or civil service.

The influence of money on politics

The pernicious influence of money on politics is yet another factor that leads political advisors astray within a highly politicised context. In an era of declining party membership, political parties have become more reliant on donations from individuals, unions or corporations to raise funds. A political advisor in the Rivard affair was influenced by a promised large political donation from a drug smuggler to the extent that he engaged in illegal behaviour to try to get the potential donor out of jail, including through intimidation and bribery. In the Sponsorship Scandal, the desire to reward party supporters led Canadian political advisors to improperly channel sponsorship funds to party loyalists. A lobbyist also organised kickbacks from commissions on securing sponsorship contracts for agencies to go to the Liberal Party fund.

Lobbyists who work on behalf of individuals or corporations have also featured in these scandals. As lobbyists have extensive connections within government, they are at times able to influence political advisors to engage in conduct that may engender a conflict of interest. In the United Kingdom, political advisor Adam Smith communicated extensively with a lobbyist for News Corporation and divulged confidential information although his Minister was engaged in a quasi-judicial role. Adam Werritty, who pretended to be former Minister Liam Fox's political advisor although he was not officially employed as such, had his activities funded by lobbyists and his Minister had to resign for requesting donors to channel money through Werritty's company.

Following the large-scale scandals involving corruption in Canada, there is now Canadian legislation regulating conflict of interest and lobbying by political advisors, including post-separation employment provisions and significant disclosure requirements (to be discussed in chapter five). This is administered by an independent statutory officer, the Conflict of Interest and Ethics Commissioner.

Lack of legal or political regulation

Many of the scandals in the Westminster jurisdictions occurred due to lack of legal or political regulation of ministerial advisors at the time of the controversies. As seen in Table 4.1 on p. 104, Canada has the largest variety of significant scandals, including where political advisors have transgressed the law. This could be attributable to the fact that it is the first jurisdiction to have political advisors entrenched into the system, and that Canada has the largest numbers of political advisors. Because of these major scandals, Canada has now developed a sophisticated legal and regulatory system for political advisors. For example, after the Sponsorship Scandal erupted, the *Federal Accountability Act* was enacted in 2006 which stringently regulates political advisors in terms of conflict of interest, lobbying and post-employment activity (to be discussed in chapter five). Loopholes such the ability of former political advisors to be appointed to the Canadian public service without competition were closed.

At the other end of the spectrum, New Zealand remains relatively untainted by the emergence of political advisors in the system, with only one significant scandal at the time of writing. This could be attributed to the low numbers of advisors, the cooperative political culture and cosy village-like democracy in New Zealand. Concomitantly, until recently, the legal and political regulation in New Zealand was underdeveloped compared to other Westminster jurisdictions, with regulation previously being primarily through the private law mechanism of employment contracts, rather than a strong legislative framework with enforceable sanctions. This has now changed with the introduction of a code of conduct for ministerial staff in 2017. The legal and political regulation of advisors in the Westminster jurisdictions will be discussed in more detail in the next chapter.

References

Books and journal articles

Blick, A, 2004, *People Who Live in the Dark*, Politico, London.

Blumler, J G, and Kavanagh, D, 1999, 'The Third Age of Political Communication: Influences and Features' *Political Communication*, vol. 163), pp. 209–230.

Burton, B, 2007, *Inside Spin: The Dark Underbelly of the PR Industry*, Allen & Unwin, Crows Nest, NSW.

Connaughton, B, 2010, 'Glorified Gofers, Policy Experts or Good Generalists: A Classification of the roles of the Irish Ministerial Adviser', *Irish Political Studies*, vol. 25(3), pp. 347–369.

Connaughton, B, 2015, 'Navigating the Borderlines of Politics and Administration: Reflections on the Role of Ministerial Advisers', *International Journal of Public Administration*, vol. 38(1), pp. 37–45.

Craft, J, 2015, 'Conceptualizing the Policy Work of Partisan Advisers', *Policy Sciences*, vol. 48(2), pp. 135–158.

Daintith, T, 2001, 'Spin: A Constitutional and Legal Analysis' *European Public Law*, vol. 7(4), pp. 593–623.

Hager, N, 2014, *Dirty Politics: How Attack Politics is Poisoning New Zealand's Political Environment*, Craig Potton Publishing, Nelson.

Heclo, H, 2000, 'Campaigning and Governing: A Conspectus' in N J Ornstein and T E Mann (eds), *The Permanent Campaign and its Future*, American Enterprise Institute and Brookings Institution, pp. 1–37.

Lawson, Nigel, 1992, *The View from No. 11: Memoirs of a Tory Radical*, Bantam Press, London.

Lock, D, 2013, 'Special Advisers and Public Allegations of Misconduct 1997–2013' The Constitution Unit, UCL. Available at: https://constitution-unit.com/2013/06/06/spads-gone-bad-public-allegations-of-special-adviser-misconduct/.

Marland, A, 2016, *Brand Command: Canadian Politics and Democracy in the Age of Message Control*, University of British Columbia Press, British Columbia.

McBride, D, 2013, *Power Trip: A Decade of Policy, Plots and Spin*, Biteback Publishing, London.

Mill, J S, 1861, *Considerations on Representative Government*, Parker, Son and Bourn, London.

Ng, YF, 2016, *Ministerial Advisers in Australia: The Modern Legal Context*, Federation Press, Sydney.

Plasse, M, 1994, *Ministerial Chiefs of Staff in the Federal Government in 1990: Profiles, Recruitment, Duties, and Relations with Senior Public Servants*, Canadian Centre for Management Development, Ottawa.

Schultz, J, 1998, *Reviving the Fourth Estate: Democracy, Accountability and the Media*, Cambridge, Cambridge University Press.

Seymour-Ure, C, 2003, *Prime Ministers and the Media: Issues of Power and Control*, Blackwell Publishing, Malden.

Shaw, R, and Eichbaum, C, 2014, 'Ministers, Minders and the Core Executive: Why Ministers Appoint Political Advisers in Westminster Contexts', *Parliamentary Affairs*, vol. 67(3), pp. 584–616.

Swanson, D L, 2003, 'Political News in the Changing Environment of Political Journalism' in P J Maarek and G Wolfsfeld (eds), *Political Communication in a New Era: A Cross-national Perspective*, Routledge, London and New York, pp. 11–32.

Tiffen, R, 1989, *News and Power*, Allen & Unwin, Sydney.

Yeung, K, 2006, 'Regulating Government Communications', *Cambridge Law Journal* vol. 65(1), pp. 53–91.

Yong, B, and Hazell, R, 2014, *Special Advisers: Who They Are, What They Do and Why They Matter*, Hart Publishing, Oxford.

Zussman, D, 2009, *Political Advisers*, OECD, Paris.

Legislation, codes, case law, government and parliamentary reports

Australia, Senate, Select Committee for an Inquiry Into a Certain Maritime Incident, 2002, *A Certain Maritime Incident*, Senate Printing Unit, Canberra.

Benoit, L, 2006, 'Ministerial Staff: The Life and Times of Parliament's Statutory Orphans', *Restoring Accountability Research Studies Volume 1: Parliament, Ministers and Deputy Ministers*, Commission of Inquiry into the Sponsorship Program and Advertising Activities, Canadian Government Publishing, Ottawa, pp. 145–252.

British Columbia, Office of the Information and Privacy Commissioner, 2015, Access Denied: Record Retention and Disposal Practices of the Government of British Columbia, Investigation Report F15-03.

British Columbia, Office of the Premier, 2013, *Review of the Draft Multicultural Strategic Outreach Plan*. Available at: https://thetyee.ca/Documents/2013/03/14/Review%20of%20the%20Draft%20Multicultural%20Strategic%20Outreach%20Plan.pdf.

Canada, Auditor-General, 2003, Report of the Auditor-General of Canada to the House of Commons, Office of the Auditor-General, Canada.

Canada, Commission of Enquiry into the Actions of Canadian Officials in relation to Maher Arar, 2006, Report of the Events Relating to Maher Arar: Analysis and Recommendations, Public Works and Government Services Canada, Ottawa.

Canada, Commission of Inquiry into the Sponsorship Program and Advertising Activities, 2005, Who is Responsible? Volume 1: Fact Finding Report, prepared by Justice J H Gomery, Public Works and Government Services Canada, Ottawa.

Canada, Dorion Inquiry, 1965. Special Public Inquiry 1964, Report of the Commissioner, prepared by the Honourable Frederic Dorion, Chief Justice of the Superior Court for the Province of Quebec, Privy Council Office, Canada.

Canada, Federal Accountability Act 2006.

Canada, House of Commons, Standing Committee on Access to Information, Privacy and Ethics, 2010, *Evidence*, 13 May 2009.

Canada, House of Commons, Standing Committee of External Affairs of Trade, 1991, *First Report of the 3rd Session of the 34th Parliament*.

Canada, Office of the Conflict of Interest and Ethics Commissioner, 2017, The Wright Report. Available at: http://ciec-ccie.parl.gc.ca/Documents/English/Public%20Reports/Examination%20Reports/The%20Wright%20Report.pdf.

Canada, Office of the Ethics Commissioner, 2005, *The Sgro Inquiry: Many Shades of Grey*, Prepared by B J Shapiro, Office of the Ethics Commission, Ottawa.

Canada, Office of the Information Commissioner of Canada, 2011, Interference with Access to Information, Special Report Part 1, prepared by S Legault, Information Commission of Canada.

Canada, Senate, 2013, *Debates*, 22 October.

Egan v Willis (1998) 195 CLR 424.

Canada, House of Commons, 1964, *Debates*, 23 November.

New South Wales Ombudsman, 2009, *Opening up Government: Review of the Freedom of Information Act 1989: A Special Report to Parliament under s 31 of the Ombudsman Act 1974*. Ombudsman, New South Wales.

New Zealand, Official Information Act 1982.

New Zealand, Office of the Inspector-General of Intelligence and Security, 2014, *Report into the Release of Information by the New Zealand Security Intelligence*

Service in July and August 2011, Public Report, Prepared by C Gwyn, Inspector-General of Intelligence and Security.

New Zealand, Office of the Ombudsman, 2015, *Not a Game of Hide and Seek: Report on an Investigation into Central Government Agencies for the Purpose of Compliance with the OIA*, prepared by Dame B Waken, Chief Ombudsman.

New Zealand, Privileges Committee, 2013, Question of Privilege regarding use of Intrusive Powers within the Parliamentary Precinct: Interim Report of the Privileges Committee.

Ontario, Archives and Recordkeeping Act 2006, SO 2006, c 34.

Ontario, Freedom of Information and Protection of Privacy Act 1990, RSO 1990.

Ontario, Office of the Information and Privacy Commissioner, 2013, *Deleting Accountability: Records Management Practices of Political Staff: A Special Investigation Report*, prepared by A Cavoukian, Information and Privacy Commissioner, Ontario.

Phillis, B, 2004, *An Independent Review of Government Communications*, House of Commons Select Committee on Communications, Cabinet Office.

R v Duffy (2016) ONCJ 220.

Thomas, P G, 2009, 'Who is Getting the Message? Communications at the Centre of Government', in *Public Policy Issues and the Oliphant Commission Independent Research Studies*, Commission of Enquiry into Certain Allegations Respecting Business and Financial Dealings between Karlheinz Schreiber and the Right Honourable Brian Mulroney', Minister of Public Works and Government Services, Canada, pp. 77–136.

United Kingdom, Committee on Standards in Public Life, *Public Hearings*, 9 July 2002.

United Kingdom, House of Commons, Public Administration Select Committee, 2003, These Unfortunate Events: Lessons of Recent Events at the Former DTLR, Eighth Report of Session 2001–2002, The Stationery Office, London.

United Kingdom, House of Commons, Public Administration Select Committee, 2000, The Government Information and Communication Service *(2000–1)*, HC 511, Minutes of Evidence, 17 May.

United Kingdom, House of Commons, Public Administration Select Committee, 2012, Special Advisors in the Thick of It, Sixth Report of Session 2012–2013, The Stationery Office Ltd, London.

United Kingdom, Information Commissioner's Office, 2012, *Freedom of Information Act 2000 Decision* Notice FS50422276. The Leveson Inquiry, 2012, *An Inquiry into the Culture, Practices and Ethics of the Press Report*, Volume III, The Stationery Office, London.

United Kingdom, Committee on Standards in Public Life, 2003, Defining the Boundaries within the Executive: Ministers, Special Advisers and the Permanent Civil Service. Ninth Report, CM5775, The Stationery Office, London.

Victoria, Legislative Council, Standing Committee on Finance and Public Administration, 2010, Inquiry into Victorian Government Decision Making, Consultation and Approval Processes, Second Interim Report, Government Printer, Victoria.

Newspaper articles

Battersby, S, 2015, 'Stephen Harper Insists Nigel Wright was Alone to Blame in Duffy Affair', The Star, 7 September. Available at: www.thestar.com/news/federal-election/2015/09/07/stephen-harper-insists-nigel-wright-was-alone-to-blame-in-duffy-affair.html.

Bishop, G, 1974, 'Labour's private army in Whitehall', New Statesman, 10 May.
Blatchford, C, 2017, 'McGuinty Aide was Warned not to Delete Gas Plants Emails, Trial Told', National Post, 29 September. Available at: http://nationalpost.com/opinion/christie-blatchford-mcguinty-aide-was-warned-not-to-delete-gas-plants-emails-trial-told.
Brogan, B, 2002, 'Mottram's Oath-laden Prediction comes True' The Telegraph, 30 May. Available at: www.telegraph.co.uk/news/uknews/1395782/Mottrams-oath-laden-prediction-comes-true.html.
Eichbaum, C, 2017, 'Chris Eichbaum: Free and Frank Advice Fast Disappearing', The Dominion Post, 8 August 2017. Available at: www.stuff.co.nz/national/politics/95499693/chris-eichbaum--free-and-frank-advice-fast-disappearing.
Martin, L, 2006, 'Ottawa's "Bubble Boy" is Courting Conflict', The Globe and Mail, 30 March. Available at: https://beta.theglobeandmail.com/opinion/ottawas-bubble-boy-is-courting-conflict/article1097026/?ref=http://www.theglobeand mail.com&.
Shaw, R, 2016, 'Former Political Aide George Gretes fined $2,500 for Misleading B.C.'s Privacy Commissioner', Vancouver Sun, July 14. Available at: http://vancouversun.com/news/local-news/former-political-aide-george-gretes-fined-2500-for-misleading-b-c-s-privacy-commissioner.
Sparrow, A, 2001, 'Sept 11: 'A Good Day to Bury Bad News', The Telegraph, 10 October. Available at: www.telegraph.co.uk/news/uknews/1358985/Sept-11-a-good-day-to-bury-bad-news.html.
Tomazin, F, 2012, 'Staffers Vet FOI Requests: Report', The Age, 16 December. Available at: www.theage.com.au/victoria/staffers-vet-foi-requests-report-20121215-2bghs.html.
Whelan, C, 2000, 'Time No 10 Cleaned Up Old Pals Act', Mirror, 3 July.

5 Legal and political regulation

The scandals and controversies in the preceding chapter have sparked an impetus to regulate the actions of political advisors. This chapter examines the legal and political regulation of political advisors in each jurisdiction. Legal mechanisms range from legislation setting out sanctions and recourse to external adjudicators to 'soft law' such as codes of conduct and guidance. Political regulation through parliamentary scrutiny can also enhance the accountability of political advisors in explaining their public actions and decisions. In recent times, oversight bodies have become an important force in holding advisors to account.

United Kingdom

Legal regulation

The *Constitutional Reform and Governance Act 2010* puts the position of British special advisors on a legislative footing. It provides that special advisors are temporary civil servants that are appointed by Ministers personally, and whose appointments are approved by the Prime Minister. The terms and conditions of their appointment are set out by the Civil Service Minister. Under the Act, the Civil Service Minister is required to annually report to Parliament the number and cost of special advisors (s 16), and this requirement is echoed in the Ministerial Code (para 3.4). Importantly, this sets up a legislative framework for ministerial accountability to Parliament for expenditure on advisors. The names and numbers of advisors are also regularly reported in the British media. This extensive scrutiny, combined with a cap on the number of advisors stipulated by the Ministerial Code of a maximum of two special advisors per Minister, apart from the Prime Minister and Deputy Prime Minister (para 3.2), has kept the number of political advisors in the UK low compared to other jurisdictions. Although the Prime Minister has the discretion to authorise additional appointments and the caps have not been strictly complied with despite the fervent vows of incoming Prime Ministers, the very existence of a political cap may explain the low numbers of advisors in the UK.

Special advisors are appointed under terms and conditions set out in the *Model Contract for Special Advisers* and the *Code of Conduct for Special Advisers*. The *Constitutional Reform and Governance Act 2010* requires that the Minister for the Civil Service publish a Code of Conduct for special advisors (s 8). The Act stipulates that the code must prohibit special advisors from authorising the expenditure of public funds or having responsibility for budgets, or otherwise exercising any statutory or prerogative power (s 8(5)). In addition to this, the Code of Conduct prohibits special advisors from asking civil servants to do anything that is inconsistent with their obligations under the Civil Service Code or the standards of their department (*Code of Conduct for Special Advisers*, para 5). Special advisors are also prevented from exercising any management power over the civil service, but may manage other special advisors. However, a 2015 amendment to the Code stated that special advisors could convey Ministers' instructions to officials (*Code of Conduct for Special Advisers*, para 4). Civil servants argued that this could effectively give special advisors managerial power, by allowing the advisors to give instructions to the bureaucracy.

Special advisors are also bound by the *Civil Service Code* (UK, Civil Service Commissioner 2010), with the exception of appointment on merit and being required to act with political impartiality (*Code of Conduct for Special Advisers*, para 8). The *Civil Service Code* provides for internal review of potential breaches of the Code, as well as external review by the Civil Service Commission. However, civil servants are generally reluctant to put their case to the Civil Service Commission as this would be the 'nuclear option' (UK, Public Administration Select Committee 2003, p. 17). In practice, at first instance, the permanent secretary will investigate the issue and make recommendations to the Minister. Ultimately Ministers are responsible for managing and disciplining their own special advisors (Ministerial Code, para 3.3). Ministers are accountable to the Prime Minister, Parliament and the public for their actions and decisions about their special advisors. The Prime Minister may intervene and adjudicate on difficult cases as he/she has the overarching ability to terminate the employment of a special advisor (UK, Committee on Standards in Public Life, 2000b, Chap. 6).

Both the Ministerial Code (para 3.3) and the Code of Conduct (para 2) were amended in 2010 to provide that special advisors are employed to serve the Prime Minister and the government as a whole, not just their appointing Minister. This reflected the political reality at the time of a minority government, but has been retained. The provision can also be applied to the endemic problem of advisors behaving in a factional way of promoting their Minister, possibly at the expense of the government. This was underscored by a period of pervasive leaks to the media (discussed in chapter four), resulting in a series of new media requirements in the Code. A provision was inserted cautioning special advisors against leaking official information that has been communicated in confidence in government. It also condemns the preparation or dissemination of inappropriate material or personal attacks in the conduct of public life. Any special advisor found to be disseminating inappropriate material will be disciplined and perhaps dismissed. The Ministerial Code has a special provision about advance copies of select committee reports not being inappropriately disclosed by special advisors and civil servants (para 9.7). Special advisors are also enjoined not to take public part in political controversy, through any form of public statement, whether in speeches, newspaper articles, books, social media, articles or leaflets. According to the Code, advisors must be discreet and make public comment with moderation, avoiding personal attacks, and would not normally publicly speak for their Minister or the department (*Code of Conduct for Special Advisers*, para 14).

To add to transparency in dealing with the media, departments will publish on a quarterly basis details of special advisors' meetings with newspaper and other media proprietors, editors and senior executives, as well as any hospitality received by special advisors (*Code of Conduct for Special Advisers*, para 15). There is prime ministerial office control over media management. Special advisors must work with Number 10 to ensure the proper coordination of announcements, media appearances and other interviews, articles and interventions made by their Minister (*Code of Conduct for Special Advisers*, para 12). Thus, the Prime Minister's Office vets and centrally coordinates media management.

In short, the British regulatory scheme is very detailed and substantive compared to those of other jurisdictions. Strict requirements are legislated, coupled with extensive rules set out in the Code of Conduct with deep disclosure requirements. In practice, Ministers are responsible for any breaches by special advisors, and advisors primarily answer to their Minister.

Parliamentary scrutiny

There has been extensive parliamentary scrutiny of special advisors in Britain compared to other jurisdictions. The Public Administration Select Committee remarked that: 'rarely can such a small group, fewer than ninety ... have received such disproportionate attention' (Public Administration Select Committee 2008, para 112). There have been at least 11 parliamentary committee reports discussing the role of special advisors in the last 15 years. In particular, the Committee on Standards in Public Life made recommendations regarding the interaction between Ministers, civil servants and special advisors no less than three times (UK, Committee on Standards in Public Life 1995, 2000a, 2003), while the Public Administration Select Committee considered various aspects of the regulation of advisors nine times (UK, Public Administration Select Committee 1998, 2001, 2003, 2005, 2007, 2008, 2010, 2012, 2013). The extensive parliamentary scrutiny and recommendations from committees led to incremental changes in the regulation of special advisors over the years. This has resulted in the current sophisticated interlocking regulatory system of legislation, codes of conduct for Ministers, civil servants and special advisors, alongside contracts of employment for special advisors.

In the UK, it is clear that special advisors can be called to appear before parliamentary committees according to the Osmotherly Rules, which is an executive document that has not been approved by Parliament (UK, Cabinet Office 2005). The Osmotherly Rules provide for civil servants to give evidence to select committees on behalf of the Minister and under the direction of the Minister, as it is the role of select committees to ensure 'the proper accountability of the Executive to Parliament' (cl 1). Previously the Osmotherly Rules were silent on the position of special advisors. The Rules were revised in 2005 to create a presumption that where a parliamentary committee called a named official, including a special advisor, the named official will appear where possible (cl 12). For instance, where a parliamentary committee wished to call a special advisor or retired civil servant who specifically worked on a project, this would be possible:

> Where a Select Committee indicates that it wishes to take evidence from a particular named official, including special advisors, the presumption should be that Ministers will agree to meet such a request. However, the final decision on who is best able to represent the Minister rests with the Minister concerned and it remains the right of a Minister to suggest an alternative civil servant to that named by the Committee if he or she feels that the former is better placed to represent them. In the unlikely event of there being no agreement about which official should most appropriately give evidence, it is open to the Minister to offer to appear personally before the Committee.
>
> (UK, Cabinet Office 2005 cl 12)

This rule was retained when the Osmotherly Rules were revised in 2014. This development represents a positive step towards providing select committees with access to special advisors, with a presumption in favour of a named special advisor appearing. Where the special advisor does not appear and there is no other appropriate official who can appear, the Minister should appear personally to fulfil the requirements of ministerial responsibility. This model is intended to ensure that at least one public official appears before the parliamentary committee, and reinforces the position that the Minister bears ultimate responsibility for deciding which official appears before committees.

Previously there was a precedent of special advisors failing to appear before a select committee. In 1986, Thatcher's advisors Charles Powell and Bernard Ingram did not appear before the Defence Committee investigating the dispute about the future of Westland Helicopters company that led to the resignation of two Cabinet Ministers, Michael Heseltine and Leon Brittan. The Cabinet Secretary stated that the two advisors had already been questioned in depth by him and offered to appear before the committee instead. The Committee rejected this reason, stating: 'We are not satisfied that a private internal inquiry which is not fully reported to Parliament constitutes accountability' (UK, House of Commons, Defence Committee 1986).

This precedent of refusal to appear was disrupted by Alastair Campbell, then chief media advisor to Tony Blair, who appeared before the Public Administration Select Committee in 1998 (UK, House of Commons, Public Administration Select Committee 1998). Likewise Andrew Hood, special advisor to the Foreign Minister, appeared before the Committee on Standards and Privileges investigating the leaking to the executive of a draft parliamentary committee report on Sierra Leone (UK, Committee on Standards and Privileges 1999). Hood explained the circumstances in which he had possession of the report. The leak was ultimately found to be by one of the committee members.

Nevertheless, there were subsequent significant refusals by special advisors to appear before committees. Jonathan Powell, then chief of staff to Tony Blair, refused to appear before the Public Administration Select Committee in 2000 on the basis that there was no precedent for the cross-examination of a civil servant 'about himself and what he did' (UK, Public Administration Select Committee 2000a, Q 397; Public Administration Select Committee 2001, para 21). Richard Wilson, Cabinet Secretary and Head of the Home Civil Service, appeared instead. Both Alastair Campbell and Jonathan Powell declined to give evidence before the Committee on Standards in Public Life in 2002 (UK, Public Administration Select Committee 2007, p. 39).

Even after the Osmotherly Rules were revised in 2005 to include special advisors, there continued to be resistance. The Public Administration Select Committee issued a report complaining that, despite the change in the Osmotherly Rules, they faced continual difficulties in accessing witnesses from Number 10 on long-term strategic matters (UK, Public Administration Select Committee 2005). In particular, the Prime Minister's Strategy Advisor, Lord Birt, an unpaid position, declined to give evidence to the committee. In addition, the Prime Minister's senior policy advisor, Julian Le Grand, declined to give evidence to the committee in 2004 on the basis that there was a policy that it was inappropriate for the Prime Minister's special advisors to give evidence.

The situation has changed, however, due to the intense scrutiny of the British decision to go to war in Iraq based on false allegations that the Iraqi government had weapons of mass destruction, as well as the revelations that a British newspaper hacked the mobile phone of a murdered schoolgirl. The British decision to go to war in Iraq resulted in a deluge of parliamentary and judicial inquiries. At the heart of the controversy were allegations from an initially anonymous source quoted by BBC reporter Andrew Gilligan that Alastair Campbell, Blair's chief media advisor, 'sexed up' intelligence documents to make a case for war. Campbell insisted in his diaries that a controversial dossier of evidence published in the run up to the Iraq War had to be altered to be 'revelatory' (Campbell and Hagerty 2012, p. 293). This dossier became a persuasive document for the invasion of Iraq.

In 2003, Alastair Campbell voluntarily appeared before the Foreign Affairs Committee to discuss his role in briefing for war (UK, House of Commons, Foreign Affairs Committee 2003). His appearance was authorised by the

Prime Minister, as the committee's focus was on communications policy, which was an area of Campbell's responsibility as Chair of the cross-departmental Iraqi Communications Group. Campbell also appeared as a witness for the Hutton Inquiry, which was a judicial inquiry investigating the circumstances surrounding the death of David Kelly, a biological warfare expert and former United Nations weapons inspector in Iraq (Hutton 2004). Kelly was found dead after he had been named as the source of quotations used by BBC journalist Andrew Gilligan. Campbell resigned in 2003 during the Hutton Inquiry. In 2004, Jonathan Powell, chief of staff to Blair, appeared as a witness before the Butler Review, which examined the intelligence on Iraq's weapons of mass destruction. The review found that some of the intelligence relied upon was 'seriously flawed' and that 'the language of the dossier may have left with readers the impression that there was fuller and firmer intelligence behind the judgements than was the case' (UK, Committee of Privy Counsellors 2004, para 464). In 2009, following the withdrawal of British troops from Iraq, Prime Minister Gordon Brown set up the inquiry into the Iraq War, chaired by Sir John Chilcot. Both Alastair Campbell and Jonathan Powell appeared as witnesses. Although the inquiry found that there was no evidence that Number 10 influenced the text of the dossier, it reached the damning verdict that the intelligence 'had *not* established beyond doubt that Saddam Hussein had continued to produce chemical and biological weapons' (UK, Committee of Privy Counsellors 2016, p. 116).

Special advisors also appeared before inquiries investigating British media practices. Alastair Campbell appeared before the Phillis Review investigating government communications and resigned from his position during the course of the review (Phillis 2004). Several former special advisors appeared as witnesses before the 2012 Leveson inquiry, a judicial inquiry set up to investigate the culture, practices and ethics of the press, after outrage over the phone hacking of a murdered schoolgirl by *News of the World*. The key witnesses included Alastair Campbell, Adam Smith (former special advisor implicated for interfering in a quasi-judicial inquiry discussed in chapter four) and Andy Coulson (former Chief Press Secretary of David Cameron, implicated for being Editor of *News of the World* at the time of the phone hacking) (The Leveson Inquiry 2012). Alastair Campbell issued two witness statements for the Leveson inquiry, but not before he leaked drafts of his witness statements to the press, which were published online by a blogger before the actual inquiry hearing.

As part of the changed trend from his previous refusal, Jonathan Powell has since appeared as a witness before the Public Administration Select Committee in 2009 (UK, Public Administration Select Committee 2010) and 2013 to comment on the broader functioning of the civil service and special advisors (UK, Public Administration Select Committee 2013). Former special advisor Patrick Diamond also appeared before the 2013 committee.

Thus, the British Parliament has been vigilant in investigating and scrutinising the actions and misdemeanours of special advisors, as well as more broadly assessing their position within the system of executive government. It can be seen that since the Osmotherly Rules were amended in 2005, there have been significant appearances by special advisors before parliamentary committees. There is now a well-established precedent, reinforced by executive rules, that special advisors can be called and will appear before parliamentary committees.

Scrutiny by oversight bodies

Oversight bodies in the UK have not been very active in pursuing the actions of special advisors, perhaps due to the high levels of parliamentary and media scrutiny. One exception is where the Information Commissioner investigated the actions of then Education Minister Michael Gove's special advisors in 2011 for using private email accounts to hide information from civil servants and avoid scrutiny under the freedom of information legislation (UK, Information Commissioner's Office 2012). The Commissioner ruled that all emails sent by special advisors concerning government business are subject to freedom of information laws.

Besides this isolated investigation, there has otherwise not been much activity by British oversight bodies. This could be attributable to the extensive legal, parliamentary and media scrutiny that exists for special advisors in the UK, which means that it is less necessary for oversight bodies to step in and initiate investigations.

Canada

Legal regulation

The catalyst for the current comprehensive and stringent regulation of political advisors in Canada was the explosive Sponsorship Scandal and the subsequent Gomery Commission investigation that revealed widespread abuse of powers by political advisors (discussed in chapter four). Consequently, the *Federal Accountability Act* was introduced in 2006, which sought to regulate political advisors in terms of post-employment restrictions, conflict of interest and enhanced disclosure requirements.

The *Public Service Employment Act* (SC 2003, c 22, sections 12, 13) authorises Ministers to employ political staff (termed 'exempt staff'), and confirms that these staff lose their position 30 days after the Minister vacates his or her position (sections 128–9). Until 2007, political staff who were employed by Ministers for at least three years were entitled to be appointed as public servants on an equivalent level without competition after their appointment as political staff ceased. This feature enabled political staff to enter the bureaucracy through a 'back door'. Some of these staff rose to senior positions in the public service, including the top position of deputy minister (departmental head) (Aucoin 2010, p. 68), which may have politicised the bureaucracy. Nevertheless, Benoit found that the option to enter the public service was seen to be one of last resort, exercised only by eight per cent of political staff in 2006. By contrast, becoming a lobbyist was seen as the preferred option for ex-political staff due to the high pay and prestige, alongside the ability to maintain partisan affiliations (Benoit 2006, p. 219). In 2007, following the Sponsorship Scandal, where two of the political staff implicated gained priority access to the public service, this provision was removed by an amendment to the *Public Service Employment Act*, and political staff were prohibited from being lobbyists for five years after ceasing their employment (*Lobbying Act*, s 10.11).

The Privy Council Office (equivalent to Prime Minister's Department) has issued guidance that delineates the relationship of exempt staff with the department, allowing them to liaise with the department for information or communication, but prohibiting them from exercising the delegated authority of Ministers and directing public servants on their responsibilities, operational matters or the management of departmental resources (Canada, Privy Council Office 2015, E3). It also states that exempt staff should not withhold departmental advice or briefing material from the Minister or impede direct communication between the deputy minister and the Minister, but may supplement departmental advice or briefing material with their own advice. This goes towards preventing ministerial staff from 'funnelling' advice from the department. Ministers and deputy ministers are also enjoined to be vigilant in ensuring that the appropriate parameters of interaction between officials and exempt staff are observed. Nevertheless, although Privy Council Office and Treasury guidelines and the code of conduct state that 'normally' and 'to the extent practicable', interactions between officials and exempt staff should occur through the deputy minister, Craft's recent study found that this was not representative of actual practice, as it was impractical to only limit contact to the deputy minister, due to the hectic pace of policy-making in modern governance. A deputy minister stated:

> You know, you can't have a choke point in the system. You have to have a kind of a little bit of a distributive relationship between the minister's office and the department. So not everything funnels through me or my office. That would be just impossible.
>
> (quoted in Craft 2016, p. 165)

This was particularly the case in the line departments (as distinct from central agencies), where advisors were briefed not only by the deputy minister, but also by more junior departmental officers, and got more into the details of the policy advice (Craft 2016, p. 192).

Political staff are also subject to a code of conduct. The *Code of Conduct for Ministerial Exempt Staff* (Canada, Privy Council Office 2015, Annex I) allows ministerial staff to engage in party-political work, as long as it is not on paid time. It reiterates the Privy Council guidance that political staff do not have the authority to direct public servants in their own right, and recognises that political staff do not have a role in departmental operations, including exercising legal powers and functions, expending public funds and managing the department. The Code also rejects ministerial staff funnelling or blocking advice, by providing that ministerial staff will not suppress or supplant the advice prepared for the Minister by departmental public servants, beyond commenting on the advice. Further, ministerial staff are prevented from taking action that would undermine the deputy minister's authority as the Minister's primary source of public service advice for the portfolio. Ministerial staff must also comply with the *Ethical and Political Activity Guidelines for Public Office Holders* (Canada, Privy Council Office 2015, Annex I), which enjoins them to behave with honesty and integrity.

In addition, political staff are subject to conflict of interest and post-employment obligations under the *Conflict of Interest Act* (S.C. 2006, c. 9) and *Lobbying Act* (R.S.C., 1985, c. 44 (4th Supp)), introduced as part of the package of *Federal Accountability Act* reforms. The Conflict of Interest and Ethics Commissioner administers these schemes and is able to investigate breaches of these Acts and order political advisors to comply with the legislation. Under these regimes, political staff are subject to extensive disclosure requirements. They must confidentially disclose to the Commissioner all assets and liabilities they have and all firm offers of employment. Ministerial staff are prevented from engaging in conduct that would conflict with their public duties, such as making decisions that further their personal or family interests, or giving preferential treatment to others. Political advisors also have to publicly disclose all gifts above $200 that are not from friends or relatives, as well as their travel and hospitality expenses for public duties (*Conflict of Interest Act*, s 23).

The budget for political staff for each Minister is capped each year by the Treasury Board. To exceed this budget, approval is needed from the Prime Minister's Office and Treasury Board (Canada, Treasury Board 2011). Previously it was possible to circumvent the budget limits on hiring political staff through 'personal service contracts' allowing Ministers to employ additional staff with expertise or skills outside the public service (Williams 1980). For example, former Minister Lloyd Axworthy had 100 staff in his ministerial office employed through personal service contracts, with 20 exempt staff and the remainder seconded or fixed-term public servants (Bakvis 1991, p. 191). Axworthy used the large number of staff to bypass officials at any rank who were seen to be unsympathetic or simply too slow in responding to requests (Bakvis 1991, p. 192). This practice no longer applies in contemporary times due to enhanced disclosure requirements that apply to Ministers. Since 2006, the *Federal Accountability Act* requires Ministers to publicly disclose their office budgets. In addition, under the *Guidelines on the Proactive Disclosure of Contracts*, all contracts above $10,000 have to be publicly disclosed, meaning that issuing personal service contracts through departments would be publicly scrutinised, including by the media.

Thus, political staff in Canada are subject to very stringent regulation through an elaborate interlocking scheme of legislation and ethical codes, combined with strong disclosure requirements, with oversight by an independent commissioner.

Parliamentary scrutiny

The Canadian parliamentary structure consists of an elected lower house (the House of Commons) and an appointed upper house (the Senate). The Canadian Senate is supposed to be a 'chamber for sober second thought' but, for most of Canadian history, appointments to the Senate were made by the Prime Minister based on patronage (Simpson 1988, pp. 311–330). Since 2016, appointments are recommended by the non-partisan Independent Advisory Board for Senate Appointments based on merit, but it may take some time for the effects of merit appointments to filter through the system. Because of its lack of democratic legitimacy, the Canadian Senate has had very low credibility, with many calls to abolish the Senate (Boyer 2014). This has been exacerbated by the Senate expenses scandal that exploded in 2012, where several Senators were found to be abusing their expenses claims (the Duffy expenses scandal is discussed in chapter four). Due to the poor public perception of the Senate, Senators have been less willing to take action against the elected House of Commons, meaning that the Canadian Senate has generally not been an effective mechanism of executive scrutiny.

The legal powers of the Canadian Parliament are strong. Following the 1985 McGrath report on reform of the House of Commons, standing committees of Parliament were given authority to call anyone to answer questions. The report demanded that deputy ministers be directly accountable to the House of Commons, as deputy ministers rather than Ministers were the persons who were responsible for what goes on in a department and ought to be accountable for administration, including policy implementation (Canada, Special Committee on the Reform of the House of Commons 1985, p. 20). Accordingly, since 1987, parliamentary committees have been able to summon deputy ministers to provide information about the management of a department (Bourgault 2006, p. 261). Public servants have appeared regularly before parliamentary committees for the past three decades. Normally they voluntarily appear but there have been several instances where they have been summoned (Thomas 2010, p. 122).

In 1991, the House of Commons Standing Committee on External Affairs and International Trade investigated the Al-Mashat Affair (discussed in chapter four), where Al-Mashat, who had links to the Iraqi dictatorship, was granted a visa to enter Canada. The Committee took evidence from four Ministers, two political advisors and about 20 public servants. The committee was able to question all actors in depth about their actions.

More recently, however, political staff have been obstructed from appearing before parliamentary committees in Canada. In 2010, amid growing controversy about political staff interference in the administration of the *Access to Information Act*, the House of Commons Standing Committee on Access to Information, Privacy and Ethics examined allegations of systemic political interference by ministerial offices, who blocked, delayed or obstructed the release of documents under Access to Information requests. Three political staffers appeared before the committee. First, the Prime Minister's Chief of Staff, Guy Giorno, appeared. Second, Director of Parliamentary Affairs at Department of Public Works and Government Services, Sébastien Togneri, who was implicated in the media for blocking the release of a governmental report, appeared when summoned and testified twice before the committee. Togneri admitted he had sent a 'stupid email' and that it had been a mistake on his part. He also indicated it had been an isolated incident. Third, Ryan Sparrow, Director of Communications of the Minister of Human Resources and Skills Development, appeared with his Minister to address allegations he tried to suppress the cost of the Olympic advertising campaign. The figure was finally released after three weeks. In the committee hearing, the Minister sought to answer questions on behalf of Sparrow, but the committee disallowed this as they wished to question the staffer, rather than the Minister, who had already given evidence before the committee. Sparrow stated that he acted on behalf of the Minister in altering 22 per cent of responses by departmental staff to media inquiries (or 51 changes to 235 requests in six months) (Canada, House of Commons, Standing Committee on Access to Information, Privacy and Ethics 2010).

During the course of the hearings in 2010, however, the committee was impeded by a new government policy that political staff should not testify at committees and that Ministers should attend on their behalf (Canada, House of Commons Standing Committee on Access to Information, Privacy and Ethics 2010). Jillian Andrews, policy advisor to Natural Resources Minister Christian Paradis, and Dimitri Soudas, Prime Minister Stephen Harper's Director of Communications, were summoned to give evidence to the parliamentary committee but refused to appear. Togneri also declined to appear for the third time. Instead the Minister of Natural Resources and Minister of Justice appeared before the committee. The committee concluded that a potential breach of parliamentary privilege may have occurred and reported the matter to the House. However, a motion on privilege was defeated in the House of Commons.

Although there has been obstruction in terms of advisors appearing before parliamentary committees, the Minister in these instances appeared on their behalf. This means that ministerial responsibility was fulfilled in the sense that the Ministers fronted the committees to take responsibility for and justify their own decisions and actions.

Even with the alleged government ban, in a later incident, a political advisor did appear before a parliamentary committee. In 2011, Kasra Nejatian, advisor to Immigration Minister Jason Kenny, appeared before the Standing Committee on Access to Information, Privacy and Ethics (Canada,

House of Commons, Standing Committee on Access to Information, Privacy and Ethics 2011). Nejatian distributed a letter with the Minister's parliamentary letterhead seeking partisan donations from Conservative MPs. Under the conflict of interest rules, parliamentary or government resources are not to be used for partisan activities. However, the advisor mistakenly sent a letter intended for John Duncan, a Conservative MP, to New Democrat MP Linda Duncan asking for $200,000 to fund a media strategy to attract ethnic votes to the Conservative party. The Minister contacted the ethics commissioner and the speaker of the House, apologised for the error and took corrective action. The advisor explained the details of the mistake to the parliamentary committee and took responsibility for his actions. He apologised to the Minister and committee, stating that the mistake was entirely his own and in contravention of his Minister's directions. Although Nejatian resigned as a result of this gaffe, he was rehired by his Minister two months later. Thus, in Canada there is precedent for both obstruction and cooperation in terms of political staffers appearing before parliamentary inquiries.

Scrutiny by oversight bodies

In recent times, independent statutory office-holders in Canada have started to investigate and report on the actions of political staff. For instance, the Information Commissioner has become active in examining the actions of political staff. The Information Commissioner is an independent officer of Parliament who conducts administrative investigations into federal institutions' compliance with the *Access to Information Act*, makes findings of fact and provides recommendations to government institutions. The Commissioner has significant coercive powers, including the power to summon and enforce the appearance of persons, examine persons under oath, enter premises and order the production of documents (s 36). Despite this, the Commissioner does not have the power to order the release of records or compel the implementation of his or her recommendations. Although ministerial offices and political staff are excluded from the application of the *Access to Information Act* (*Canada (Information Commissioner) v Canada (Minister of National Defence)*, 2011 SCC 25), the Commissioner is able to examine the actions of political staff where they impact on departmental operations. This is because the Supreme Court determined that records located in a Minister's office are nonetheless 'under the control' of the related government institution when they concern departmental matters.

In 2011, the Information Commissioner, Suzanne Legault, reported on the actions of a political staffer at Public Works and Government Services Canada, Sébastien Togneri, who interfered in a departmental decision to release a report on the government's real estate portfolio under the *Access to Information Act*. This was following the failure of a parliamentary committee to compel a number of political staffers, including Togneri, to appear following a change in government policy, as discussed above. The Commissioner found that Togneri interfered with the release of records under the Act by instructing officials to retrieve the original release package and then directing them to release only one chapter of the report. Political staffers have no authority to make any decision under the Act or give any direction to officials. The Commissioner also found that political staff were able to influence decision-making 'due to the fact that political staff members wield the influence associated with the Minister's office and may purport to speak on behalf of the Minister' (Canada, Information Commissioner of Canada 2011, p. 15). Togneri resigned following this finding. As a corrective measure, the department changed its protocols for Access to Information requests to provide information to the ministerial office 'for information only' and removed ministerial office representation in meetings discussing the files.

In 2014, the Information Commissioner conducted a further investigation into the processing of Access to Information requests by Public Works and Government Services Canada (Canada, Office of the Information Commissioner 2014). The Commissioner summoned witnesses to give evidence, including political staff who refused to give evidence before a parliamentary committee on the same issue (Jillian Andrews and Sébastien Togneri), as discussed above. After some resistance from the ministerial office about producing documents, the Commissioner used her coercive powers to order the production of documents. The Commissioner concluded that there was systemic interference by political staff into departmental processing of Access to Information files. The Commissioner also found that political staffers exerted pressure on and gave instructions to departmental employees on what to release or suppress. The departmental officials only released information when approved by the Minister's office. As a result of the Commissioner's report, the department put into place new protocols that clarified that political staff were not to interfere with the administration of the *Access to Information Act*, and training was instituted for political staff to ensure they knew the boundaries of their role.

Following these reports, a parliamentary committee (Canada, House of Commons, Standing Committee on Access to Information, Privacy and Ethics 2016, Recommendation 3) and the Information Commissioner (Office of the Information Commissioner of Canada 2015, Recommendations 1.2–1.3) recommended that the *Access to Information Act* be amended to apply to ministerial offices. The Trudeau government (2015–present), however, did not implement this suggestion of providing full right of access to documents in ministerial offices. Rather, in 2017, the government instituted a more limited proactive disclosure regime, where the government was able to choose what was to be disclosed, and the jurisdiction of the Information Commissioner was expressly excluded (Canada, Bill C-58 2017, s 36). Ministerial offices are now expected to proactively disclose Minister's briefing materials upon assuming office, the title and tracking numbers of monthly memoranda prepared for the Minister by a government institution, monthly question period packages prepared by a government institution for the Minister, and briefing materials for parliamentary appearances of the Minister, as well as expense reports (within 120 days of the end of the fiscal year), travel expenses (monthly), hospitality expenses (monthly), and contracts over $10,000 (quarterly). However, this scheme was criticised by the Information Commissioner as being a regression from the existing regime, as the same materials were already able to be accessed under the existing scheme with Commissioner oversight (Canada, Office of the Information Commissioner of Canada 2017). The jurisdiction of the Information Commissioner has thus been diminished under the new scheme, which will reduce the level of independent oversight over access to information in Canada.

At the provincial level in Ontario and British Columbia, as discussed in chapter four, the Information Commissioners have been active in investigating political staff who have destroyed documents and regularly deleted emails in contravention of legislative requirements.

In recent times, the Conflict of Interest and Ethics Commissioner has also become active in scrutinising the actions of ministerial staff. This office was created as part of the *Federal Accountability Act 2006*, expanding the scope of duties of the previous Ethics Commissioner. The Commissioner is an independent officer of Parliament with significant coercive powers, including the power to summon witnesses and require them to give evidence under oath, as well as order the production of documents.

Formerly the jurisdiction of the Ethics Commissioner was confined to Members of the House of Commons based on their obligations under the Members' Code. The Commissioner could only conduct inquiries under the *Conflict of Interest and Post-Employment Code for Public Office Holders* into the conduct of Ministers of the Crown, Ministers of State and Parliamentary Secretaries – not that of political staff. Accordingly, former Ethics Commissioner Bernard Shapiro repeatedly took the position that political advisors were outside of his remit, stating 'the Prime Minister is ultimately responsible to Parliament for the actions of [his Chief of Staff]' (quoted in Doyle 2005). Consequently, the Commissioner refused to directly investigate complaints against a couple of political advisors: Ihor Wons, policy advisor and later Chief of Staff to former Immigration Minister Judy Sgro (the scandal is discussed in chapter four) and Tim Murphy, Chief of Staff to the Prime Minister, for his role in a leaked tape scandal.

Following the *Federal Accountability Act*, the Commissioner's jurisdiction has been legislatively extended through the *Conflict of Interest Act* to encompass all current and former political staff. The Commissioner is able to initiate own-motion inquiries into breaches of the Act, in addition to a reference from a MP. The sanctions for breaches of the Act are limited to imposing administrative monetary penalties, issuing compliance orders and conducting examinations with recommendations.

Under the new regime, the Conflict of Interest and Ethics Commissioner, Mary Dawson, found that a former political staffer, Michael Bonner, breached the Act in 2015 when he was a senior policy advisor in the Office of the Minister of Employment and Social Development (Canada, Office of the Conflict of Interest and Ethics Commissioner 2015). Bonner had accepted gifts of invitations to galas and fundraisers from stakeholders of Human Resources and Skills Development Canada. The Commissioner found that accepting the gifts from stakeholders gave the perception of influence in the exercise of Bonner's official duties. In addition, George Rae, senior advisor to the Minister of Employment and Social Development, was found by the Ethics Commissioner to have breached the *Conflict of Interest Act* by accepting a gala ticket from the Forest Products Association of Canada in 2013 (Canada, Conflict of Interest and Ethics Commissioner 2015). The Commissioner issued a compliance order against Rae, directing him to 'refrain from accepting any gift or other advantage in similar circumstances without seeking approval from my Office while you are a public office holder'. This was the first time that a compliance order had been issued against a political advisor.

Thus, Canadian independent statutory officers have started to investigate the conduct of political advisors and, through the use of their coercive powers, have discovered irregularities in the interactions between advisors and officials. Their investigations have been widely reported in the media. These office-holders are likely to become important sources of accountability in the future.

Australia

Legal regulation

Australian ministerial advisors are employed under the *Members of Parliament (Staff) Act* 1984 (Cth) as personal staff employed by Ministers. The employment terms and conditions of ministerial advisors are determined by their employing Minister, and can be varied by the Prime Minister (s 14(1)). There is no legislative requirement for the government to provide details about the employment of ministerial advisors. Nevertheless, since 2007–08, successive governments have tabled annual reports providing information about the numbers of ministerial advisors employed, their classification levels, salaries and benefits.

Ministerial advisors are subject to an unlegislated *Statement of Standards for Ministerial Staff* (formerly the Code of Conduct), which sets out the standards they are expected to meet in performing their duties. These Standards acknowledge that ministerial staff do not have the power to direct public servants in their own right. It also recognises that executive decisions are the preserve of Ministers and public servants, and not ministerial staff acting in their own right. Further, ministerial advisors have the duty to facilitate direct and effective communication between their Minister's department and their Minister. The Statement of Standards seems to suggest that ministerial advisors have a very limited role and are merely conduits between the

Ministers and the public service. However, this is untrue as contemporary ministerial advisors have very wide-ranging roles and operate with a great deal of autonomy. As such, a Senate Committee found that 'it can no longer be assumed that [ministerial] advisors act at the express direction of ministers and/or with their knowledge and consent. Increasingly, advisors are wielding executive power in their own right' (Australia, Senate Select Committee 2002, p. xxxvii). Implementation and sanctions under the Standards are handled internally by the executive through the Prime Minister's Office and the Government Staffing Committee, which is constituted by senior Ministers, and sometimes senior political advisors. This means that any breaches of the Standards by ministerial advisors would be handled behind closed doors, without the scrutiny of Parliament or any external bodies.

There have been two publicly known investigations of Australian ministerial advisors under the Code of Conduct. These were for relatively minor issues. The first related to the failure of a ministerial advisor to notify her Parliamentary Secretary of her attempt to divest her shareholdings. The Code of Conduct mandated that ministerial staff should divest themselves of any interests in public and private companies involved in the area of their Ministers' portfolio responsibilities. The ministerial advisor had notified the Parliamentary Secretary about the shares and had proactively requested that the company where she owned shares take steps to divest her holdings. Thus, the Government Staffing Committee found that there was no breach of the Code of Conduct. Nevertheless, the Committee found that the ministerial advisor should be counselled for failing to bring to the Parliamentary Secretary's attention her attempt to divest her shareholding to avoid a potential conflict of interest.

The second investigation under the Code of Conduct related to the conduct of two ministerial advisors in relation to a government media management contract that was awarded to CMAX Communications (Australia, Auditor-General 2009, p. 10). The CMAX Communications employee providing the services was married to the Defence Minister's Media Advisor, Christian Taubenschlag. Taubenschlag was at the time the sole shareholder and Managing Director of CMAX Communications. The company name was later transferred to a new entity owned by his spouse without an interest by him. There were concerns about the procurement process, where the engagement of CMAX Communications followed a suggestion from a Senior Advisor in the Prime Minister's Office, Annie O'Rourke.

The Auditor-General investigated the matter and concluded that while there was scope for improvements in the engagement process by the Prime Minister's Department, there was no evidence of external pressure being applied to the Department to engage CMAX Communications or that the fee charged by CMAX was unreasonable. The final decision of the Government Staffing Committee is not on the public record as these decisions are handled completely internally within the veil of the executive.

Besides these investigations, it is unknown whether there have been other investigations into the ministerial staff Statement of Standards (or former Code of Conduct), due to the secretive nature of investigations under the Standards. It is unknown on what bases the Government Staffing Committee makes decisions and what those decisions are. Breaches of the Standards are not legally enforceable in the courts. It is easy for the executive to bury controversies out of public view despite the existence of the Standards.

Thus, there is limited legal regulation of ministerial advisors in Australia. The legislation governing their employment is sparse and is limited to affirming the Ministers' powers to employ their advisors. Beyond this, there is no legislative requirement for ministerial advisors to adhere to certain rules of behaviour. By contrast, the United Kingdom legislation employing special advisors is more detailed and substantive, providing for reporting requirements to Parliament about advisors and requiring a Code of Conduct for special advisors (UK, *Constitutional Reform and Governance Act* 2010 sections 8, 16). The UK legislation also requires the Code to prohibit special advisors from authorising the expenditure of public funds, exercising any management power over the civil service, or exercising any executive or statutory power except in relation to another special advisor (s 8). A special advisor's Code of Conduct is legislatively deemed to be part of their employment terms and conditions. The Australian Statement of Standards for ministerial advisors is handled completely within the executive, without independent oversight. By contrast, there is a more principled method of investigating breaches of the Code of Conduct in the United Kingdom, which includes the possibility of review by an independent Civil Service Commissioner, although there may be a general culture of reluctance to make complaints to the Commissioner in the UK.

Parliamentary scrutiny

In Australia, there has been an abject failure in parliamentary scrutiny of the actions of ministerial advisors. Ministerial advisors have been used as scapegoats to enable Ministers to evade political responsibility to Parliament in relation to incidents such as the 'Children Overboard' affair at the Commonwealth level and the 'Hotel Windsor' incident at the Victorian level (discussed in chapter four). In these incidents, Ministers forbade their advisors from appearing before the parliamentary committee, claiming that there was a constitutional convention that ministerial advisors do not appear. This allowed Ministers to completely escape accountability for controversial actions and decisions. Despite this, ministerial advisors have appeared before parliamentary committees in the States of New South Wales, Western Australia and South Australia (Ng 2016a).

Scrutiny by oversight bodies

Independent statutory office holders in Australia have lagged behind compared to New Zealand and Canada in holding ministerial advisors to account. The jurisdiction of the Australian federal Ombudsman does not cover the actions and decisions of ministerial offices, which means that the Commonwealth Ombudsman is unable to investigate the actions of ministerial staff. By contrast, the Victorian Ombudsman's jurisdiction is wider than that of the Commonwealth Ombudsman, as the Victorian Ombudsman is able to investigate matters involving ministerial advisors that are referred by a House of Parliament or a parliamentary committee (Victoria, *Ombudsman Act* 1973 (Vic) s 16).

The Ombudsman has strong powers to compel the attendance of witnesses and the production of documents, as well as to interview witnesses under oath. This is likely to enhance the explanatory accountability of the actions of ministerial advisors, where they explain their actions, which better enables their Ministers to be held accountable. This was exhibited in the 'Hotel Windsor' incident discussed in chapter four, where the Victorian Ombudsman stepped in to investigate the matter and was able to interview the Minister, ministerial advisors and public servants, as well as discover all relevant emails where the parliamentary committee failed to do so, due to his strong powers under legislation (Victorian Ombudsman 2011). Thus, the Ombudsman is effectively able to compel answerability or explanatory accountability. Nevertheless, the Ombudsman's powers are limited to persuasion and the ability to table adverse reports before a House of Parliament, which is a significant limitation. The Ombudsman does not have the power to make binding determinations, impose sanctions or seek remedial action from government agencies. This means that amendatory accountability in the form of remedial action is absent even where the Ombudsman investigates a matter and makes an adverse finding. However, the combination of the power to table a report in a House of Parliament and media scrutiny may at times be sufficient to change governmental practices.

At the State level, the New South Wales Ombudsman investigated the processing of FOI requests, and found a practice of all ministerial offices providing the Premier's Department with a fortnightly report about the status of its portfolio agencies' new and contentious FOI applications. Departmental FOI processing was delayed as the determinations were not finalised until the agency heard back from the ministerial offices. The Ombudsman stated:

> FOI staff were often unclear what they are waiting for and delays could run into weeks. This is not appropriate and raises questions about the role Ministers' offices are playing in the FOI process. Of even more serious concern is the practice of sending draft determinations to a Minister's office. We have recently had cause to make such conduct the subject of a formal investigation under the Ombudsman Act and have made a series

> of recommendations about the inappropriateness of such a practice including that it should cease immediately.
>
> (New South Wales Ombudsman 2009, p. 38)

The federal Australian Information Commissioner has issued a set of Guidelines under the Commonwealth *Freedom of Information Act* (FOI Act) that govern documents of ministerial advisors (Australia, Office of the Australian Information Commissioner 2010, pp. 9–10). Ministers and agencies are legislatively required to take these Guidelines into account when performing a function or exercising a power under the *Freedom of Information Act 1982* (Cth) (s 93A(2)). The Commissioner's Guidelines state that documents in the possession of the Minister are to be interpreted broadly as being in the Minister's office, and may be constructively possessed if the Minister is entitled to access a document that has passed from their possession. The Guidelines affirm case law at the Victorian level, where the Court of Appeal held that the Premier's chief of staff's diary was accessible via the FOI Act (*Office of the Premier v Herald and Weekly Times Pty Ltd* (2013) 38 VR 684). This means that documents bearing a direct or indirect relationship to affairs of a government department or other agencies can be accessed through FOI processes. Due to these recent developments, FOI may become an increasingly powerful avenue to access documents of ministerial advisors in the future.

New Zealand

Legal regulation

New Zealand's regulatory regime for ministerial advisors has recently been boosted by the introduction of an unlegislated code of conduct for ministerial staff by the State Services Commissioner in 2017 (NZ, *Code of Conduct for Ministerial Staff*). Previously there was no code that applied specifically to NZ political advisors. The new code itself is rather terse, merely stating that ministerial staff should be fair, professional, responsible and trustworthy. The guidance issued by the State Services Commission (NZ State Services Commission 2017), however, does elaborate on these principles.

The guidance stipulates that, in communicating with agencies, ministerial staff should be aware that executive decisions are the preserve of Ministers and public servants. The guidance also states that major decisions should usually be discussed between the Minister and senior public servants, rather than communicated through ministerial staff, to help ensure there is clarity of message and that it is backed by full authority. This is an aspirational statement, rather than a firm requirement. There are also requirements of honesty and integrity, requiring ministerial staff not to mislead Parliament, Ministers, public servants or the general public.

Ministerial staff are subject to conflict of interest requirements, and must take reasonable steps to avoid any real or perceived conflicts of interest from secondary work, political activity, offers of employment, financial or family interests. As such, ministerial staff should decline any gifts or hospitality that place them under any obligation or perceived influence. Any potential conflicts, gifts or hospitality that are offered or accepted must be declared to their employing department.

To guard against partisan behaviour, the guidance provides that ministerial staff should only make media or public comment when authorised to do so, and should not make political party comment and not be involved in the preparation or dissemination of inappropriate material or personal attacks. In addition, if ministerial staff wish to undertake work for a political party, they must do this outside of paid work hours and must not use official resources for political party activity. Ministerial staff also must maintain the confidentiality of official information.

The State Services Commissioner is responsible for the code and may conduct investigations and make reports on matters of integrity and conduct relating to ministerial staff. As the code has only just been introduced, it is unclear how the Commissioner will exercise his/her powers and whether breaches of the code will be publicised.

In addition to the *Code of Conduct for Ministerial Staff*, political advisors must also comply with any codes of conduct, policies and procedures issued by the Department of Internal Affairs, which is the employing department of all ministerial staff in NZ. As ministerial staff are employees of the Department of Internal Affairs, they are directly accountable to the Department for their public spending decisions. They must be able to demonstrate that the travel and hospitality expenses they incur are within rules set out in the Ministerial Staff Handbook. The Auditor-General has criticised the lack of clarity on ministerial staff spending, as the spending rules can be waived by the departmental Assistant General Manager (New Zealand, Controller and Auditor-General 2010, pp. 57–59). Further, the rules give too much discretion to political advisors to determine what reasonable expenditure is. The Handbook is not a legal document and breaches are not legally enforceable.

The New Zealand *Cabinet Manual* 2017, which is an authoritative guide to the uncodified constitutional system, also imposes certain responsibilities on political advisors. It specifies that advisors must take care to ensure that they do not improperly influence matters that are the responsibility of others (cl 3.23). Ministerial staff and public servants are both enjoined to avoid actual and perceived conflicts of interest and ensure that their personal interests or activities do not interfere with, or appear to interfere with, their obligation to serve the aims and objectives of their employer (cl 3.62), a requirement that is reiterated in the ministerial staff code of conduct. The Manual also puts some responsibility on Ministers to ensure that their advisors understand the principles governing the Minister's role, the Minister's relationship with public service officials (cl 3.23) and the *Official Information Act* (cl 8.30). The Manual provides that while Ministers may involve political advisors in policy development and other areas of work normally performed within the

Minister's department, the Minister and the departmental head must establish a clear understanding to ensure that departmental officials know the extent of the advisors' authority, and that proper accountability exists for financial requirements under the *Public Finance Act 1989* (cl 3.26). These mechanisms set up a form of managerial accountability which requires Ministers in conjunction with the department to reach an agreement on the scope of the authority of political advisors. Nevertheless, the Cabinet Manual is not a formal legal document with enforcement mechanisms and any breach of its principles is not justiciable in courts.

In New Zealand, public sector employment of both public servants and political staff are covered by the *State Sector Act 1988*, which was amended in 2013 to more explicitly account for the employment conditions of ministerial advisors. Ministerial staff are employed by the Chief Executive of the Department of Internal Affairs, but Chief Executives must have regard to the Minister's wishes for their ministerial staff (s 59(5)). In recognition of their partisan and political roles, ministerial staff are exempt from the standard public service appointment provisions, including the requirement of appointments being on merit (s 66).

In short, legal regulation of ministerial advisors in New Zealand has recently been boosted by a code of conduct, which brings it into alignment with the other Westminster jurisdictions. However, the requirements under the code are less stringent compared to Canada and the United Kingdom, and it remains to be seen how the new regime will be enforced.

Parliamentary scrutiny

Like the other Westminster jurisdictions, New Zealand operates within the constitutional framework of individual ministerial responsibility for departmental actions (New Zealand, Cabinet Office 2017, cl 3.27). Ministers are accountable to Parliament for the actions of a department when errors are made, even when the Minister had no knowledge of, or involvement in, those actions. Public servants regularly appear before parliamentary committees in New Zealand. The guidance for officials appearing before select committees issued by the State Services Authority applies broadly to employees of the state sector, which include ministerial staff (New Zealand, Controller and Auditor-General 2010). The intention is for officials to appear before select committees to enable Parliament to more effectively scrutinise the executive, subject to the 'no surprises' principle that Ministers are informed about the appearance.

Despite the permissive regulatory framework, unlike the United Kingdom, the New Zealand Parliament has been silent on the issue of political advisors. Partly this is the result of institutional arrangements. In New Zealand, there is a unicameral House of Parliament, and thus no Upper House scrutiny exists akin to the situation in Australia. The parliamentary system in New Zealand was particularly weak before the change of the electoral system to mixed member proportional representation (MMP) – between 1951–1978 governments recessed parliament for up to eight months to avoid scrutiny (Wanna 2005, p. 167). This deficiency was remedied by the *Constitution Act 1986*, which required Parliament to meet no later than six weeks after the return of the writs of a general election (s 19). In addition, the parliamentary committee system has been strengthened post-MMP, as the norm now is to have a coalition of parties on the committees based on proportional representation (New Zealand, House of Representatives 2014). With the revitalisation of parliamentary committees, particularly select committees where the government does not have a majority, there is an increased prospect for parliamentary scrutiny of the activities of advisors. In fact, precedent exists in New Zealand for political advisors appearing before parliamentary committees. Wayne Eagleson, Prime Minister Key's Chief of Staff, appeared before the Privileges Committee in 2013 (New Zealand Privileges Committee 2013). Eagleson gave evidence about the release of ministerial emails and meta-data to the David Henry inquiry into the leak of a sensitive report. This shows that there is no impediment to ministerial staff appearing before parliamentary committees in New Zealand.

Scrutiny by oversight bodies

Independent statutory office-holders in New Zealand are starting to play a role in holding ministerial advisors to account. This is an effective scrutiny mechanism as statutory office-holders such as the Ombudsman and the Auditor-General are officers of Parliament in New Zealand and are thus independent of the executive. In addition, certain office-holders have strong coercive powers to summon witnesses and question them under oath.

For instance, following the revelations in the Nicky Hager book discussed in chapter four (Hager 2014), which exposed potential manipulation of *Official Information Act* (OIA) processes by a political advisor, the Inspector-General of Intelligence and Security and the Ombudsman initiated investigations into this issue. The Inspector-General of Intelligence and Security, who has coercive powers under legislation, summoned and questioned several political staff in the Prime Minister's Office as witnesses, including the Chief of Staff, Deputy Chief of Staff, senior advisors and senior media advisors. This enabled the Inspector-General to make findings about the actions of ministerial staff who leaked information to a private blogger to smear the Opposition.

The Ombudsman also initiated an inquiry, although her jurisdiction was limited, being unable to specifically investigate the actions of ministerial advisors under the OIA. Nevertheless, the Ombudsman received full cooperation from the agencies she surveyed, including from Ministers, chiefs of staff, political advisors, chief executives and agency staff, who completed surveys, provided material or made themselves available for interview. As a result, the Ombudsman was not required to utilise her coercive powers under legislation to require the production of documents, summons witnesses and put officials on oath.

In terms of financial expenditure, the Auditor-General has scrutinised spending on ministerial and parliamentary support in response to specific issues as well as at a general level (New Zealand, Controller and Auditor-General 2010). In all these inquiries, the Auditor-General had the full cooperation of both Ministers and their staff, which is different from all of the other jurisdictions, where oversight bodies faced stiff opposition from government when they conduct their inquiries.

In short, the oversight system in New Zealand will become increasingly relevant as future controversies surface over the years. Compared to other jurisdictions, Ministers and political staff in New Zealand show a remarkably high degree of cooperation with investigations of statutory officers. While statutory officers in other jurisdictions complain bitterly that their investigations have been thwarted due to executive intransigence, New Zealand statutory officers are more likely to thank the Ministers and their staff for their cooperation and transparency and are less likely to need to resort to their coercive powers. This may reflect the general transparent nature of governance in New Zealand, where Cabinet minutes and the advice of the bureaucracy are published and there is a more open culture in releasing information through the OIA, which is a commendable aspect of the political culture in New Zealand.

Adequacy of legal and political regulation

The legal and political regulation of political advisors varies dramatically across the Westminster countries. Although each country started from a similar base of Westminster traditions and has faced similar challenges in the rise of political advisors, the countries have adopted divergent regulatory trajectories in governing political advisors. Australia's regulation can be characterised as minimalist legal regulation, with legislation setting out the basic employment framework, combined with an internally policed code of conduct for ministerial advisors, alongside contracts of employment. On the other hand, the United Kingdom and Canada have a comparatively high regulatory intensity, with a detailed regulatory framework setting out explicit requirements in a combination of legislation, codes of conduct and contracts of employment. New Zealand has recently enhanced its regulatory framework with the introduction of an unlegislated code of conduct overseen by the State Services Commissioner, alongside an unenforceable Cabinet Manual and private contracts of employment. With this change, New Zealand's framework is slightly more robust than Australia, as its code is overseen by an independent statutory officer, but still lags behind the United Kingdom and Canada in terms of disclosure requirements.

There are a few forms of regulation of advisors that can be observed. The first are restrictions on the employment of advisors, either through a cap on the numbers of advisors, as in the United Kingdom, or a cap on the total budget for advisors, as in Canada. Second, there are restrictions on the actions of advisors themselves, such as prohibiting advisors from exercising executive power (UK) or recognising that advisors should not exercise executive power (Canada, Australia, NZ), prohibiting advisors from expending public funds (UK, Canada), leaking confidential or sensitive information (UK) or engaging in conduct that conflicts with the public interest (Canada, NZ). Canada has post-employment restrictions banning advisors from becoming lobbyists five years after ceasing their employment. Third, transparency measures also exist, such as requirements that departments disclose all meetings that advisors have with the media (UK) and what hospitality these advisors receive (UK, Canada, NZ). In Canada, advisors have to further disclose to the Conflict of Interest and Ethics Commissioner all assets and liabilities they possess and all firm offers of employment. Finally, there are attempts to regulate advisors' interactions with the bureaucracy, such as prohibiting advisors from directing the civil service (UK, Canada, Australia, NZ).

A major issue with the legislative frameworks and codes of conduct regulating political advisors is the level of enforcement of these requirements. For instance, although there are caps on the numbers of advisors in the UK, these have not been strictly enforced and can be circumvented. In addition, breaches of codes of conduct that are policed internally within the core executive can be easily hidden, as can be seen in Australia. Even in jurisdictions that allow for the codes of conduct to be policed externally through an independent commissioner, there might be a cultural predisposition not to have recourse to these mechanisms, such as in the UK with the Civil Service Commissioner. Canada has the most independent regulatory framework in this regard, with conflict of interest and lobbying provisions being policed by the Conflict of Interest and Ethics Commissioner, who has generally been more independent than the core executive.

Within the core executive, it is difficult to police adherence to the letter and spirit of the law, as many of the players, whether they are Ministers, public servants or political staff, have the incentive to hide controversies wherever possible. As such, it is necessary to consider external regulatory mechanisms beyond the core executive, such as parliamentary scrutiny and the scrutiny of oversight bodies such as ombudsmen and commissioners. The judiciary has been largely absent in the debate about regulating political advisors, as most of the actions of advisors in policy-making, administration and interactions with stakeholders within and outside of government fall outside the ambit of legal action. It is only where political advisors actually exercise executive power (e.g. sign visa decisions), or fall foul of the law (e.g. breach criminal law) that the courts will intervene and adjudge the actions of advisors (Ng 2016b). Courts in Australia (Ng 2016b) and Canada have also ruled on statutory regimes such as Freedom of Information legislation to allow for documents of political staff to be accessible through those regimes. Beyond this limited scope, courts have not entered into the fray of regulating the actions of political advisors.

As such, it falls to the other arm of government, Parliament, to be the main body that scrutinises political advisors. This is consistent with the traditional Westminster doctrine of ministerial responsibility that stipulates that Ministers are responsible to Parliament for the actions of their advisors. However, as seen above, parliamentary scrutiny of the actions of advisors has been patchy across the jurisdictions. It is particularly weak in Australia, where Ministers have avoided appearing before parliamentary committees, as well as prevented political advisors from appearing before committees. At the other end of the spectrum, the United Kingdom Parliament has been the most vigilant in investigating the actions of special advisors, with 11 inquiries over the last 15 years and executive rules stipulating that there is a presumption that political advisors should appear before committees. The rules have eventually led to a change in governmental practice, from intransigence about advisors appearing before committees, to a situation where advisors have appeared before parliamentary committees in significant controversies as well as for inquiries into the general functioning of the system of governance. Canadian governments have exhibited both cooperation and obstruction in terms of advisors appearing before parliamentary committees. The issue of political advisors appearing before parliamentary committees has not loomed large in New Zealand, but one advisor has voluntarily appeared before a committee without any impediment.

As vertical accountability through Parliament is weak or at best inconsistent, we have to look to horizontal accountability mechanisms to police the actions of political advisors. Oversight bodies in the form of ombudsmen, auditors-general and commissioners have become a significant avenue for investigating the actions of political advisors in Westminster jurisdictions. Investigations on advisors have been conducted by the Ombudsman (NZ), Auditor-General (NZ), Information Commissioner (Canada, Australia), Conflict of Interest and Ethics Commissioner (Canada), and Inspector-General of Intelligence and Security (NZ). The Australian federal Ombudsman is impaired by jurisdictional issues, but the Victorian State Ombudsman has successfully questioned political advisors where a parliamentary committee failed to compel the advisors to appear. The Canadian Information Commissioner was likewise able to interview political advisors under oath, although these advisors refused to appear before a parliamentary committee. The integrity bodies have thus at times achieved more success than Parliament in holding political advisors to account. In this vein, it becomes imperative to ensure that the legislation empowering these oversight bodies gives them jurisdiction to investigate the actions of political advisors. This is illustrated by the initial refusal of the Canadian Conflict of Interest and Ethics Commissioner to investigate political advisors until the Commissioner's jurisdiction was expanded to explicitly encompass them, which led to the activation of the role in subjecting advisors to scrutiny.

Exceptionally, the United Kingdom has exhibited strong parliamentary scrutiny compared to other Westminster jurisdictions. Perhaps as a result,

British oversight bodies have not been as active in pursuing special advisors compared to Canada and New Zealand. This suggests that where vertical accountability through Parliament is sufficient, there is less need to activate horizontal accountability mechanisms such as oversight bodies. The issues of vertical accountability through Parliament and horizontal accountability through oversight bodies will be more fully ventilated in the next chapter.

References

Books and journal articles

Aucoin, P, 2010, 'Canada', in C Eichbaum and R Shaw (eds), *Partisan Appointees and Public Servants: An International Analysis of the Role of the Political Adviser*, Edward Elgar, Cheltenham, pp. 64–93.

Bakvis, H, 1991, *Regional Ministers: Power and Influence in the Canadian Cabinet*, University of Toronto Press, Toronto.

Boyer, J P, 2014, *Our Scandalous Senate*, Dundurn, Toronto.

Campbell, A, and Hagerty, B, 2012, *The Alastair Campbell Diaries. Volume 4, The Burden of Power: Countdown to Iraq*, Hutchinson, London.

Craft, J, 2016, *Backrooms and Beyond: Partisan Advisers and the Politics of Policy Work in Canada*, University of Toronto Press, Toronto.

Eichbaum, C, and Shaw, R, 2010, 'New Zealand' in C Eichbaum and R Shaw (eds), *Partisan Appointees and Public Servants: An International Analysis of the Role of the Political Adviser*, Edward Elgar, Cheltenham, pp. 114–147.

Eichbaum, C and Shaw, R, 2008, 'Revisiting Politicization: Political Advisers and Public Servants in Westminster Systems', *Governance*, vol. 21(3), pp. 337–363.

Hager, Nicky, 2014, *Dirty Politics: How Attack Politics is Poisoning New Zealand's Political Environment*, Craig Potton Publishing, Nelson.

Ng, YF, 2016a, 'Dispelling Myths about Conventions: Ministerial Advisers and Parliamentary Committees', *Australian Journal of Political Science*, vol. 51(3), pp. 512–529.

Ng, YF, 2016b, *Ministerial Advisers in Australia: The Modern Legal Context*, Federation Press, Sydney.

Simpson, Jeffrey, 1988, *Spoils of Power: The Politics of Patronage*, Collins, Toronto.

Thomas, P, 2010, 'Parliament and the Public Service' in Christopher Dunn (ed), *The Handbook of Canadian Public Administration*, 2nd edn, Oxford University Press, Ontario.

Wanna, J, 2005, 'New Zealand's Westminster Trajectory: Archetypal Transplant to Maverick Outlier' in H Patapan, J Wanna and P Weller (eds), *Westminster Legacies: Democracy and Responsible Government in Asia and the Pacific*, UNSW Press, Sydney, pp. 153–185.

Williams, B, 1980, 'The Para-political Bureaucracy in Ottawa' in H D Clark (ed), *Parliament, Policy and Representation*, Methuen, Toronto, pp. 215–229.

Legislation, codes, case law, government and parliamentary reports

Australia, Auditor-General, 2009, CMAX Communications Contract for the 2020 Summit: Department of the Prime Minister and Cabinet, Audit Report No 19, 2008–2009 Performance Audit.

Australia, Freedom of Information 1982 (Cth).

Australia, Members of Parliament (Staff) Act 1984 (Cth).

Australia, Office of the Australian Information Commissioner, 2010, Guidelines issued by the Australian Information Commissioner under s 93A of the Freedom of Information Act 1982. Available at: www.oaic.gov.au/freedom-of-information/foi-guidelines/.

Australia, Senate, Select Committee for an Inquiry into a Certain Maritime Incident, 2002, *A Certain Maritime Incident*, Senate Printing Unit, Canberra.

Australia, Special Minister of State, 2013, Statement of Standards for Ministerial Staff. Available at: www.smos.gov.au/resources/statement-of-standards.html.

Benoit, L, 2006, 'Ministerial Staff: The Life and Times of Parliament's Statutory Orphans', *Restoring Accountability Research Studies Volume 1: Parliament, Ministers and Deputy Ministers*, Commission of Inquiry into the Sponsorship Program and Advertising Activities, Canadian Government Publishing, Ottawa, pp. 145–252.

Bourgault, J, 2006, 'The Deputy Minister's Role in the Government of Canada: His Responsibility and His Accountability', *Restoring Accountability Research Studies, Volume 2: The Public Service and Accountability*, Commission of Inquiry into the Sponsorship Program and Advertising Activities, Canadian Government Publishing, Ottawa, pp. 253–296.

Canada, *Bill C-58* (2017), An Act to amend the Access to Information Act and the Privacy Act and to make consequential amendments to other Acts, 42nd Parliament, 1st Session.

Canada, Code of Conduct for Ministerial Exempt Staff (2015).

Canada, Commission of Inquiry into the Sponsorship Program and Advertising Activities, 2005, *Who is Responsible? Volume 1: Fact Finding Report*, prepared by Justice J H Gomery, Public Works and Government Services Canada, Ottawa.

Canada, Conflict of Interest Act, SC 2006, c. 9.

Canada, Conflict of Interest and Ethics Commissioner, 2015, Compliance Order under Section 30, Conflict of Interest Act. Available at: http://ciec-ccie.parl.gc.ca/Documents/English/Public%20Reports/Compliance%20Orders/Compliance%20Order%20-%20G.%20Rae.pdf.

Canada, Ethical and Political Activity Guidelines for Public Office Holders (2015).

Canada, Federal Accountability Act 2006.

Canada, Guidelines on the Proactive Disclosure of Contracts (2013).

Canada, House of Commons, Standing Committee on Access to Information, Privacy and Ethics. 2010, *Evidence*, 13 May.

Canada, House of Commons, Standing Committee on Access to Information, Privacy and Ethics, 2011, *Evidence*, 21 March.

Canada, House of Commons, Standing Committee on Access to Information, Privacy and Ethics, 2016, *Review of the Access to Information Act*. Available at: www.ourcommons.ca/DocumentViewer/en/42-1/ETHI/report-2/page-45#8.

Canada (Information Commissioner) v Canada (Minister of National Defence), 2011 SCC 25 ('PM's Agenda Case').

Canada, Lobbying Act RSC, 1985, c 44 (4th Supp).

Canada, Office of the Conflict of Interest and Ethics Commissioner, 2015, Referral from the Public Sector Integrity Commissioner: The Bonner Report.

Canada, Office of the Information Commissioner of Canada, 2011, Interference with Access to Information, Special Report Part 1, prepared by S Legault, Information Commission of Canada.

Canada, Office of the Information Commissioner of Canada, 2014, Interference with Access to Information, Special Report Part 2, prepared by S Legault, Information Commission of Canada.
Canada, Office of the Information Commissioner of Canada, 2015, Striking the Right Balance for Transparency, prepared by S Legault, Information Commission of Canada. Available at: www.oic-ci.gc.ca/telechargements-downloads/userfiles/files/eng/reports-publications/Special-reports/Modernization2015/OIC_14-418_Modernization%20Report.pdf.
Canada, Office of the Information Commissioner of Canada, 2017, Failing to Strike the Right Balance for Transparency: Recommendations to improve Bill C-58: An Act to Amend the Access to Information Act and the Privacy Act and to Make Consequential Amendments to Other Acts, prepared by S Legault, Information Commission of Canada. Available at: www.ci-oic.gc.ca/eng/rapport-special-c-58_special-report-c-58.aspx.
Canada, Privy Council Office, 2015, Open and Accountable Government.
Canada, Public Service Employment Act SC 2003, c 22.
Canada, Special Committee on the Reform of the House of Commons, 1985, Report of the Special Committee on Reform of the House of Commons, Third Report, Chair J A McGrath, Canadian Government Publishing Centre, Ottawa.
Canada, Treasury Board, 2011, Policies for Ministers' Offices. Available at: www.canada.ca/en/treasury-board-secretariat/services/policies-ministers-offices-january-2011.html.
Herald and Weekly Times Pty Limited v Office of the Premier (2012) VCAT 967 [22].
Hutton, Lord, 2004, Report of the Inquiry into the Circumstances Surrounding the Death of Dr David Kelly CMG, The Stationery Office, London.
The Leveson Inquiry, 2012, An Inquiry into the Culture, Practices and Ethics of the Press Report, Volume III, The Stationery Office, London.
New South Wales Ombudsman, 2009, Opening up Government: Review of the Freedom of Information Act 1989: A Special Report to Parliament under s 31 of the Ombudsman Act 1974, Ombudsman, New South Wales.
New Zealand, Cabinet Office, 2017, Cabinet Manual 2017, Department of Prime Minister and Cabinet, Wellington, NZ.
New Zealand, Constitution Act 1986.
New Zealand, Controller and Auditor-General, 2010, How the Department of Internal Affairs Manages Spending that could give Personal Benefit to Ministers: Part 2 of the Auditor-General's Inquiry into certain types of Expenditure in Vote Ministerial Services. Available at: www.oag.govt.nz/2010/ministerial-spending/docs/ministerial-spending.pdf.
New Zealand, House of Representatives, 2014, Standing Order 185(1).
New Zealand, Official Information Act 1982.
New Zealand Privileges Committee, 2013, Question of Privilege regarding use of Intrusive Powers within the Parliamentary Precinct: Interim Report of the Privileges Committee.
New Zealand, Public Finance Act 1989.
New Zealand, State Sector Act 1988.
New Zealand, State Services Commission, 2017, Code of Conduct for Ministerial Staff. Available at: www.ssc.govt.nz/sites/all/files/code-of-conduct-ministerialstaff-nov17.pdf.

New Zealand, State Services Commission, Explaining the Code of Conduct for Ministerial Staff, 2017. Available at: www.ssc.govt.nz/sites/all/files/explaining-code-of-conduct-ministerialstaff-nov17.pdf.

Office of the Premier v Herald and Weekly Times Pty Ltd (2013) 38 VR 684.

Phillis, Bob, 2004, An Independent Review of Government Communications ('Phillis Review').

United Kingdom, *Civil Service Order in Council* 1991.

United Kingdom, *Civil Service (Amendment) Order in Council* 1997.

United Kingdom, Constitutional Reform and Governance Act 2010.

United Kingdom, Cabinet Office, 2005, Departmental Evidence and Response to Select Committees ('Osmotherly Rules').

United Kingdom, Cabinet Office, Giving Evidence to Select Committees: Guidance for Civil Servants (2014).

United Kingdom, Cabinet Office, Code of Conduct for Special Advisers (2016).

United Kingdom, Cabinet Office, Ministerial Code (2016).

United Kingdom, Cabinet Office, Model Contract for Special Advisers (2016).

United Kingdom, Civil Service Commissioner, Civil Service Code 2010 (amended 2015).

United Kingdom, Committee of Privy Counsellors, 2004, Review of Intelligence on Weapons of Mass Destruction: Report of a Committee of Privy Counsellors, 14 July, HC 898 Chair, The Rt Hon The Lord Butler, The Stationery Office, London.

United Kingdom, Committee of Privy Counsellors, 2016, The Report of the Iraq Inquiry, 6 July, HC264, Chair, Sir John Chilcot, The Stationery Office, London.

United Kingdom, Committee on Standards and Privileges, 1999, Premature Disclosure of Reports of the Foreign Affairs Committee, HC 607, Eighth Report of Session 1998–1999.

United Kingdom, Committee on Standards in Public Life, 1995, Members of Parliament, Ministers, Civil Servants and Quangos, First Report.

United Kingdom, Committee on Standards in Public Life, 2000a, Reinforcing Standards, Sixth Report.

United Kingdom, Committee on Standards in Public Life, 2000b, Reinforcing Standards 18–084, Sixth Report: Government's Response to the Sixth Report from the Committee on Standards in Public Life.

United Kingdom, Committee on Standards in Public Life, 2003, Defining the Boundaries within the Executive: Ministers, Special Advisers and the Permanent Civil Service, Ninth Report.

United Kingdom, House of Commons, Defence Committee, 1986, Westland plc: The Government's Decision-making, HC-519, Fourth Report of Session 1985–1986, HMSO, London.

United Kingdom, House of Commons, Foreign Affairs Committee, 2003, The Decision to go to War in Iraq. Ninth Report of Session 2002–2003.

United Kingdom, Constitutional Reform and Governance Act 2010.

United Kingdom, House of Commons, Public Administration Select Committee, 1998, Minutes of Evidence, 23 June.

United Kingdom, Information Commissioner's Office, 2012, Freedom of Information Act 2000, Decision Notice FS50422276, 9th October.

United Kingdom, Public Administration Select Committee, 1998, The Government Information and Communications Service, Sixth Report of Session 1997–1998.

United Kingdom, Public Administration Select Committee, 2000a, *Making Government Work*, Minutes of Evidence, 1 November.
United Kingdom, Select Committee on Public Administration. 2000b. 'The Government Information and Communication Service' (2000–2001) HC 511, Minutes of Evidence, 17 May.
United Kingdom, Public Administration Select Committee, 2001, Special Advisers: Boon or Bane?, Fourth Report of Session 2000–2001.
United Kingdom, Public Administration Select Committee, 2003, These Unfortunate Events: Lessons of Recent Events at the Former DTLR, Eighth Report of Session 2001–2002.
United Kingdom, Public Administration Select Committee, 2005, The Attendance of the Prime Minister's Strategy Adviser before the Public Administration Select Committee, First Special Report of Session 2005–2006.
United Kingdom, Public Administration Select Committee, 2007, Politics and Administration: Ministers and Civil Servants, Third Report of Session 2006–2007.
United Kingdom, Public Administration Select Committee, 2008, Constitutional Renewal: Draft Bill and White Paper, Tenth Report of Session 2007–2008.
United Kingdom, Public Administration Select Committee, 2010, Goats and Tsars: Ministerial and other appointments from outside Parliament, Eighth Report of Session 2009–2010.
United Kingdom, Public Administration Select Committee, 2012, Special Advisers in the Thick of It, Sixth Report of Session 2012–2013.
United Kingdom, Public Administration Select Committee, 2013, Truth to power: How Civil Service Reform Can Succeed, Eighth Report of Session 2013–2014.
Victoria, Ombudsman Act 1973 (Vic).
Victoria, Ombudsman, 2011, Ombudsman Investigation into the Probity of the Hotel Windsor Redevelopment. Available at: www.ombudsman.vic.gov.au/getattachment/753dfb69-1001-4cd6-8b6b-3c9a52f0539f//reports-publications/parliamentary-reports/ombudsman-investigation-into-the-probity-of-the-ho.aspx.
Wintringham, M, 2002, Annual Report of the State Services Commissioner, State Services Commission, Wellington.

Newspaper articles

Doyle, Simon, 2005, 'Martin, Chief of Staff Face Ethics Investigation,' *Star-Phoenix* (Saskatoon), 22 June, A11.

6 Realigning Westminster

The Westminster principles of ministerial responsibility and the politics/administration dichotomy were conceived of in a past era where Ministers were administering small departments and the only relevant relationship was that of the Minister and the civil service. These concepts have become problematised as political advisors have been added as a 'third wheel' in the system. It is undeniable that political advisors play an important and essential role in government, and are now firmly integrated as a prominent part of the executive in Westminster systems. Nevertheless, the insertion of political advisors in the system has been rocky, with recurring controversies that have not subsided over time.

This chapter discusses how the Westminster system could be realigned to accommodate political advisors, as relatively new actors within the executive. I argue that in the context of weak vertical or parliamentary accountability, horizontal accountability mechanisms, such as oversight bodies and the media, have become increasingly important to ensure the accountability of political advisors.

The Westminster legacy

There is no definitive statement on the characteristics of Westminster systems. Indeed, the quest to find an 'ideal model' of Westminster is muddied by the different and shifting institutional foundations of each country: even Britain has moved away from its Westminster roots. New Zealand has transformed from an archetypical form of Westminster, proclaimed by Arend Lijphart as 'more Westminster than Westminster itself' (Lijphart 1994, pp. 16, 21), to an outlier through a change in electoral system to mixed member proportional representation in 1993, which altered the constitutional dynamic between the executive and legislature. But the Westminster legacy remains pervasive in political discourse and as a way of describing countries with a common constitutional and legal heritage.

Yet there is much to doubt about the Westminster legacy. Rhodes, Wanna and Weller have argued that the concept of Westminster is a myth. Westminster can be seen as 'nostalgic nirvana'; an era 'where politicians were principled, where unconstrained debate could examine each piece of legislation on its merits, where the executive behaved itself and kept parliament informed, where spin was unknown' (Rhodes, Wanna and Weller 2009, p. 226). Of course, this nirvana never really existed, despite the speeches of former politicians and former senior public servants lamenting that everything has gone downhill since they retired.

Another narrative of Westminster that can explain the accountability failings is Westminster being used as a political tool: 'the expedient cloak worn by governments and politicians to defend themselves and criticise opponents' (Rhodes, Wanna and Weller 2009, p. 223). In a system 'so infused with convention and precedent', the concept of Westminster is invoked opportunistically by political participants to justify their actions by claiming that whatever they are proposing or opposing upholds the traditional standards and is 'consistent with Westminster' (Rhodes, Wanna and Weller 2009, p. 227). Thus, politicians cynically manipulate the malleable conventions of Westminster to evade responsibility for their actions. Similarly, the concept of Westminster and the Northcote–Trevelyan Report can also be used by senior public servants as a legitimising tool to defend their position and traditional roles (Rhodes, Wanna and Weller 2009, p. 228).

This book has focussed on the Westminster tradition relating to executive organisation and its relationship to the legislature and civil service. This includes the notion of ministerial responsibility, that is, the executive being responsible to the legislature. In addition, the concept of an impartial civil service serving a partisan Minister has generated the theory of the strict politics/administration dichotomy. The insertion of political advisors as part of the executive has challenged these two fundamental precepts of the Westminster system. As Eichbaum and Shaw argue, the Westminster ideal assumes a 'bilateral monopoly' between the 'political and administrative arms of the executive' (Eichbaum and Shaw 2007, p. 615). As we have seen in chapter five, with the addition of a third actor in the executive, Ministers are able to circumvent their own responsibility to Parliament by utilising political advisors as scapegoats for their actions or inactions. Political advisors also blur the politics/administration dichotomy, as they take on roles traditionally allocated to Ministers and the civil service. Although their role is to give partisan political advice, they also undertake policy and administrative functions and, if their role is not properly delineated, they may interfere with bureaucratic processes. I will critically analyse the main convention that underpins the politics/administration dichotomy, that is, ministerial responsibility, both in ideal form and reality.

Individual ministerial responsibility: theory and practice

The principle of ministerial responsibility originated from the United Kingdom in the nineteenth century, and was later adopted by other Westminster jurisdictions. According to this principle, Ministers are responsible to

Parliament for the acts of their department (Woodhouse 1994, p. 38). Under this doctrine, the Minister absorbs the mistakes of civil servants. Sir William Armstrong, then Head of the Home Civil Service, penned a memorandum stating that 'the civil service … has no constitutional personality or responsibility, separate from the duly elected Government of the day' (Armstrong Memorandum 1985). This denoted the unity of mind between civil servants and Ministers. Hence civil servants operate as an *alter ego* of their Minister. Christopher Hood and Martin Lodge dub this the 'directed bargains', where civil servants have 'no independent liability or responsibility of their own' (Hood and Lodge 2006, p. 45). This means that Ministers should take responsibility for all actions of the agent, even those that the Ministers did not authorise. Sir Ivor Jennings wrote that the 'act of every civil servant is by convention regarded as the act of the Minister' (Jennings 1938, p. 184), while Lord Morrison proclaimed that the 'Minister is responsible for every stamp stuck on an envelope' (quoted in Heard 1991, p. 52). Nonetheless, it is doubtful that this principle has ever reflected reality. Following the high point of the British Crichel Down episode in 1954, where Sir Thomas Dugdale, Minister for Agriculture, resigned for the faults of his department, it has since become rare for Ministers to resign or even accept responsibility for the actions of their department where they were not personally involved (Finer 1989, pp. 124–5; Thompson and Tillotsen 1999).

Further, contrary to the proclamations of the indivisibility of the civil service, senior British civil servants did have an independent responsibility from Ministers for departmental finances, as all British permanent secretaries of departments are designated as 'Accounting Officers'. This is a movement that predates ministerial responsibility, from Gladstone's time as Chancellor of the Exchequer, where he established the powerful and prestigious Public Accounts Committee in 1861, which began to refer to permanent secretaries as accounting officers in 1870 (Burnham and Horton 2013, p. 231). The designation of 'Accounting Officer' means that the official has a personal responsibility for the propriety and regularity of departmental finances and is directly answerable to Parliament and parliamentary committees for areas of their responsibility (Franks 2004, pp. 3–4). This concept is now given legislative expression by the *Government Resource and Accounts Act 2000*, which provides that the Treasury is able to appoint an officer from each department as an accounting officer, and stipulates that the appointed person shall be responsible for the departmental accounts (s 5). The accounting officer concept means that Ministers and civil servants are not indivisible, rather senior civil servants have their own personal sphere of responsibility.

The convention of ministerial responsibility developed a century ago, when the role of government was limited and departmental sizes were small, meaning that a competent Minister could be assumed to have personal control of a department (Gay and Powell 2004, p. 7). In that context, demanding the resignation of a Minister for faults in a department is reasonable. However, as the executive increased in size, scale and complexity in each jurisdiction, and the bureaucracy became vast and entrenched, with hundreds of thousands of staff, it became less feasible for a Minister to be abreast of all actions of the department. As Margaret Hodge MP, then chair of the House of Commons Public Accounts Committee, stated:

> When Haldane established the constitutional convention that Ministers are accountable to Parliament and civil servants are accountable to Ministers, there were 28 civil servants in the Home Office. Now, despite the changes and the growth of the Ministry of Justice, there are 34,000. The idea that one Cabinet Minister can be accountable for the actions of some 34,000 people is, I think, mistaken.
>
> (UK, House of Lords 2012)

In this context, conceptions of ministerial responsibility started to shift. Diana Woodhouse argued that in the United Kingdom, the convention of individual ministerial responsibility requires resignation or 'sacrificial responsibility' for personal fault or private indiscretion by the Minister, or departmental fault where the Minister was personally involved or should have known about the issue (Woodhouse 1994, p. 38). However, where there was maladministration within a department that the Minister was unaware of and which could not be attributed to the Minister's negligence, the Minister's responsibility is limited to explanatory or amendatory accountability, with no requirement for resignation. Explanatory responsibility requires the Minister to explain or account for his/her own behaviour and the department's behaviour, while amendatory responsibility involves the Minister making amends for his/her own or departmental failings. This approach has also been adopted in Australia, where there is pressure to resign only when a Minister is personally culpable for actions within the department, while resignation may not be necessary without ministerial culpability (Killey 2012, pp. 104–13). From 1901–1996, resignations for personal fault in a public or private capacity amounted to 27 per cent of resignations in the United Kingdom and 40 per cent in Australia, while resignations due to accepting blame for public servants accounted for only five per cent of resignations in the United Kingdom and none in Australia (Butler 1997, p. 6). Similarly, in Canada, out of 150 ministerial resignations between 1867 to 1990, there were only two ministerial resignations for maladministration in the portfolio (Sutherland 1991, p. 102). In New Zealand, only two resignations out of 23 scandals over the last 40 years was for departmental fault (Farrar 2012). In the Cave Creek scandal, after 14 people were killed by the collapse of a government-built viewing platform, two Ministers resigned from the relevant portfolio for departmental faults, but still remained Ministers. Thus, ministerial responsibility for faults that occurred within the department has always been weak across all the Westminster jurisdictions in terms of resignations or sacrificial responsibility. There has never been a conventional practice of ministerial resignation for faults within their department where they are not personally culpable. The only requirement for resignation is where there the Minister is caught in the act with a 'smoking gun' in their hand (Thompson and Tillotsen 1999, p. 57). Finer put it more strongly, stating that resignations only occur if 'the minister is yielding, his Prime Minister unbending, and his party is out for blood' (Finer 1956).

Ministerial responsibility in the post-NPM era

The concept of ministerial responsibility is predicated upon a departmental structure where the Minister has full control over the department and should thus be aware of departmental activities under their remit. The Haldane report affirmed that the best way to ensure ministerial responsibility is through departmental structures with the Minister being solely responsible, to avoid responsibility being dispersed (UK, Ministry of Reconstruction 1918, p. 11). However, the relationship between Ministers and civil servants was fundamentally altered by the 'New Public Management' (NPM) movement that swept through the Westminster jurisdictions in the 1980s, which focussed on instilling private sector managerial principles into the public sector and sought to separate between policy and service delivery through the creation of new agency structures, as well as contracting out and outsourcing (Hood 1991).

NPM disrupts the traditional relationship between Ministers and civil servants through the proliferation of new agencies and contractors, which disperses responsibility amongst numerous entities. In addition, NPM delineates different areas of responsibility for Ministers and civil servants, making responsibility more diffuse and amorphous. In this new division of responsibilities, civil servants take on additional areas of responsibility, such as the responsibility for departmental finance and management of their departments. This is embodied by the Accounting Officer model introduced in Canada, where civil servants are explicitly made responsible for departmental spending (*Financial Administration Act* R.S.C., 1985, c. F-11 s 16.4), although responsibility still ultimately lies with the Minister. As discussed above, in the United Kingdom, the Accounting Officer concept has a longer provenance before NPM, where senior civil servants have a specific area of personal responsibility to Parliament for the propriety and regularity of the public finances. In Australia and New Zealand, the equivalent practice has developed of public servants appearing before estimates committees to give an account of departmental expenditure, although the Minister retains overall responsibility. However, it is only in the United Kingdom that there is a separate sphere of personal responsibility for senior civil servants, while under the conception of ministerial responsibility in Australia, New Zealand and Canada, the civil servant's role is merely to account for their actions, while retaining the traditional notion that Ministers retain the ultimate responsibility.

This idea of a division of responsibility within departments between Ministers and senior civil servants clearly prevails today in executive practice. There is a marked contrast here with the traditional notion of ministerial responsibility, which received judicial endorsement in the *Carltona* case in 1943, that in decision-making, public servants acted as the *alter ego* of their Minister, but the Ministers retained legal and political responsibility for those decisions (*Carltona Ltd v Commissioners of Works* (1943) 2 All ER 560, 563). Ministers, the court said, may have agents who are authorised to carry out certain tasks without having a formal delegation to do so. The agent's decision is deemed to be the Minister's decision. Ministers remain responsible and answerable to Parliament for anything their officials have done under the Ministers' authority; thus, ministerial responsibility is maintained. The *Carltona* principle was a pragmatic recognition by the judiciary of the need for efficiency in the functioning of the State by means of comprehensive informal delegation of decision-making power.

Despite the *Carltona* principle, in all Westminster jurisdictions, there is a continuing trend towards more formal delegation and distribution of departmental powers and functions. Formal legislative delegation provisions can provide Ministers with the ability to delegate their powers, or specify that a senior civil servant is to exercise powers under statute. Under instruments of delegation, the civil servant exercises power independently on their own behalf, and are not merely acting as the Minister's *alter ego*. It is now evident that the conception that civil servants are merely the extension of the Minister is less applicable today. Their relationship has evolved into what Hood and Lodge call the 'delegated agency bargain', where the political principal and civil servant agree on a framework set by the principal, where the civil servant is given 'a zone of discretion … in exchange for direct responsibility for outcomes within that zone of discretion' (Hood and Lodge 2006, p. 56). The delegation and financial accountability principles mark the distance travelled in the last few decades, from the notion that the civil servant is the mere *alter ego* of an omnipresent Minister to a mode of governance in which the activity of portfolio Ministers is focussed on policy direction, on securing a fair share of legislative and financial resources, and on public and parliamentary representation.

Codification of ministerial responsibility

In recent times, there have been attempts to codify the responsibility of Ministers and civil servants through various codes of conducts, standards, guides and manuals (Brenton 2014, p. 472). These codes, particularly ministerial codes, are usually vaguely worded, but may seek to delineate the responsibility of Ministers and civil servants to Parliament. On the one hand, the Australian Ministerial Statement of Standards is the sparsest in terms of imposition on Ministers. Although the Standards emphasise that Ministers must accept the full implications of the principle of ministerial responsibility, they only oblige Ministers not to mislead Parliament, which is a rather low bar (Australia, Prime Minister and Cabinet 2015, cl 5.1).

At the other end of the spectrum, the New Zealand Cabinet Manual reiterates the traditional principle of ministerial responsibility, stating that

Ministers are responsible for determining and promoting policy, defending policy decisions and answering to Parliament for both policy and operational matters, while officials are responsible to their Minister (New Zealand, Cabinet Office 2017, cl 3.5). The concept of individual ministerial responsibility is also further elucidated:

> Ministers are accountable to the House for ensuring that the departments for which they are responsible carry out their functions properly and efficiently. On occasion, a Minister may be required to account for the actions of a department when errors are made, even when the Minister had no knowledge of, or involvement in, the actions concerned.
>
> (New Zealand, Cabinet Office 2017, cl 3.27)

This provision obliges Ministers to account for the actions of their department, even when the Minister had no knowledge of these actions. In addition to their departmental obligations, Ministers in New Zealand are also responsible for the financial expenditure and strategic direction of Crown entities within their portfolio, which are arms-length bodies where the government has a controlling interest (New Zealand, Cabinet Office 2017, cl 2.24).

The Canadian Code states that Ministers are not presumed to have knowledge of every departmental matter, but nevertheless stresses the requirement for Ministers to account to Parliament for all departmental actions in terms of explaining matters, responding to questions and undertaking remedial action:

> Ministerial accountability to Parliament does not mean that a Minister is presumed to have knowledge of every matter that occurs within his or her department or portfolio, nor that the Minister is necessarily required to accept personal responsibility for every matter. It does require that the Minister attend to all matters in Parliament that concern any organizations for which he or she is responsible, including responding to questions. It further requires that the Minister take appropriate corrective action to address any problems that may have arisen, consistent with the Minister's role with respect to the organization in question.
>
> (Canada, Privy Council 2015, cl 1.3)

Arguably the Canadian position may be broadly equivalent to the New Zealand position, as it requires the Minister to give a full account to Parliament for all matters, impliedly including matters where they do not have personal knowledge and responsibility, and requires Ministers to take corrective action to rectify any issues. The Canadian Code also provides that Ministers should be responsible for arms-length organisations in their portfolio, such as agencies, tribunals and Crown corporations, although a high-level strategic oversight is sufficient to satisfy this responsibility.

The UK Ministerial Code also retains the full responsibility of Ministers to Parliament, even over agencies they do not directly control, although there is a devolution of power to civil servants in terms of the Accounting Officer model. The UK Code states that Ministers have a duty to Parliament to account, and be held to account, for the policies, decisions and actions of their departments and devolved executive agencies (UK, Cabinet Office 2016, cl 1.2). This echoes a House of Commons resolution in 1997, which puts the responsibility on Ministers to account to Parliament for actions of departments under their direct control, as well as executive agencies, which are constitutionally, legally and managerially separate from Ministers and not subject to direct ministerial control. In addition, the UK Code states that Ministers should require civil servants who give evidence before parliamentary committees on their behalf and under their direction to be as helpful as possible in providing accurate, truthful and full information (UK, Cabinet Office 2016, cl 1.2). The Code also enshrines the Accounting Officer model, providing for a separate personal accountability of senior civil servants.

Thus, the codes put varying levels of responsibility on Ministers, with the Australian code being the most lax. The New Zealand code is the firmest on ministerial responsibility in explicitly providing that Ministers are responsible to account to Parliament even for departmental actions they are not aware of. The UK and Canadian codes highlight the comprehensive nature of ministerial responsibility, which may imply that Ministers are also responsible to account to Parliament for departmental matters they are unaware of. The UK code also carves out a separate area of responsibility to civil servants based on the Accounting Officer concept. In New Zealand, UK and Canada, there is acknowledgement that Ministers maintain some form of responsibility over arms-length executive agencies created as a result of NPM. It can thus be seen that, despite NPM, ministerial responsibility remains the lynchpin of Westminster constitutional systems.

In all jurisdictions, the codes emphasise the pre-eminence of the Prime Minister in determining how ministerial responsibility is to be enforced. This is particularly pronounced in Canada, where power is strongly centralised in the Prime Minister. Canadian departmental heads and political advisors are appointed by the Prime Minister, who also influences their careers. In Canada, therefore, 'ministerial responsibility can only be understood and appreciated as a ruling concept against the backdrop of prime ministerial government' (Smith 2006, p. 123).

There is a disjuncture, however, between the NPM reforms and codification of responsibilities between Ministers and civil servants that have led to disputes about whether accountability can be evaded if it is diffused amongst various actors, or alternatively whether Ministers are able to use the new structures to evade ultimate responsibility for scandals and controversies by blaming their officials and advisors. Questions have been raised about whether senior departmental figures have become scapegoats and taken the blame for certain incidents. For instance, in the United Kingdom, politicians have sought to delineate between policy and operational matters, and have claimed that civil servants should be responsible for operational issues (Gay and Powell 2004, p. 12). Margaret Hodge, former chair of the Public Administration Committee, has advocated strongly for civil servants to appear before parliamentary committees, but has also claimed that civil servants should shoulder increasing responsibility. Hodge stated to the House of Lords Select Committee on the Constitution in 2012:

> I think that you just have to accept the reality that Ministers cannot be accountable for much that happens. To take an example of a procurement decision, the NHS IT system was a complete shambles that cost £6 billion. Can you really say that Ministers were accountable for that? Big procurement decisions are one example. I think that we have to try to move to a definition where Ministers are responsible for policy formulation and there is greater accountability of the civil service for policy implementation. That is difficult and blurred, and there will no doubt be areas where disagreements will arise, but select committees are actually pretty adept at sorting out where responsibility and accountability lie. That is hugely important.
>
> (quoted in Gay 2012, pp. 9–10)

These opportunistic positions, given the difficulties in separating between policy and administration, have led to British Ministers blaming civil servants for operational failures. For example, British Ministers blamed prison escapes on the operational failings of the Prison Service, rather than their policy decisions for which they could be held responsible (Barker 1998, p. 1; Gay and Powell 2004, pp. 21–5). These actions are consistent with 'public choice' theory, which predicts that politicians have the incentive to deflect all the blame that comes in their direction, while accepting the credit for anything that goes right towards achieving 'the political nirvana of a system of executive government in which blame flows downwards in the bureaucracy while credit flows upwards to ministers' (Hood and Lodge 2006, p. 59). Of course, there are exceptions where Ministers have remarkably high personal ethics and integrity; however, by and large Ministers have the overriding incentive to shift blame to another locus.

The media and public expectations of ministerial responsibility

In the constitutional vacuum left by Ministers not being held to account, the mass media have become a potent force in scrutinising ministerial responsibility. This may signal a shift in the location of accountability, away from politicians and Parliament, to the media (Woodhouse 2004, p. 16). If an embattled Minister is on the headlines of the news for a prolonged period, sucking up political oxygen, and loses the support of the

Prime Minister, the Minister will ultimately resign. Rodney Brazier states that the media can be seen as possessing a unique capacity to enforce ministerial responsibility:

> For Parliament cannot collectively remove an erring Minister (for when did a Minister last resign at the clear behest of Parliament?), nor can the ranks of the Opposition do so (for it is the job of the Opposition to criticize, and its criticisms can be discounted as partisan; even when the attack had merit, the Government's Commons majority will beat off the attack). Nor can the courts police the doctrine of ministerial responsibility, for the fitness for office of a Minister is not a justiciable issue. To the extent that some Ministers, in effect, have been forced from office by the media, the media can claim that they have moved into a constitutional lacuna and have fulfilled a useful public service.
>
> (Brazier 1997, p. 271)

The media's definition of ministerial responsibility is usually more stringent than self-enforced ministerial codes of conduct, where sometimes explanatory responsibility or amendatory responsibility is sufficient. The media often demand the Minister's scalp:

> Resignation is the measure and the meaning of ministerial responsibility – to the media, who need only to fix their focus on an individual, and to the public, who take their understanding of ministerial responsibility largely from the media.
>
> (Smith 2006, p. 107)

Thus, the media and the public still demand ministerial resignation to satisfy a metaphorical 'public hanging' or 'shooting gallery mentality' (Smith 2006, p. 107) – a symbolic gesture of the person at the top taking ultimate blame.

There is therefore a disjuncture in the theory, practice, reality, codification and public expectations in terms of ministerial responsibility. The theory suggests a strong form of ministerial responsibility, where Ministers are responsible for the actions of their department and advisors, even those they did not authorise. The practice indicates that Ministers only resign over events where they are personally culpable, and sometimes Ministers do not resign even if they are culpable. Some ministerial codes suggest an increasing division between what Ministers and their department are responsible for. Nevertheless, public expectations reinforced by the media are that Ministers resign over departmental blunders, with other gestures seen as too weak. As a convention, ministerial responsibility is easily malleable and cynically circumvented by politicians towards achieving short-term political ends. There is no wonder that the doctrine has become so confused and easily manipulated over time.

Political advisors and parliamentary accountability

So, how does the concept of ministerial responsibility apply to political advisors? As an extension of the concept of ministerial responsibility, Ministers should also technically take responsibility for the actions of advisors in their own offices, who are at an even higher level of direct ministerial control than departments. Even more than civil servants, advisors are seen to be acting as *alter egos* of their Ministers. This means that Ministers should account to Parliament for the actions of their advisors, even those they did not authorise. However, the theory of ministerial responsibility has never matched the practice, where Ministers have generally not resigned over the actions of their advisors. Indeed, Ministers have instead used their advisors as scapegoats and blamed them for controversial events.

The next question is: what is the relationship of political advisors to Parliament in upholding the principle of ministerial responsibility? In this respect, an analogy can be made with civil servants appearing before parliamentary committees. Civil servants routinely appear before parliamentary committees. Apart from Accounting Officers in the United Kingdom, who have an independent personal responsibility, the presence of civil servants is to give an account of their actions to Parliament, that is, provide explanatory accountability, while responsibility for their actions falls on their Minister, who may be censured in Parliament. The appearance of political advisors before parliamentary committees would be similarly to provide an account of their actions, while the Minister would remain answerable to Parliament for any remedial action and subject to any sanctions by Parliament.

Civil servants do exercise statutory power and manage the expenditure of public funds, while political advisors in general do not. This justifies the attendance of civil servants at estimates committees scrutinising the expenditure of public funds. Nevertheless, where there is a controversy and it is necessary to work out relevant factual information, political advisors and civil servants occupy the same position in relation to Ministers through the principle of responsible government. Yet civil servants as a general rule do appear before parliamentary committees, while political advisors sometimes resist. There is little rationale for political advisors not appearing, as there is no reason to distinguish political advisors from civil servants in establishing factual information regarding controversies.

As discussed in chapter five, in the United Kingdom, it is clear that special advisors can be called to appear before parliamentary committees according to the Osmotherly Rules, which were revised in 2005 to create a presumption that where a parliamentary committee called a named official, including a special advisor, the named official will appear where possible (UK, Cabinet Office 2005, cl 12). However, the Minister is given discretion to decide who should ultimately appear, including an alternate civil servant – or the Minister may choose to appear themselves. This reinforces the Minister's ultimate responsibility, but facilitates the committees' inquiries to obtain factual information as needed. There is no such explicit acknowledgement of the responsibility of political advisors to Parliament in other jurisdictions.

The latest ministerial codes are generally silent about the responsibility of Ministers for the actions of their personal staff, apart from a previous incarnation of the Australian ministerial code, the Howard government's 1996 'Guide on Key Elements on Ministerial Responsibility', which states:

> Ministers' direct responsibility for actions of their personal staff is, of necessity, greater than it is for their departments. Ministers have closer day-to-day contact with, and direction of the work of, members of their staff. Furthermore ministerial staff do not give evidence to parliamentary committees, their actions are not reported in departmental annual reports, and they are not normally subject to other forms of external scrutiny, such as administrative tribunals ... Ultimately, however, ministers cannot delegate to members of their personal staff their constitutional, legal or accountability responsibilities. Ministers therefore need to make careful judgments about the extent to which they authorise staff to act on their behalf in dealings with departments.
>
> (Australia, Office of the Prime Minister and Cabinet 1996, cl 6)

Thus, the previous Australian code provided that Ministers had a higher direct responsibility for ministerial advisors compared to their department due to the higher level of direct control. The code also stated that advisors should not be subject to external accountability mechanisms, such as parliamentary committees and administrative tribunals, which is contrary to what is argued in this book. The code suggested that Ministers should restrain the level of responsibility given to their staff, which has not eventuated in practice, given the dramatic expansion of the roles of advisors over time. This provision was later removed, meaning that there is no longer any clarity on these issues.

As seen in chapter five, in most Westminster jurisdictions, there has been some level of intransigence towards advisors appearing before parliamentary committees. In the United Kingdom, a number of Margaret Thatcher's and Tony Blair's advisors refused to appear before committees (UK, Public Administration Select Committee 2007, p. 39), although this practice changed following the amendment to the Osmotherly Rules, which over time led to political advisors appearing before various large-scale inquiries such as on the British participation in the Iraq War (UK, House of Commons, Foreign Affairs Committee 2003). In Canada, the government issued a new policy in 2010 that political staff should not testify before committees and that Ministers should attend on their behalf (Canada, House of Commons Standing Committee on Access to Information, Privacy and Ethics 2010). The Canadian position still reinforces the traditional view of ministerial responsibility where Ministers appear before parliamentary committees to account for the actions of their advisors. Even after the change in government policy, an advisor appeared before a parliamentary committee (Canada,

Standing Committee on Access to Information, Privacy and Ethics 2011). This can be contrasted with the complete lack of accountability in Australia, where in the 'Children Overboard' incident, political advisors were banned from appearing before parliamentary committees, and Ministers refused to appear before the Senate committee on the basis that they were not a member of that House (Australia, Senate Select Committee for an Inquiry 2002). In the Australian system, Ministers tend to be in the Lower House, while parliamentary committees are, as a rule, only active in the Upper House where the government rarely holds the majority due to the proportional representation voting system. As a result, neither Ministers nor advisors appeared before the Senate committee investigating the 'Children Overboard' incident to provide explanation, accept a sanction or undertake remedial action. Therefore, Australia has the weakest system of parliamentary accountability in this field. In the United Kingdom, Canada and New Zealand, Ministers routinely appear before parliamentary committees for issues of controversy, even when they are not compelled to do so. The issue of political advisors and parliamentary committees has not featured strongly in New Zealand, although an advisor appeared before a parliamentary committee in 2013 without any outcry (New Zealand Privileges Committee 2013).

Thus, at differing points, there have been varying interpretations of how ministerial responsibility should operate in the context of political advisors appearing before parliamentary committees, with the United Kingdom and New Zealand being the most principled in allowing advisors to appear, Canada being more obstructive but still maintaining ministerial responsibility, while Australia has subverted the notion of ministerial responsibility by allowing both Ministers and political advisors to completely escape accountability to committees.

I will now consider in what circumstances political advisors should appear before parliamentary committees. The Senate Committee on ministerial staff following the Australian 'Children Overboard' incident identified situations where ministerial advisors should appear before committees, including where there are administrative problems, such as information not passing from the advisor to the Minister or the advisor acting without the Minister's authority, as well as situations where the Minister has not assumed responsibility, such as by refusing to appear before committees or distancing themselves from the actions of their advisors (Australia, Senate Finance and Public Administration References Committee 2003). In 2004, Labor and Democrat Senators called on the Liberal government to implement the Committee's recommendation that ministerial staff be required to appear before parliamentary committees where important information has emanated from a Minister's office but not from the Minister (Australia, Senate, 2004, p. 3216). These are all appropriate circumstances for political advisors to appear before parliamentary committees.

In addition, if a political advisor engages in some form of illegal or improper conduct, this should be scrutinised by a parliamentary committee.

For example, if a political advisor made a policy recommendation where they had a personal financial conflict of interest, this would be a matter that should be scrutinised and the advisor should appear. More broadly, if there was any suggestion of improper behaviour by the Minister or their advisor, this may necessitate questions being asked although policy issues are involved. For instance, it is improper to run a sham public consultation as it is a fraud on those participating in it and a waste of taxpayer money to run a consultation process when the outcome has already been decided. Further, there may be situations where the facts on significant issues are only within the knowledge of the ministerial advisor. For example, in the Australian 'Hotel Windsor' incident, only the political advisor herself could confirm if she was acting on instruction of her Minister, the Premier, or the Premier's chief media advisor.

Accordingly, political advisors should appear before parliamentary committees in at least the following situations:

- where a Minister has renounced a political advisor's action or refused to appear to answer questions regarding the conduct of their advisor;
- where critical information has been received in a Minister's office but is not communicated to a Minister;
- where critical instructions have emanated from a Minister's office and not the Minister;
- where a government programme is administered to a significant extent by a political advisor;
- where there are facts within the personal knowledge of only the political advisor that are relevant to a significant issue; or
- where advice by the political advisor involves some form of illegal or improper conduct, including policy advice (Ng 2016).

If neither Ministers nor their advisors appear before parliamentary committees in these circumstances, Ministers are able to escape scrutiny for their actions and deny responsibility for events or policies. This creates an accountability deficit where no one takes explanatory or amendatory responsibility for public controversies. Consequently, the basic tenet of ministerial responsibility that seeks to ensure executive accountability is undermined. This is a failure at a systemic level, where Ministers are able to utilise political advisors to avoid their own responsibility to Parliament.

Towards a new accountability framework: vertical and horizontal accountability

The decline of vertical accountability

The traditional conception of ministerial responsibility under which Ministers answer to Parliament for all actions of their department implies a strong hierarchical structure where control over all decisions can if necessary be exercised at the top and the relevant information can be readily transmitted up and down. The idea that responsibility implies ministerial resignation in the case of departmental errors, including those that Ministers did not authorise or of which they were not personally aware has never held sway in the United Kingdom, Canada, Australia and New Zealand.

The traditional Westminster accountability framework is predicated on ministerial responsibility and responsible government: a form of *vertical* accountability, that is, a top-down hierarchical accountability of Ministers to Parliament to answer for their actions and decisions. The role of advisors and civil servants in this context is generally to give an account for their actions, while responsibility for their actions rests with the Minister. However, particularly in Australia, this vertical accountability mechanism focussing on the accountability of Ministers to Parliament has been undermined by party politics and the self-interested actions of politicians. Due to the partial fusion of the executive and legislature in Westminster systems, the executive often has the majority to block inconvenient parliamentary scrutiny. In addition, Parliament is often hamstrung when dealing with political advisors who refuse to appear before parliamentary committees at the instruction of their employer, the Minister. Although Parliament has strong powers to punish those who do not comply, including the power of imprisonment (Jack et al 2011, pp. 192–193), it is rather harsh to imprison a person who is following the directions of their employer. Parliamentary accountability in Westminster jurisdictions has been unreliable at best. In instances where the Minister is not directly culpable, parliamentary accountability has never really existed. Thus, vertical accountability has always been weak and may be declining with the entrenchment of political advisors within the Westminster system.

The rise of horizontal accountability

As such, we now have to look to *horizontal* accountability mechanisms, that is broadly parallel institutions, to capture the actions of advisors (Scott 2000, p. 42). These include traditional public law oversight mechanisms such as the Ombudsman and Auditor-General, as well as the media.

Oversight bodies

The rise of the administrative state in the 1970s has seen the proliferation of a plethora of oversight bodies or office-holders to monitor the executive, such as ombudsmen, auditors, commissions and tribunals; or what Hood et al colourfully called the 'waste watchers, quality police and sleaze busters' (Hood et al 1999, p. 11). Within their legislative mandate, these watchdog bodies have a continuing function of review or enquiry in relation to particular aspects of executive activity. They often have a high level of independence from the executive, sometimes achieved through a relationship with the legislature, and significant coercive powers to enter premises of public organisations, question witnesses under oath and compel the production of documents. Among these the longest established and most indispensable are the Auditors-General, whose audits of departmental and agency spending, encompassing both regularity and quality of performance, are an essential support for parliamentary supervision of public finance. Ombudsmen have also become a permanent point of resort for citizens complaining of maladministration, and may have systemic investigatory powers, either instigated on their own motion or by government. Information Commissioners have been introduced more recently to police freedom of information regimes. Although these bodies lack the coercive power to change governmental practices, the publicity of their reports may encourage government agencies to respond in a positive and productive way. Thus, regulatory powers are deliberately divided among separate bodies, with regulatory agencies exercising restricted powers focussed on monitoring and initiating enforcement actions, with only advisory roles in relation to rule-making, which is the preserve of legislatures or Ministers exercising delegated powers (Scott 2014, p. 359). These arms-length scrutineers insulate regulatory decision-making from both the self-interested structures of self-regulation inside government, as well as the self-interested structures of politics (Scott 2014, p. 357).

The introduction of the administrative state was met with equal measures of celebration and derision. For example, in Australia, a package of administrative law mechanisms was introduced in the 1970s that included statutory judicial review, a generalist merits review tribunal, the ombudsman and freedom of information. Dennis Pearce hailed the new system as the 'vision splendid' of the means by which an affected citizen would be able to test Commonwealth government decisions (Pearce 1987, p. 15). Many bureaucrats predictably reacted with hostility. In 1993, the then Secretary of the Australian Department of Veterans' Affairs stated that administrative law was no longer necessary and its practitioners should be searching for a new role (Woodward 1993, pp. 49–50).

Oversight bodies subvert the Westminster tradition of secrecy within government. The growth of these bodies as part of the 'audit explosion' can be attributed to the rise of 'new public management' with its diffusion of power, increased demands for government accountability and transparency, as well as the rise of quality assurance models of organisational control (Power 1994; Power 2000, p. 111). The audit explosion was thus 'not only the explosion of concrete practices, it was also and necessarily the growth and intensification of an idea about audit in a number of spheres' (Power 2000, p. 112). At the same time, the proliferation of oversight bodies was paradoxically accompanied by the 'new public management' destabilisation and reduction in numbers of the bureaucracy. In the United Kingdom, for example, drastic cuts to the civil service were accompanied by dramatic increases in the budget of oversight agencies. Between 1976 and 1995, staffing in the British civil service was cut by 30 per cent, while the staffing in public sector regulators grew by 90 per cent (Hood et al 1999, pp. 29–31). Over time, the oversight bodies grew in reputation, stature and public recognition, and are now a well-established feature of liberal democratic regimes.

Oversight bodies have become an increasingly effective force in holding political advisors to account. Where parliamentary committees have failed, independent scrutineers have succeeded. For instance, in the 'Hotel Windsor' incident in the Australian State of Victoria, where the ministerial advisor accidentally sent an email to a journalist at the Australian Broadcasting Corporation stating that the Minister intended to run a sham public consultation on the redevelopment of the Hotel Windsor, the parliamentary committee failed to compel the ministerial advisor to appear due to government intransigence. At this point, the committee referred the matter to the Victorian Ombudsman, who stepped in to investigate the matter. Using his strong legislative coercive powers, the Ombudsman was able to interview the Minister, ministerial advisors and public servants, as well as discover all relevant emails, where the parliamentary committee failed to do so (Victoria, Ombudsman Victoria 2011, p. 19). It is paradoxical that although Parliament is the supreme law-making body and has strong coercive powers, the Ombudsman, who is an officer created by Parliament, was able to gain better access to ministerial advisors than the parliamentary committee itself.

Likewise, in Canada, the Information Commissioner has been active in inquiring into the actions of ministerial staff. The Commissioner investigated the handling of access to information requests in the Department of Public Works. In the course of the investigation, the Commissioner summoned witnesses to give evidence, including political staff who refused to give evidence before a parliamentary committee on the same issue, Jillian Andrews and Sébastien Togneri. The Commissioner concluded that there was systemic interference by political staff into departmental processing of Access to Information files and that civil servants were swayed from performing their legislative duties to please ministerial staff (Canada, Office of the Information Commissioner of Canada 2011, p. 15).

There are several reasons why oversight bodies have proved to be more effective than parliamentary committees in uncovering issues relating to advisors. For one, these monitoring bodies are seen to be more impartial than a parliamentary committee, as the officers are non-partisan, and more likely to treat people with fairness. By contrast, parliamentary committees are highly partisan avenues of conflict and drama, where each parliamentarian tries to grandstand, score points and get media coverage for their own benefit or that of their political party. Another reason why political advisors have been more cooperative with the oversight bodies is because the questioning of these scrutineers is often not in the public forum, compared to appearances before parliamentary committees, where a single slip of the tongue can be pounced upon by the media. Although the final report of these oversight bodies is usually made public, the finer details of the questioning are not.

Even apart from supplementing parliamentary processes, monitoring bodies have been active in pursuing the actions of political advisors, including the Canadian Conflict of Interest and Ethics Commissioner, who found that several ministerial staff breached the *Conflict of Interest Act* (Canada, Office of the Conflict of Interest and Ethics Commissioner 2015), as well as the New Zealand Inspector-General of Intelligence and Security, who made findings about the actions of ministerial staff in leaking information to a private blogger to smear the Opposition (New Zealand, Office of the Inspector-General of Intelligence and Security 2014).

There are, however, limitations to these statutory oversight bodies. Apart from the inherent constraints of their position of only having the power of recommendation rather than enforcement, there are issues of structural protections of integrity bodies. For one, appointments are made by the executive, so governments may seek to appoint compliant commissioners or make partisan appointments of those who share their political ideology. These watchdogs are ordinarily appointed for a fixed term of between 5–10 years, sometimes with the possibility of reappointment. If a statutory officer was vying for reappointment, they might not seek to ruffle too many feathers in government. In addition, funding for these bodies is dependent on government, meaning that they can be defunded by a hostile government. An ignominious example is the Australian Information Commissioner, who in 2016 was defunded by a conservative government, to the extent that the Commissioner was forced to shut his office and work from home, clearly hampering the Commissioner's ability to satisfactorily perform his statutory functions (Mulgan 2015). Nevertheless, despite the limitations of their roles, oversight bodies are starting to be very effective in holding political advisors to account and are likely to become increasingly important in the future.

Media

The mass media are another form of horizontal accountability that have become a potent force in holding government to account, through the medium of broadcast, print and online journalism. Unlike oversight bodies, which have a direct accountability relationship with government, the media are a more diffuse mechanism of achieving accountability through the broader political process. Despite this, much of political activity, such as legislative debate, is conducted with the hope that the media will report on it to achieve a wider public audience. Reports of oversight bodies condemning government practices may also achieve greater outcomes through media publicity leading to public outrage, particularly since these bodies are unable to compel changes in government agencies.

The mass media are both a *vehicle* and a *player* in the public policy space. The media are used by politicians and their media advisors strategically through 'spin' and leaking documents to gauge public reactions. Leaking by public servants is seen to be a deviation from proper process and is thus uncontrolled and disapproved of within the bureaucracy. Lobby groups use the media as a platform for debate and public awareness. But the media are not just a conduit for other groups; rather the media have their own agenda and run campaigns against politicians and political regimes, which may lead to Ministers resigning or a change in government. The media have thus become an independent political player and agent of accountability in their role as the 'fourth estate' (Mulgan 1998, p. 68). Specialised journalists report on politics and government, called the lobby in the United Kingdom and the press gallery in Australia, New Zealand and Canada, in addition to journalists who specialise in particular policy issues. Nevertheless, there is a tension between the media fulfilling an idealised political 'fourth estate' role and their functions based on commercial imperatives (Schultz 1998, p. 1), with 'its head in politics and its feet in commerce' (Boyce 1978). As such, media coverage tends to be on what would appeal to a broad audience, with a preference for sensationalism in the form of the dramas of politics, disputes, strategies and blunders, rather than subtlety or complexity (Schultz 1998, p. 140). As such, political reporting tends to focus on 'conflict rather than cooperation and scandals rather than abstract issues and general policies' (Mulgan 1998, p. 71). Nevertheless, free and independent media are crucial in achieving government accountability in criticising governmental actions, policies and incompetence, as well as increasing public awareness and mobilisation on contentious issues.

As noted above, the media are able to promote ministerial responsibility by pressuring for Ministers or advisors to resign over major scandals, as resignation is the measure of ministerial responsibility to the media. The media can promote accountability by enhancing transparency about any problematic issues with advisors. Public outrage may lead to the resignation of Ministers or their advisors. Jonathan Powell, Tony Blair's former chief of staff, explained the way the media puts pressure on politicians embroiled in scandals:

> One of the less attractive features of the British press is the feeding frenzy that develops when journalists smell blood. If politicians have been wounded politically by scandals, the press gather in a pack and savage them until either they have brought them to the ground and finished them off or the politicians in question have managed to limp away into safety.
> (Powell 2010, p. 220)

However, the media are not an uncontroversial mechanism to ensure accountability compared to traditional public law mechanisms. The media can be a tool for advisors to try to take down their political opponents, through damaging leaks and 'off the record' briefings, some of which may be fabricated (or in the more contemporary parlance: 'fake news' or 'alternative facts'). In particular, the completely unregulated domains of social media and blogs can be avenues for fake news. As discussed in chapter four, Damian McBride is a salutary example, as a special advisor who plotted to create a private blog that would fabricate sexual rumours to tarnish British Opposition MPs (McBride 2013). In New Zealand, the Prime Minister's senior advisor channelled sensitive governmental information damaging to the Opposition to a private blogger (Hager 2014). Similarly, Dominic Cummings and Henry De Zoete, special advisors to the British Education Minister, used an anonymous Twitter account to attack the Opposition (as discussed in chapter four). Thus, the media is an important, if imperfect, mechanism of horizontal accountability for advisors.

References

Books and journal articles

Barker, A, 1998, 'Political Responsibility for UK Prison Security: Ministers Escape Again', *Public Administration*, vol. 76(1), pp. 1–23.

Boyce, G, 1978, 'The Fourth Estate: A Reappraisal' in G Boyce, J Curren and P Wingate (eds), *Newspaper History: From the 17th Century to the Present Day*, Constable, London.

Brazier, R, 1997, *Ministers of the Crown*, Clarendon Press, Oxford.

Brenton, S, 2014, 'Ministerial Accountability for Departmental Actions Across Westminster Parliamentary Democracies', *Australian Journal of Public Administration*, vol. 73(4), pp. 467–481.

Burnham, J, and Horton, S, 2013, *Public Management in the United Kingdom: A New Introduction*, Palgrave Macmillan, Basingstoke.

Butler, D, 1997, 'Ministerial Accountability: Lessons of the Scott Report', *Papers on Parliament No 29*.

Campbell, A, and Stott, R (eds), 2007, *The Blair Years: Extracts from the Alastair Campbell Diaries*, Hutchinson, London.

Daintith, T, and Page, A, 1999, *The Executive in the Constitution: Structure, Autonomy, and Internal Control*, Oxford University Press, Oxford.

Eichbaum, C, and Shaw, R, 2007, 'Ministerial Advisers, Politicization and the Retreat from Westminster: The Case of New Zealand', *Public Administration*, vol. 85(3), pp. 609–640.

Finer, S E, 1956, 'The Individual Responsibility of Ministers' *Public Administration*, vol. 34(4), pp. 377–396.

Finer, S E, 1989, 'The Individual Responsibility of Ministers' in G Marshall (ed), *Ministerial Responsibility*, Oxford University Press, Oxford, pp. 115–26.

Franks, CES, 2004, 'Accountability to Parliament for Financial Matters in the British System', Unpublished, 8 December 2004, pp. 3–4.

Gay, O, 2012, 'Individual Ministerial Accountability' Parliamentary and Constitution Centre Briefing Paper for Members of Parliament, SN06467, 8 November 2012.

Gay, O and Powell, T, 2004, 'Individual Ministerial Responsibility – Issues and Examples', Parliament and Constitution Centre, Research Paper 04/31, 5 April 2004.

Hager, Nicky, 2014, *Dirty Politics: How Attack Politics is Poisoning New Zealand's Political Environment*, Craig Potton Publishing, Nelson.

Heard, A, 1991, *Canadian Constitutional Conventions, The Marriage of Law and Politics*, Oxford University Press, Toronto.

Hood, C, 1991, 'A Public Management for all Seasons?', *Public Administration*, vol. 69(1), pp. 3–19.

Hood, C, and Lodge, M, 2006, *The Politics of Public Service Bargains: Reward, Competency, Loyalty–and Blame*, Oxford University Press, Oxford.

Hood, C, James, O, Jones, G, Scott, C and Travers, T, 1999, *Regulation inside Government: Waste-watchers, Quality Police, and Sleaze-Busters*, Oxford University Press, Oxford.

Jack, M et al (eds), 2011, *Erskine May's Treatise on the Law, Privileges, Proceedings and Usage of Parliament*, 24th edn, LexisNexis, London.

Jennings, W I, 1938, *The Law and the Constitution*, University of London Press, London.

Killey, I, 2012, *Constitutional Conventions in Australia: An Introduction to the Unwritten Rules of Australia's Constitution*, 2nd edn, Australian Scholarly Publishing, North Melbourne.

Lijphart, A, 1994, *Democracies*, Yale University Press, New Haven.

McBride, D, 2013, *Power Trip: A Decade of Policy, Plots and Spin*, Biteback Publishing.

Mulgan, R, 1998, *Holding Power to Account: Accountability in Modern Democracies*, Palgrave Macmillan, Basingstoke.

Ng, YF, 2016, 'Dispelling Myths about Conventions: Ministerial Advisers and Parliamentary Committees' *Australian Journal of Political Science*, vol. 51(3), pp. 512–529.

Pearce, D, 1987, 'The Fading of the Vision Splendid? Administrative Law: Retrospect and Prospect' *Canberra Bulletin of Public Administration*, vol. 58, pp. 15–24.

Powell, J, 2010, *The New Machiavelli: How to Wield Power in the Modern World*, Bodley Head, London.

Power, M, 1994, *The Audit Explosion*, London, Demos.

Power, M, 2000, 'The Audit Society: Second Thoughts' *International Journal of Auditing*, vol. 4(1), pp. 111–119.

Rhodes, R A W, Wanna, J and Weller, P, 2009, *Comparing Westminster*, Oxford University Press, Oxford.

Schultz, J, 1998, *Reviving the Fourth Estate: Democracy, Accountability and the Media*, Cambridge University Press, Cambridge.

Scott, C, 2000, 'Accountability in the Regulatory State', *Law and Society*, vol. 27(1), pp. 38–60.

Scott, C, 2014, 'Evaluating the Performance and Accountability of Regulators', *Seattle University Law Review*, vol. 37, pp. 353–374.

Smith, D E, 2006, 'Clarifying the Doctrine of Ministerial Responsibility as it applies to the Government and Parliament of Canada,' *Restoring Accountability Research Studies Volume 1*, Commission of Inquiry into the Sponsorship Program and Advertising Activities, Canadian Government Publishing, Ottawa, pp. 101–143.

Sutherland, S, 1991, 'Responsible Government and Ministerial Responsibility: Every Reform is its Own Problem', *Canadian Journal of Political Science*, vol. 24(1), pp. 91–120.

Thompson, E and Tillotsen, G, 1999, 'Caught in the Act: The Smoking Gun View of Ministerial Responsibility', *Australian Journal of Public Administration*, vol. 58(1), pp. 48–57.

Woodhouse, D, 1994, *Ministers and Parliament: Accountability in Theory and Practice*, Clarendon Press, Oxford.

Woodhouse, D, 2004, 'UK Ministerial Responsibility in 2002: The Tale of Two Resignations', *Public Administration*, vol. 82(1), pp. 1–19.

Woodward, L, 1993, 'Does Administrative Law expect too much of the Administration?' in S Argument (ed), *Administrative Law and Public Administration: Happily Married or Living Apart under the Same Roof?*, AIAL, Canberra, pp. 36–50.

Legislation, codes, case law, government and parliamentary reports

Armstrong Memorandum. 1985. HC Deb Vol 74, cols 128–130 (WA), 26 February 1985, revised HC Deb Vol 123, cols 572–575 (WA), 2 December 1985.

Australia, Office of the Prime Minister and Cabinet, 1996, *Guide on Key Elements on Ministerial Responsibility*, Canberra.

Australia, Prime Minister and Cabinet, 2015, Statement of Ministerial Standards.

Australia, Public Finance, Governance and Accountability Bill 2013 Explanatory Memorandum.

Australia, Public Governance, Accountability and Performance Act 2013 (Cth).

Australia, Public Service Act 1999 (Cth).

Australia, Senate, 2004, *Journals of the Senate*, No 138. Australian Federal Police Commissioner: Ministers and Ministerial Staff, 24 March.

Australia, Senate, Finance and Public Administration References Committee, 2003, *Staff employed under the Members of Parliament (Staff) Act 1984*, Senate Printing Unit, Canbesrra.

Australia, Senate, Select Committee for an Inquiry into a certain Maritime Incident, 2002, *A Certain Maritime Incident*, Senate Printing Unit, Canberra.

Canada, Financial Administration Act R.S.C., 1985, c. F-11.

Canada, House of Commons Standing Committee on Access to Information, Privacy and Ethics, 2010, *Evidence*, 25 May.

Canada, House of Commons, Standing Committee on Access to Information, Privacy and Ethics, 2011, *Evidence*, 21 March.

Canada, Office of the Conflict of Interest and Ethics Commissioner, 2015, Referral from the Public Sector Integrity Commissioner: The Bonner Report, made under the Conflict of Interest Act.

Canada, Office of the Information Commissioner of Canada, 2011, Interference with Access to Information, Special Report Part 1, prepared by S Legault, Information Commission of Canada.

Canada, Privy Council, 2015, Open and Accountable Government, Privy Council Office.

Carltona Ltd v Commissioners of Works (1943) 2 All ER 560.

New Zealand, Cabinet Office, 2017, *Cabinet Manual 2017*, Department of Prime Minister and Cabinet, Wellington, NZ.

New Zealand Privileges Committee. 2013. Question of Privilege regarding use of Intrusive Powers within the Parliamentary Precinct: Interim Report of the Privileges Committee.

New Zealand, Office of the Inspector-General of Intelligence and Security, 2014, Report into the release of information by the New Zealand Security Intelligence Service in July and August 2011. Available at: www.igis.govt.nz/assets/Inquiries/FINAL-REPORT-INTO-THE-RELEASE-OF-INFORMATION-BY-NZSIS-IN-JULY-AND-AUGUST-2.pdf.

United Kingdom, Cabinet Office, 2005, Departmental Evidence and Response to Select Committees, July 2005.
United Kingdom, Cabinet Office, 2016, Ministerial Code.
United Kingdom, Government Resource and Accounts Act 2000.
United Kingdom, House of Commons, Foreign Affairs Committee, 2003, The Decision to Go to War in Iraq. Ninth Report of Session 2002–2003.
United Kingdom, House of Lords, Select Committee on the Constitution, 2012, The Accountability of Civil Servants, 6th Report of session 2012–2013, The Stationery Office, London.
United Kingdom, Ministry of Reconstruction, 1918, Report of the Machinery of Government Committee, Prepared by Viscount R Haldane, Machinery of Government Committee, HMSO, London.
United Kingdom, Public Administration Select Committee, 2007, Politics and Administration: Ministers and Civil Servants, Third Report of Session 2006–2007, HC 122-I.
United Kingdom, Select Committee on Public Administration, 2000, 'The Government Information and Communication Service' (2000–2001) HC 511, Minutes of Evidence, 17 May.
Victoria, Ombudsman Victoria. 2011. Ombudsman Investigation into the Probity of the Hotel Windsor Redevelopment. Available at: www.ombudsman.vic.gov.au/getattachment/753dfb69-1001-4cd6-8b6b-3c9a52f0539f//reports-publications/parliamentary-reports/ombudsman-investigation-into-the-probity-of-the-ho.aspx.

Newspaper articles

Farrar, D, 2012, 'Parliamentary Resignations', New Zealand Herald, 23 March 2012.
Mulgan, Richard, 2015, 'The Slow Death of the Office of the Australian Information Commissioner', The Canberra Times, 1 September. Available at: www.canberratimes.com.au/national/public-service/the-slow-death-of-the-office-of-the-australian-information-commissioner-20150826-gj81dl.html.

7 Conclusion

In the last 40 years, political advisors have become a potent force in Westminster advisory systems. Their numbers have multiplied over successive governments, and their roles have expanded from predominantly administrative tasks to more substantive policy-based roles. With the advent of the 24-hour media cycle, their grip over the media has tightened, giving them the ability to cajole, shape and direct Ministers in their media appearances and presentation.

The numbers of advisors differ across the Westminster jurisdictions, with the Canadian and Australian systems having the largest numbers of advisors and the highest degree of support for Ministers, while New Zealand and the United Kingdom have low numbers of advisors and far less support for each Minister. Despite this variance, there is a distinct uniformity in the reasons that political advisors have come to prominence and the roles that they undertake in our contemporary system of governance.

Governments who have been out of power for a long time tend to be suspicious of the behemoth of the bureaucracy and try to shore up personal support through increasing the numbers of political advisors. In addition, where minority or coalition governments are elected, there is a need for a larger number of advisors to broker positions and coordinate the uneasy alliance between different political parties. The roles of advisors in all jurisdictions span across handling administrative matters, media management and both the procedural and substantive aspects of policy-making, as well as dealing with stakeholders both within and outside of government.

Political advisors wield influence due to their privileged position within the Westminster advisory system. As the most proximate advisors to Ministers, they have unprecedented access to their Ministers and are the final port of call for Ministers seeking advice. In addition, the roles that they play in mediating and gate-keeping between the Minister and other stakeholders, be they departmental bureaucrats or external stakeholders such as interest groups, give them the ability to sift priorities and make independent decisions about what information eventually reaches the Minister. More amorphously, political advisors are influential because of the relationship of trust and confidence they have with their Minister. In a hot-house, high-pressure environment where the Minister feels besieged on all fronts by enemies in the form of political factions, the Opposition, the hungry media or perhaps a cold, inscrutable bureaucracy, they turn to their trusted partisan advisors for advice and emotional support. This creates a relationship forged in fire – leading to an unparalleled intimacy, trust and confidence between Ministers and their advisors.

External factors can also explain the increasing influence of political advisors at the expense of the civil service. For one, to varying extents across the Westminster jurisdictions, the civil service has been deeply destabilised by the advent of the 'new public management' movement that swept through Western democracies in the 1980s. At the same time, political advisors were institutionalised into the system, as an overt move to increase the 'responsive competence' of the bureaucracy. In addition, the frantic 24/7 media cycle has fundamentally changed the pace and operation of politics, such that politicians have to respond almost immediately to the news headlines. Prime Ministers tend to centralise media management and seek to tightly control ministerial media appearances to more carefully craft and curate the messages that they send to the public, a practice pejoratively called 'spin'. In this environment, media advisors have become prominent figures with the ability to direct and instruct Ministers to present themselves in certain ways. The combination of internal and external factors has led to the entrenchment, solidification and institutionalisation of political advisors within the Westminster system of governance.

The integration of political advisors into the Westminster system has not been seamless, with the jurisdictions being inundated with various scandals and controversies. There are several commonalities in the types of controversies involving political advisors. Political staff have acted independently beyond their authority without the knowledge of their Minister or failed to communicate properly with their Minister or the civil service. Further, the politics/media interface has become a dominant problem in many countries, with the prevalence of leaking information to smear factional opponents or the Opposition, as well as the use of the completely unregulated domains of private blogs and social media. The strong focus on spin, in combination with highly partisan behaviour, has led to many controversies involving political advisors. This is particularly prevalent in the United Kingdom.

In addition, political advisors have had a tendency to inappropriately interfere with bureaucratic decision-making, particularly in Freedom of Information requests, by blocking or delaying requests for information, or expediting the release of information to favoured channels that will embarrass the Opposition. This reflects the government's agenda to restrict and control information that is disseminated to the public. At the extreme end of the spectrum, political advisors in Canada have engaged in behaviour that is either illegal or contrary to legislative requirements such as mass deletion of emails and document destruction to avoid public scrutiny. Information Commissioners and Ombudsmen play an important role in bringing these actions to light, while the courts are able to police actions that transgress the law.

These controversies can be attributed to issues arising at the faction/opposition interface, compounded by incompetent appointments through patronage. Excessively zealous partisan behaviour has led advisors to overstep their role and interfere with the bureaucracy, or engage in improper or illegal behaviour. Some advisors have sought to protect their Minister at all costs and tried to discredit opposing factions or the Opposition. Others have sought to promote their party's electoral prospects or boost the coffers of their political party. The influence of money on politics cannot be denied. In an era of declining public trust in political institutions and a reduction of party membership, politicians have become increasingly reliant on political donations and campaign financing by individuals, unions and corporations. As a result, Ministers and their advisors may be susceptible to improper influence by individual or corporate donors or lobbyists representing these donors.

The rise and increasing influence of political advisors has taken a generally uniform route throughout the Westminster jurisdictions. The regulatory trajectory for each country, however, has charted a unique path. In Canada, large-scale scandals involving corruption and illegal behaviour by advisors have led to sophisticated regulation of political advisors through an interlocking scheme of legislation overseen by independent commissioners, codes of conduct and the scrutiny of oversight bodies. Canada was the first jurisdiction to develop the position of political advisors and has the largest number of advisors. Perhaps due to the large numbers of advisors, further scandals have continued to erupt despite the high regulatory intensity in Canada.

The United Kingdom also has detailed regulation with strong requirements set out in legislation and codes of conduct, alongside extensive parliamentary and media scrutiny of advisors. The UK has the lowest number of advisors of all the jurisdictions, which may be due to the cap of two advisors per Minister, coupled with extensive parliamentary and media scrutiny. Problems, however, still abound as there are many media issues that have surfaced, including prevalent leaking and utilising social media against the Opposition. The UK is characterised by an aggressive tabloid media culture that may exacerbate these problems.

In Australia, there is minimal regulation of political advisors, with largely unenforceable legislation and codes of conduct. In addition, Australian Ministers have refused to appear before parliamentary committees and have blocked their advisors from appearing. Thus, legal regulation and parliamentary scrutiny is generally weak in Australia. This has led to major scandals, such as the 'Children Overboard' incident, where Ministers claimed ignorance for perpetuating lies about asylum seekers throwing their own children overboard.

New Zealand has recently introduced a new code of conduct in 2017, to supplement the requirements of the Cabinet Manual and contracts of employment. It is too early to tell how the new regime will be implemented. To date,

New Zealand has largely escaped the major controversies that have plagued the other Westminster jurisdictions. This could potentially be attributed to the small numbers of advisors and the more cooperative political culture that exists in New Zealand. However, there is no cause to be complacent as a recent scandal has exposed the dark underbelly of the actions of a political advisor in the Prime Minister's Office, who provided confidential information to a private blogger to attack the Opposition. As a result, oversight bodies in New Zealand have become increasingly active in investigating issues relating to political advisors.

There are a few regulatory methods that have been adopted by the Westminster jurisdictions. The first is government-wide restrictions on the employment of advisors, either in terms of numbers of advisors or budget limits on advisors' salaries. The second is regulation targeted at the advisors themselves, including positive requirements set out in legislation or codes of conduct, such as the requirement to act ethically, to avoid conflicts of interest and to make financial disclosures. Negative stipulations on advisors can also be observed, such as prohibitions on advisors exercising executive power, expending public funds or directing civil servants.

A major issue in regulating political advisors is the enforceability of these provisions. 'Soft law' such as codes of conduct may be policed completely within the executive. However, members of the core executive such as Ministers, advisors and the civil service benefit when problematic issues are quietly buried or hidden from public view. Legislative provisions may lack 'teeth' in the sense that there might not be proper enforcement mechanisms. The most robust regulation tends to be where there is an independent commissioner overseeing compliance with legislation. But this is no guarantee of an effective regulatory framework. Even with external policing of regulatory frameworks in the United Kingdom through the Civil Service Commissioner overseeing codes of conduct, there is a cultural predisposition not to take the 'nuclear option' of reporting issues to the Commissioner. By contrast, the Canadian Conflict of Interest and Ethics Commissioner is more independent and active in monitoring adherence to legislative provisions. Given the difficulty in enforcing the effective regulation of political advisors, generally it is only egregious issues that come to light, including those that have been leaked to the media, investigated by oversight bodies or transgressed the boundaries of the law and have been prosecuted in the courts.

A common theme across the jurisdictions is that parliamentary accountability is a weak method of ensuring the accountability of advisors, as Ministers rarely take the blame for the actions of their advisors unless they are personally culpable, and Ministers do not always take the blame even if they are culpable. Parliamentary accountability represents a vertical form of accountability based on a chain of hierarchy dependent on the answerability of civil servants to their Minister, and Ministers' accountability to Parliament. This embodies the traditional Westminster concept of ministerial responsibility, which is highly variable in theory, practice, political and media interpretation.

As a result, vertical accountability through Parliament has been, by and large, ineffective in Westminster jurisdictions.

In a Westminster context of weakened parliamentary accountability, horizontal accountability mechanisms have become important to provide a framework of accountability for political advisors. The emphasis on horizontal accountability reflects a move from traditional hierarchical models to polycentric network-based modes of governance and accountability. It is also a shift from internal hierarchical bureaucratic line management to supervision by arms-length scrutineers, that is, regulation inside government. Regulation through the broader political process, such as the media, is an important tool for government accountability, but is not without its problems. Thus, in modern Westminster systems, an optimal framework for accountability includes a combination of vertical and horizontal accountability mechanisms operating in a complex network of governance.

This book highlights the various methods of regulating political advisors, such as legal and political frameworks, as well as scrutiny by integrity bodies and the media. It shows how in the shifting sands of the modern regulatory environment, accountability is continually renegotiated, reshaped, reconfigured. This paints a richer and more complete picture of the implications of an ever-changing executive structure. It is only through these dynamics that political advisors, as relatively new actors in government compared to Ministers and civil servants, may be held to account.

Governments may wish to adopt a purposeful reform agenda to align traditional Westminster principles to a modern world. For one, legislation and codes of conduct should be implemented to regulate the actions of political advisors. Compliance with the regulatory framework should be overseen and policed by an independent commissioner. A government-wide cap on budget or numbers of advisors could be mandated. Legislation or codes should also delineate the appropriate boundaries for political advisors in interacting with civil servants.

Secondly, parliamentary accountability can be improved by the enactment of guidelines agreed between the government and Parliament facilitating the appearances of political advisors before parliamentary committees. These guidelines should provide for the protection of advisors in providing evidence by limiting their evidence to the internal processes of administration and technical details of policies, with Ministers being responsible for discussing the merits of policies, consistent with their roles as elected representatives. In that vein, it is imperative that Ministers appear before parliamentary committees to fulfil the requirements of ministerial responsibility, contrary to the self-interested position of Australian Ministers refusing to appear before Senate committees.

Third, political advisors should be integrated into horizontal accountability mechanisms. Ombudsmen, Auditors-General, Information Commissioners and anti-corruption bodies should explicitly be given the jurisdiction to investigate the actions of political advisors and ministerial offices in their constituting legislation. This will shed light on any improper or illegal behaviour of advisors, as well as allow the oversight bodies to make recommendations to improve the administration of departments, agencies and ministerial offices.

Finally, political advisors should be given training on the legislation and codes of conduct applicable to them, as well as the appropriate boundaries of their roles. At a managerial level, Ministers and chiefs of staff should ensure that their staff work effectively in coordinating policy advice between the department and the Minister. In a modern democracy, this combination of reforms will better hold political advisors to account.

In short, this book makes a valuable contribution by adopting a comparative approach in analysing the rise in the power and significance of political advisors in the Westminster jurisdictions of the United Kingdom, Australia, New Zealand and Canada. It shows the fundamental shift of the locus of power from the neutral public service to highly political and partisan ministerial advisors. The book traces the divergent paths for legal and political regulation of political advisors in the Westminster jurisdictions and illuminates the tensions that these advisors pose within the Westminster system in terms of the media/politics and faction/opposition interfaces. This book also makes recommendations for reform and considers how the traditional Westminster principle of ministerial responsibility can be realigned to the modern world. It develops an accountability framework for political advisors based on both vertical and horizontal accountability mechanisms. Drawing on this, the book identifies strategies, institutional arrangements and practices that facilitate the accountability of political advisors, which can be used by policy-makers to improve their respective national regulatory frameworks.

To conclude, the institutionalisation of political advisors poses a challenge to the traditional Westminster system, built as it is upon a bedrock of the Northcote–Trevelyan report in the 1800s that envisages only a binary relationship between Ministers and civil servants. Nevertheless, the Westminster constitutional context of the executive is steeped in fluid convention, which allows for the gradual evolution of the practices, organisation and control of the executive. And so the significant change in the structure of the executive, with political advisors interposed between Ministers and civil servants, has been followed by legal and political regulation through legislation and codes of conduct, alongside parliamentary scrutiny and more recently the increased vigilance of oversight bodies and the media. Although scandals continue to erupt and we can expect further incremental regulation, the story of the rise of political advisors within the Westminster tradition is one of experimentation, innovation and adaptation. It shows how we are able to, sometimes imperfectly, adapt to change.

Index